THE PONZI SCHEME PUZZLE

THE PONZI SCHEME PUZZLE

A History and Analysis of Con Artists and Victims

Tamar Frankel

OXFORD
UNIVERSITY PRESS

OXFORD
UNIVERSITY PRESS

Oxford University Press

Oxford University Press is a department of the University of Oxford. It furthers the University's objective
of excellence in research, scholarship, and education by publishing worldwide.

Oxford   New York

Auckland   Cape Town   Dar es Salaam   Hong Kong   Karachi
Kuala Lumpur   Madrid   Melbourne   Mexico City   Nairobi
New Delhi   Shanghai   Taipei   Toronto

With offices in

Argentina   Austria   Brazil   Chile   Czech Republic   France   Greece
Guatemala   Hungary   Italy   Japan   Poland   Portugal   Singapore
South Korea   Switzerland   Thailand   Turkey   Ukraine   Vietnam

Oxford is a registered trade mark of Oxford University Press in the UK and certain other countries.

Published in the United States of America by
Oxford University Press
198 Madison Avenue, New York, NY 10016

Library of Congress Cataloging-in-Publication Data
Frankel, Tamar.
The Ponzi scheme puzzle: a history and analysis of con artists and victims/Tamar Frankel.
p. cm.
Includes index.
ISBN 978-0-19-992661-9 (cloth: alk. paper) 1. Swindlers and swindling. 2. Investment
advisors—Corrupt practices. 3. Corruption—Prevention. 4. Self-consciousness (Awareness) I. Title.
HV6691.F73   2012
364.16'3—dc23   2011051887

1 3 5 7 9 8 6 4 2

Printed in the United States of America
on acid-free paper

To my husband, Ray, and my children, Anat Bird
and Michael Frankel

CONTENTS

PREFACE

In 2001, I had the good fortune to meet Professor Diego Gambetta of Nuffield College at Oxford University. Having heard of my interest in and work on trust in the financial area, he suggested that I study the mimics of trustworthiness: con artists. I did, and entered the world of the cons and their victims. The journey was fascinating, as I discovered the intricate relationship between con artists and their "marks," and uncovered the games they play and the price they pay. On the way, puzzles piled up. How can con artists be so successful? How are their marks so blind? Why is this type of fraud so prevalent around the globe?

I sought the answers to these questions by drawing on the facts as the courts described them, and sometimes as the parties alleged them. There have been hundreds of U.S. court cases over the years. In addition, there is *The Rise of Mr. Ponzi,* the autobiography of Charles Ponzi, which tells us much about him and about con artists in general. There are studies about the unique characteristics of con artists, how they cooperate, and what underlies their true nature. These materials helped uncover patterns of facts and behaviors. As varied as the stories of con artists are, and as diverse as the victims' behavior seems to be, patterns began to emerge. The tales that con artists tell investors are enticing in a consistent way. The narratives hide the truth in a consistent manner. Con artists share features of their character and conduct. And so do many of their victims!

Yet the main puzzles remained. How do con artists dazzle and lure wealthy and educated individuals, and representatives of large institutions, to hand over huge sums of money? How do the con artists divert the investors' attention from the "soft" (false) spots of their stories? What kind of businesses do con artists describe to their victims? Why do they choose those business stories to gain the trust of the marks? And why is it so hard to eradicate Ponzi schemes? What kind of people are these con artists and their victims?

There are already many books and articles about Ponzi schemes. There are so many warnings and constant advice on how to detect and avoid con artists. We are told time and again: "Here is information! Use it! Educate yourself! Protect yourself from fraud!" Yet, these messages seem to do little good. Warnings go unheeded. People are endlessly caught in the net of con artists. Why can't we learn from the mistakes of others? Why don't we heed past disasters?

We can learn much by analyzing the behavior of the victims. Warnings against fraud and lists of red flags seem to offer little protection against treacherous charmers. This book suggests a somewhat different approach to investor self-protection. It is by exploring the con artists' fascinating power of persuasion and deception, and by recognizing the subtle signals that mimic truth and honesty, that knowledge can help us recognize our own vulnerability to alluring promises that cannot be fulfilled. This awareness can protect us.

Tamar Frankel
Massachusetts, 2012

ACKNOWLEDGMENTS

I owe a debt of gratitude to Professor Diego Gambetta, Professor Avner Offer, and Professor Joshua Getzler of Oxford University for their ideas, comments, and support. Much of the factual material for this book was derived from court cases and news articles. I thank William Hecker, Esq., Valentina Elson, and Leanne Chaves for their valuable research and the many Boston University School of Law students who assisted in this project throughout the years. My thanks to Connie Taylor, publisher and friend of many years, for her patience and suggestions. Energy and inspiration have always come from family: my husband, Ray; my children, Michael and Anat. They have given me the gift of love and joy, which feeds my work.

THE PONZI SCHEME PUZZLE

Introduction

The American public is better educated and better informed than ever. But here's a paradox: The more people know, the dumber and more careless they seem to get about their investments.

—Richard L. Stern and Lisa Gubernick, *"The Smarter They Are, the Harder They Fall," Forbes, May 20, 1985, at 38*

[Scientists] are absorbed by teasing out the secrets of nature. . . . But how wonderful it is also to penetrate the secrets of men's minds, to turn the chaos of human endeavor into order and bring the darkest deeds from night into daylight.

—Iain Pears, *An Instance of the Fingerpost 404 (1998)*

It takes brains to be a swindler.

—Dan Seligman, *"The Mind of the Swindler," Forbes, June 12, 2000, at 426*

I can calculate the motions of heavenly bodies, but not the madness of people.

—Nicholas Dunbar, *Inventing Money: The Story of Long-Term Capital Management and the Legends Behind It 1 (2000, quoted in Robert Prentice, Whither Securities Regulation? Some Behavioral Observations Regarding Proposals for its Future, 51 DUKE L.J., 1397–1398, 2002, "quoting Sir Isaac Newton, speaking after he lost £20,000 in the stock market")*

What are Ponzi schemes? How do they work? Whom do they affect? And why do they raise interest, awe, anger, and anguish? They are named after Charles Ponzi, who perpetrated such a scheme in the early 1920s. A Ponzi scheme defrauds investors as follows. The con artist offers investors investments that carry extraordinary returns and promise no risk or low risk. The profits are presumed to derive from some business, or product, or financial arrangement. In fact, however, there is no business or product or financial arrangement. The money to pay the investors' profits and sometimes the investments themselves is raised from new investors who are made similar promises.

Do all investors lose under the scheme? Not necessarily. Some investors gain, together with the con artist. But most investors lose heavily. Here is how one bankruptcy court decision shows the distribution of the losses and gains in a Ponzi scheme: about "924 investors, who deposited more than four million dollars with the debtors [the con artist] after June 12, 1981, received no returns and lost all of their original investments."[1] The group of first investors is likely to receive their capital and a profit of 200 percent. Somewhat later, a second group of investors is likely to receive their capital and 150 percent profits. And a third their capital and 100 percent profits, and so on, until the investors in the last group in line are likely to receive 0 capital and 0 percent return. These calculations are similar to those that predict the behavior of "herding," or a "run" in the market. Like market investors,[2] investors in Ponzi schemes follow each other, especially if they are connected in an affinity group, or if they are influenced by the growing reputation of the con artists, or by the con artists' salesmanship and that of their sales force.

Who are the victims of these schemes? Many are wealthy, well-informed, and famous individuals.[3] As one court noted: "Lest one think Ponzi schemes are too simple and obvious to bamboozle the financially savvy, an oil-drilling swindle in the 1970s duped top executives at Pepsico, Time, and General Electric, as well as the chairman of U.S. Trust, the president of First Boston Corp., and an author of several books on Wall Street finance."[4] News in May 2002 revealed that a few banks lost close to $1 billion in a classic, run-of-the-mill scheme.[5] In another case, BankAtlantic was caught in a Ponzi scheme when fraudulent loan applications were offered to the bank, and the con artists continued to make payments on the loans in order to hide the borrowers' delinquencies.[6]

In 2010, a hedge fund manager was found to have "conned some of Denver's wealthiest people."[7] His scheme lasted more than ten years; according to a report of a court-appointed receiver, this manager collected more than $71 million from about sixty-five people. He left his firm with $9.5 million in assets and $140 million in liabilities.[8] In the 1980s, a Ponzi scheme was exposed at J. David Dominelli's currency trading firm, much to the shock of San Diego's elite. About a thousand investors lost a total of $80 million in Dominelli's fraud, which promised returns on the order of 40 percent. In 1985, he was sent to prison for twenty years.[9] In Australia, the victims of another scheme included former famous football and soccer players.[10] Large institutional investors,[11] religious organizations, and their members were not spared either.[12] On December 11, 2008, Bernard Madoff, a well-known broker dealer and a former chair of NASDAQ (National Association of Securities Dealers' Automated Quotations), confessed to having defrauded his investors. The list of his investors included investment management firms, foreign banks, hedge funds, wealthy individual investors, brokerage firms, pension funds, companies, charities, universities, and insurance companies. His scheme lasted at least twenty years. The precise amount of the fraud is not yet established, but it is in the billions. He was sentenced to 150 years in prison.[13]

Thus Ponzi schemes catch in their net highly sophisticated individuals and institutions as well as low-income and middle-income investors. In New Mexico, with a population of about two million, a Ponzi case or two appear almost every year. Although New Mexico may have a distinctive character, perhaps as a place where investors might lose less "only because they had less wealth to lose," even so "when it comes to gullibility, New Mexicans proved to be no different from the swells in New York and Florida."[14]

Yet con artists treat the rich and the less affluent alike. Middle- and low-income people are caught in the net as well. As we shall see, their motivation may be mixed with religious affinity, or pride in the rising star of one of them, or total and unquestioning belief. But they too follow the con artist. In addition, there are pyramid schemes. These are somewhat similar to Ponzi schemes, except that they target the less affluent. The victims are invited to recruit salespersons to sell products that are not in fact sellable. The "buyers" of the privilege to sell pay those who recruited them. Each recruit pays for sales materials and the permission to sell the product. The recruit then seeks to sell this right to another recruit, and be paid by the latter. In reality, what is being sold is the *right to sell* a product that is rarely or never sold. New recruits pay to the parties that recruited them. Each of the recruiters keeps part of the money received from the new recruits and pays the rest of the money to the persons who recruited them. Thus, the top of the pyramid collects from all sellers below; the amount of the collection falls with the position of the person in the pyramid. Those at the lower level pay people at the higher level a percentage of the amounts their new recruits pay and receive payment from those below. At some point, the number of potential buyers of the privilege to sell is exhausted, and the scheme comes to an end.

Are Ponzi schemes unique to the United States? Not at all. These schemes have attracted investors all over the world, in different cultures and countries. They have been highly successful in Russia[15] and India[16] and resulted in investors' riots in Albania.[17] In Romania, about a hundred such schemes have operated; the largest was Caritas. Estimates of the number of Caritas investors vary from two to eight million, and the amount of money involved was in the billions—some say up to a third of the country's liquid reserves.[18] Portugal had its share when Dona Branca operated a scheme, paying 10 percent monthly interest, from 1970 to 1984.[19]

Similar stories appear with monotonous regularity. In Costa Rica, two brothers, Luis Enrique and Osvaldo Villalobos, operated a Ponzi scheme—the Brothers Fund—for twenty years. Investors, among them sixty-four hundred American retirees, invested $10,000 each and received up to 3.5 percent interest per month in cash. Costa Rican officials began to investigate the organization and discovered a "giant Ponzi scheme." When the brothers' bank accounts were frozen, it was estimated that $300 to $600 million was missing, and possibly as much as $3 billion. Osvaldo Villalobos is serving a jail sentence; Luis Enrique is a fugitive.[20] In a Haitian operation in 2001, it is estimated that more than $240 million was swindled from investors, equivalent to 60 percent of the country's GDP.[21]

On February 18, 2011, the Securities and Exchange Commission filed an emergency action against Secure Capital Funding Corporation and certain individuals to freeze their multimillion-dollar international investment scheme, which allegedly offered risk-free Swiss debentures earning from 10 to 100 percent a month. According to the commission, "[t]hese securities were fictitious and nearly $3 million of investor funds were quickly wired out of the country to accounts in Latvia and Jamaica."[22]

Do Ponzi schemes have an impact on the financial system and society? They do. The dollars that investors lose in Ponzi schemes are not trivial. In the United States, the annual losses from the schemes vary; in 2000 it was reported that American investors were losing more than $10 billion a year to investment frauds.[23] According to court cases, the year 2002 showed losses of more than $9.6 billion.[24] Each of the years 1995 and 1997 showed losses of more than $1.6 billion. The years 1996, 1990, and 1976 showed annual losses of more than $1 billion as well. But these numbers are drawn only from court cases.

Some numbers speak for themselves. "Larry Reynolds assisted Tom Petters in routing $12 billion of investor funds through Reynolds's company's California bank account. Petters had told investors that their funds were used to purchase consumer electronics, when in fact Reynolds directed that the funds be sent to Petters's company. Petters then used the funds to perpetrate a massive Ponzi scheme." Reynolds's conviction was affirmed in 2011.[25] In 2010, Randall Treadwell, Ricky Sluder, and Larry Saturday were convicted for operating "a massive four-year Ponzi scheme in which more than 1,700 investors across the United States lost over $40 million."[26]

Do these swindles die out? Not at all. After the conviction of Treadwell and his two partners, the court commented: "Despite the apparent notoriety of Ponzi schemes, they continue to dupe investors."[27] As was noted in the *New York Times* on May 2, 2011, "This kind of swindle thrived well into the 20th century."[28] But as the cited case will show, the twenty-first century is not lagging behind.

Losses from Ponzi schemes in the United States are equal to the losses from shoplifting, which is considered a vast and costly criminal behavior. According to one study, about twenty-three million Americans try to steal at shops annually.[29] Ponzi schemes cannot boast such a large number of criminals, but the schemes do compete with shoplifting on the cost side. The aggregate cost of shoplifting in 2001 to U.S. retailers was $10.23 billion,[30] compared to investment frauds (involving far fewer con artists) amounting to approximately the same sum—$10 billion.[31] One case alone resulted in losses of $9 billion.[32]

In addition, losses from Ponzi thefts are more "concentrated" than the losses of shoplifting, which are spread throughout the retailing business. In 2000, the average dollar loss per shoplifting incident was $195.73.[33] But Ponzi schemes cost each investor much more. In 2002, PinnFund defrauded 159 sophisticated high-income investors of $330 million, or more than $2 million each on average.

Ponzi schemes and investment frauds seem to have reached the proportion of an epidemic. These schemes have their share around the world; during 2001, global investment frauds amounted to about $35 billion;[34] for example, "The annual loss from all varieties of fraud in Canada is estimated to exceed 1.5 per cent of the country's $800-billion gross domestic product—or more than $12 billion a year stolen from individuals, corporations and governments."[35]

As Debra A. Valentine, general counsel for the U.S. Federal Trade Commission, stated, "Ponzi [pyramid] schemes not only injure consumers. In many cases, they affect the daily operations of banks and taint the banking industry's overall reputation for safety and soundness."[36] Charles Ponzi used a bank for his operations, opening many accounts in fictitious names and using his influence to cover overdrafts. The bank went under as Ponzi's scheme unraveled.[37]

Ponzi schemes raise many questions. What is it that makes these schemes so appealing? How do con artists entice educated, wealthy individuals and representatives of large financial institutions to hand them huge sums of money?[38] How do they tempt middle income and low income investors to follow them unquestioningly? What is it that makes this type of fraudulent scheme "international and global" like a virus that catches all humans? What is it that makes these schemes so difficult to uncover and almost impossible to eliminate?

Among the plots of confidence men, or "con artists" as they are called, there is much that is especially instructive about human weakness and antisocial behavior. Ponzi schemes are just as appealing to con artists as they are to their investing victims. For the investors, the schemes offer many enticing features, not the least of which is an incredibly high return. For con artists, the schemes provide a means of repeat "plays" with the same "marks," that is, the victims who roll over or increase their investment.[39] Some fraudulent games can be played only once or a few times, as in games with loaded dice and marked cards; these frauds are discovered fairly quickly. In contrast, a Ponzi

THE PONZI SCHEME PUZZLE

scheme can last two to three years, and in the good times of a market bubble even longer.[40] A tax consultant who "managed" his client's assets kept his scheme alive from 1978 to 1989.[41] In rare cases, a scheme may last more than ten years;[42] Madoff's case was unique and seems to have gone on for over twenty years. Perhaps he did start his business legitimately, and only later began to defraud investors. Or perhaps by drawing investors from around the world he could continue the scheme longer.

Yet the main feature of every Ponzi scheme is its *inevitable end*. As the number of investors grows, the number of new investors must grow *exponentially*. This is because as their money is used to pay the previous investors, the new investors must now be paid as well. Because one of the attractive features of a Ponzi scheme is the promise of a higher return than current market yields, payments to these new investors must be covered from yet other new investors. Therefore, a Ponzi scheme is the inverse of compounding in finance. New investors' money must cover not only the high obligations to the new investors but also the high returns to the previous investors (who covered the obligations of the investors before them).

Inevitably, when the fountain of new investors dries up, the scheme ends in a "bust."[43] Ponzi schemes usually last longer than the con artist's payment obligations suggest, because many investors are repeat players. They not only roll over their investment but also add to it, as payment of very high interest rates persists. In the case of the Baptist Foundation of Arizona, 94 percent of the investments, which were in the form of short-term loans, were reinvested when the loans came due, until the scheme came to an end.[44]

In the end, both parties lose. But each party loses in a different way. Though most investors end up losing all or much of the money they invested, there are notable exceptions among them. Ponzi schemers share the fruits of their embezzlement with the *early group of investors*. However, even the early investors may lose their profits;

they are not immune from the claims of the losing investors, as we shall learn in Chapter 6. The "winning" investors may have to repay their gains (if not all their recouped investments) to a bankruptcy trustee and share these payments with other, less fortunate, investors. Only those who managed to retrieve their capital and earnings in time—usually many years before the scheme is uncovered—may perhaps retain their investment and in some cases their gains as well. As for the con artists, if caught they may lose the money they embezzled, unless they have spent it all or managed to stash away some of it. They end up in court, and sometimes in prison.

This book analyzes the reasons for the local and global success and the longevity of such schemes and seeks to understand the nature of the con artists and their victims. Therefore, the book does not tell the story of any particular con artist. Nor does it offer statistical data even though it does occasionally cite published numbers. Instead, the book takes a middle road. It combines many stories, derived mostly from court cases, and some from studies, newspapers, and articles, to show the patterns of such frauds, the nature of the con artists, and the character of their victims. To be sure, these patterns are not without exceptions. And yet, because they are based on a sufficiently large number of cases, the patterns tell us much about human nature, about our society, and also about ourselves.

Finally, a word about the theoretical structure of this book, or lack of it. *The Ponzi Scheme Puzzle* does not belong to any particular discipline. In fact, it is the product of a mix of disciplines. The facts are drawn mostly from legal cases, but not from the legal rules that are the focus of these cases. Yet, there are few exceptions, especially in Chapter 6, which discusses the legal proceedings after the schemes are uncovered and the victims make their claims from third parties, and from other victims who fared better. The descriptions and analysis of sales by con artists and the receptivity of affinity groups draw to some extent on sociology. Psychology helps understand the character of con artists and the nature of their victims. The context combines finance and business; pyramid schemes are built on sales and advertising. Although the book does not aim at arguing about the theory of interdisciplinary work, it might demonstrate the use of drawing on many disciplines—and probably also the weakness of doing so.

Chapter 1 analyzes the design and pattern of the con artists' attractive offers and how they hide their deception. The deceptions are covered not only in the words con artists use but also in their actions, forms of payments, and misleading attitudes; a striking example of deception is the con artists' professed *reluctance* to accept the investors' money. But that is not enough; schemes must be sold. This issue leads us to Chapter 2, which deals with how Ponzi schemes are advertised and sold. It shows how con artists draw attention to themselves, and how they recruit their sales force and target the vulnerable victims. But that too is not enough; schemes must be believable. So Chapter 3 focuses on the core of con artists' success. It demonstrates how close their actions are to those of many humans—and even animals. We all "make believe." Not only adults but even children learn such behavior instinctively at a very early age. Even chimpanzees and gorillas can conspire to defraud one of their species. In addition, con artists remind us of honest people. They are similar to entrepreneurs, eternally and unshakably optimistic, and they act like (and *are*) gifted salespersons. Con artists make it hard to distinguish their schemes from lawful activities. If so, are we all con artists, or victims? The suggested answer is that the players in these games have unique and sometimes treacherous character flaws.

Chapter 4 discusses the character of con artists and their victims: the kind of people who are driven to act as con artists—mimics of trustworthiness—and why they can be mistaken for trustworthy individuals.[45] We deal with the tendency of both con artists and their victims to become addicted to the game, and we highlight the dark side of con artists—their narcissistic character disorder, lack of empathy. We examine the character traits and behavior of their victims as well: a large dose of gullibility, an inclination to risk taking, and the need for feeling special and exclusive.

Chapter 5 deals with the aftermath of a Ponzi scheme mess. We learn about the varying reactions of victims when they discover they have been defrauded. We look at how some continue to follow the defrauders, some wish to forget it ever happened, and some carry out the sad spectacle of victims fighting victims, and the attempts of the courts and the law to find the right balance among the victims' claims. This chapter ends with the public's views of the diversity of con artists and types of victims.

Chapter 6 brings us to the courts. It deals with the closure of Ponzi schemes, clearing the shambles in the relationships among the victims and reaching to the helpers of the con artists. Difficult issues arise as the trustee in the bankruptcy court and other claimants seek to collect as much money as possible to be divided equitably among the victims. Not all victims bear the same burden. Early investors may have managed to collect their investments and high returns as well. Later investors may have lost all or some of their investments. Should those who collected all repay some of the money they received, to share with those who lost all? What if the fortunate investors lost or spent their money years ago? What is the legal status of "feeders" that helped the con artists recruit new investors? These questions are clearer than the answers. Yet the discussion highlights the difficulties of dividing the assets fairly among the victims.

What lessons can we learn from these stories and analysis? The Epilogue offers a number of observations. Our attitude toward con artists is ambivalent, perhaps because their behavior is so close to that of honest people and businesses. Or perhaps because con artists act like the social leaders with whom they are likely to mingle. Or perhaps because their actions are necessary in shaking up a complacent society. Therefore, self-protection from charming and dangerous con artists must involve self-examination. The more captivating the con artists seem, the more tempting their stories and their promises are, the more vulnerable we may be to their lethal offerings. The law may help protect us. Our logic may help protect us. The warnings we hear from others may help protect us. But the most powerful protection against these enticing people, their stories, and their promises is self-awareness. It is finding out the extent to which we might be drawn to such schemes and to their attractive schemers. Once we recognize our own tendencies, we can better protect ourselves from their toxic attraction.

Chapter 1

Con Artists At Work

A. THREE STORIES OF PONZI SCHEMERS

1. Charles Ponzi

In a constant search for ideas that would appeal to investors, Charles Ponzi read in 1919 about postal stamps, redeemable by the issuing governments in their own currencies. He calculated that trading on the difference between the value of the currencies in which these stamps were issued could bring enormous profits. For example, he would buy 100 stamps for 100 Italian lire, which are worth, say, $20. If the price of the lire rose and their value increased to $30, he would surrender the stamps for the 100 lire and buy dollars with the lire, at a profit of $10—or a 50 percent return.

These calculations may have looked convincing on paper, provided the scheme was carried out with respect to a few stamps, and only some of the time; and provided, of course, the currency price differences rose in the right direction, and provided as well that the governments continued to redeem the stamps. The calculations were not correct with respect to bagsful of stamps to be carried across the ocean from Italy, and the long-term plan of collecting millions of dollars, especially if the Italian government ceased to redeem its stamps and stopped paying cash for surrendered stamps.

Nonetheless, Ponzi launched his project without hesitation and with the greatest enthusiasm, though with little long-term planning.

In business, he showed poetic tendencies. As he wrote in his autobiography: "A new rainbow had come within my range of vision. The most spectacular I ever saw. With renewed energy and enthusiasm, I chased after it. I caught up with it. When I did, I found fifteen millions of dollars at the end of it. I should have called it a day. And quitted [sic] while the quitting was good. I didn't. Hence, this story."[1] Describing how he conceived of the idea and verified it, he wrote: "In all, it had cost me less than four dollars to lay the foundation for a venture which nine months thence, had an outstanding indebtedness of $15,000,000."[2]

Ponzi convinced relatives and friends to invest in his personal notes. He promised a return of 10 percent a *month*, when banks were paying about 5 percent a *year*. As he began to pay this incredible return, other investors knocked on his door, bringing millions.

The stamp currency arbitrage could not materialize on such a scale, if it could materialize at all. It is not clear how much Ponzi invested in the venture, although one publication suggested that his investment amounted to about $30.[3] In any event, the stamp investment did not come close to the $15 million that investors had entrusted to him. The investment produced a minuscule fraction of the returns that Ponzi had promised. Revenue dried up soon after he started the venture, as governments ceased to pay cash for surrendered stamps.[4] The governments' payback in their currencies was, after all, the foundation of the proposed business.

Even though he was an incorrigible optimist, once Ponzi was holding about $5 million of investors' money, he recognized that the investment could not possibly bring the promised profits. As he explained in his book, "[My] predicament was relatively critical. With four or five million dollars in cash and every opportunity to beat it for parts not reached by extradition treaties, it could not be called critical. It was ideal. But for a stubborn cuss like me, determined to stick it out to the end, it was more than critical. It was hopeless."[5] And later: "It never occurred to me to pocket all the ready cash and duck out. If I had, I wouldn't have been called the darn fool as many times as I have been."[6] He could choose to disappear with the money or stay and continue the game. He chose to stay because, he wrote without elaborating, "what kind of life I would lead [if I disappeared]."[7] The meaning of this statement becomes clear in the later part of his autobiography. Ponzi had "an unlimited confidence in luck [and his] ability to exploit it," clinging to the belief that there was a chance of success: "I went headlong, like a bull in a china shop, to smash all precedents and principles of high finance as it was preached, but not practiced on Wall Street."[8] He hoped to invest the money in a legitimate profitable business, such as banking, while gradually lowering the promised returns.[9] In the meantime, unbeknownst to investors, he used the money raised from later investors to pay the promised return to earlier investors, cover marketing costs, and finance a lavish lifestyle.

When rumors that Ponzi was bankrupt began to circulate, investors clamored for their money. He paid them back quickly, to reduce his obligations of the enormously high returns, which were depleting his resources. But he remained $4 million short and was arrested, convicted, and sent to prison; on his release, he was deported to his homeland, Italy.[10]

A Ponzi scheme uncovered in 2000 was identical. The defendants "allegedly sold promissory notes with no source of income other than the investors' funds. The indictment alleged that, after collecting funds from investors, the defendants would facilitate the deposit of these funds into bank accounts controlled by co-conspirators. The deposited funds would then be used to further the operation of the Ponzi scheme and the personal enjoyment of the defendants."[11]

It should be noted that the investors and followers of Charles Ponzi had similar approaches to these investments and shared a similar dream. He may have instinctively offered them what they sought:

not merely a rational investment, but something that they could be proud of, an inventive investment by one of their kind—an Italian immigrant! As we shall see, the victims of Ponzi schemes are often drawn to invest by something other than rational, calculating business evaluations.

2. Bernard Madoff

Perhaps the most astonishing characteristic of Bernard Madoff's $40–60 billion (who knows?) Ponzi scheme is not its magnitude or worldwide reach, but rather the identity of his investors. Many sophisticated people and heads of large organizations were misled. Among them were investment management firms, foreign banks, hedge funds, wealthy individual investors, brokerage firms, pension funds, charities, universities, and insurance companies. All these investors relied on Madoff's reputation for "absolute returns" of profits in a down market as well as an up market. "'Bernie had a good reputation at the SEC with a lot of highly placed people as an innovator as somebody who speaks his mind and knows what's going on in the industry. I think he was seen as a valuable resource to the commission in its deliberations on things like market data,' noted Donald C. Langevoort, a Georgetown University law professor who specializes in securities regulation and served with Madoff on an SEC advisory committee."[12] One person remarked: "It's extraordinary how the hedge fund industry in some way works like Hollywood. You know, you have stars. You don't understand, but you have big stars. And you need to invest in big fund with big names, famous people. You need to invest in that thing because it's a big name."[13]

Seldom did investors dare to question Madoff's enigmatic and "proprietary" investment strategy, and those who did were given an ultimatum to either cease probing or be expelled from the select investor group—with their money. Few risked the latter option.

Moreover, investors forgot the indispensable golden rule of investment, diversification: "Don't put all your eggs in one basket." Many invested their entire life savings with Madoff.[14]

Bernard L. Madoff Investment Securities LLC, a securities trading firm founded by the father and managed by his sons and brother, perpetrated his fraud as a trader who purportedly uses a split-strike conversion strategy.[15] This is a legitimate investment strategy combining the purchase of stocks with the use of options to hedge against the risk that the price of the stocks will decline. Madoff claimed to have used this strategy to achieve uniform and higher returns for many consecutive years. He promised "11 percent annual return over the last 15 years, with only 13 losing months," losses that one "feeder fund" paid out.[16] However, the split-strike strategy is not loss-proof. For sophisticated investors, Madoff's promised returns should have raised a red flag about his operations not because the returns were very high but because they were *consistently higher than the market*.

There were other indicators that something was awry. Madoff was secretive about information that other investment managers did not consider proprietary. His secretive attitude violated the policies of certain endowments and institutional investors, policies requiring them to ask and receive this information before making any investments.[17] In addition, Madoff did not charge the usual managers' performance fees of 2 percent of assets under management and 20 percent of profits. He claimed to collect sufficient returns from trading commissions that he received,[18] and whereas fund managers capitalize on their names Madoff suspiciously prohibited his feeder funds—the ones investing their clients' money with Madoff—from disclosing his name on their prospectus.[19] He desired to remain a broker, having custody of the clients' assets, rather than an adviser-fund manager (which is more strictly regulated in some respects). By avoiding receipt of advisory fees, he seems to have escaped regulation as adviser for many years (until 2006).

So why were sophisticated investors drawn to Madoff? One explanation is that they were drawn to the privilege of investing with him. Investors begged their "connected" friends to pull strings and persuade Madoff to accept their money. Madoff's secrecy played well into this image. Few wanted to rock the boat and be forced out of the closed circle.[20] Further, few investors were willing to admit their ignorance by asking questions about how the split-strike conversion strategy actually worked. Indeed, Madoff's posture of secrecy strengthened his image as a genius.

Madoff had the endorsement of the Jewish community. Being a Jew, he had a stamp of approval from institutions supported by many of his direct investors, such as synagogues, members of Jewish congregations, prominent figures in Jewish communities, and foundations. Madoff "was God" to the investors, explained Elie Wiesel; "it was a myth that he created around him . . . the myth of exclusivity. . . . He gave the impression that maybe a hundred people belonged to his club."[21]

By the 1990s, Madoff had been introduced to a large and important investment advisory institution. This institution helped spread the Ponzi scheme to investors in Europe, and to banks and feeder funds around the world.[22] Records show that Madoff defrauded more than ten thousand investors worldwide in a scheme that is estimated to have involved between $40 and $65 billion.[23] Although Madoff's was the largest Ponzi scheme to date, it ended just as all the schemes before it had done: when investors' requests for repayment exceeded new investments.

3. Gregory Bell

In late 2001, Gregory Bell established a number of funds, which he represented in various capacities (agent, director, manager, partner). The ostensible purpose of "Funds" was to lend money to Thousand

Lakes LLC, whose purpose was to buy consumer goods from two suppliers, Enchanted Family Buying Company and Nationwide Resources International, Inc. Thousand Lakes was assumed to sell the goods to the retailers before it borrowed the money from Funds. The Funds would profit from interest payments on the Thousand Lakes notes, which were ostensibly secured by the goods held by Thousand Lakes, and by its accounts receivable and credit insurance. Added protection for the Funds was a purported "lock-box" arrangement with Thousand Lakes "which gave the Funds control over the bank account into which the retailer was supposed to wire payments for the underlying goods." This design is similar to securitization of loans. It combined financial assets such as loans and notes with real assets (consumer goods), presumably easily tradable.

> Funds provided potential investors with a Confidential Information tion Memorandum... describing the Funds' investment strategy, including the terms and protections as described here. Between 2002 and 2008, the Funds raised over $2.5 billion from individuals, retirement plans, individual retirement accounts, trusts, corporations, partnerships, and other hedge funds.
>
> But in September of 2008, it was revealed that Funds' investments were a total sham.

There were no goods, no true purchase orders, and no real invoices of goods that were purchased by retailers. Enchanted Family Buying and Nationwide Resources International did not operate real businesses. They were shell companies—empty vessels: "Early investors in the Funds were paid not out of any money raised from the sale of consumer goods but from funds invested by subsequent lenders."[24] Later investors lost. It was a classic Ponzi scheme. The context of this scheme was quite sophisticated and complex; nonetheless, and perhaps because it was complex, investors relied on the con artists'

THE PONZI SCHEME PUZZLE

salespersons rather than on what they offered in deciding to participate. Not surprisingly, complexity and secrecy have the same effect:
they make it difficult to understand and check the investment.

These three stories seem very different and deal with a variety of
businesses and business structures, involving several types of actors
and approaches. Yet fundamentally, they are all the same. As we shall
see, surprisingly, con artists and their victims are more similar than
meets the eye.

B. THE BASIC DESIGN

1. Drawing Attention to the Offer

In this chapter, we learn about the drawing power of Ponzi schemers'
offerings. One aspect of their attraction is a promise of high return
coupled with low risk (or seemingly none). A second aspect of the
drawing power is the exceptional and creative stories and explanations for the offering, devised to satisfy the curiosity of potential investors. A third aspect is that the offerings are unique and scarce.

A. HIGH RETURNS AT NO RISK

Con artists, like salespersons in general, draw the victims' attention
by means of enticing offers. The first two components of such offers
are very high returns *and* no risk. All Ponzi schemes share this very
effective draw of an unusually high promised return. An offer of
paying, for example, 10 percent a month (paid sometimes every
month, or not later than every quarter) persisting even when general
lending rates are 5–10 percent a year makes people stop in their
tracks. These fabulous promised returns vary. In one case the con
artist offered 40 percent within six to eight weeks, $9,000 on $23,000
in thirty days, $15,000 on $23,000 in four months, and 75 percent on
$40,000 within nine months.[25] On February 24, 2011, a man who

seems to have been implicated in a $326 million Ponzi scheme in Jamaica (appropriately called "Cash Plus") was accused in the United States of orchestrating another scheme that offered returns of up to 100 percent a month.[26] As the court in still another case noted, the promised return was "astronomical."[27]

Extremely high interest or profit is a hallmark of Ponzi schemes around the world. The Romanian scheme Caritas offered a return of eight times the amount invested, within three months. Even in a country beset by inflation, this was an unbelievable return.[28]

An Australian con artist offered up to 200 percent from a nonexistent commercial business in carpet contracts.[29] In yet another case, a con artist who "pretended to sell lucrative interests in oil and gas leases . . . in one case promised the investor a guaranteed *monthly* payment of $934 for every $25,000 invested."[30]

Interest can be tweaked when the promised returns vary and is reported in monthly statements, for example, showing 7 percent to 17.6 percent per month,[31] or 15 to 20 percent every ninety days, all with "little or no risk."[32] Such variations draw attention and create expectations, and more likely, excitement: "What will this month's return be?"

The stock markets, lotteries, and fabulous payments on the part of famous people make high returns believable. When markets "bubble," investors hear and read much about enormous profits made in hours or even seconds. When lotteries abound, investors may eagerly read about millions of dollars won by the lucky holders of the right lottery ticket. When sports stars, actors, corporate management, and investment bankers earn fabulous amounts, so much more than by a lifetime of hard work, investors may ask themselves, "Why not me?"

Businesspeople may even be tempted to involve their own enterprise in what turns out later to be a Ponzi scheme. A significant discount on the price of commodities that their business needs can tempt them to prepay for the commodities, but in fact end up paying a con artist. In one case, the regional sales manager of a national corporation that sold corn, bean, and alfalfa seed, offered a discount program to customers who prepaid for these products before the planting season. The "early pay" to gain a discount had to be deposited in Agri-Management Corporation, which the con artist controlled and misappropriated. In this case the customers were lucky; the corporation deducted their misappropriated payments from their bills. After all, these were customers, and the manager had been picked by the corporation.[33]

Attractive Ponzi schemes accompany the sky-high interest rate with assurance of very low risk. Madoff's scheme promised lower returns than those offered in most schemes, though they were still higher than usual. However, his scheme entailed the unbelievable feature a return consistently higher than market prices. This consistency had an effect similar to reduced risk; it lowered the anxiety of risk-averse investors and attracted conservative, long-term, nontrading investors. Madoff offered the members of his "exclusive investment club . . . steady, double-digit returns even when the market was down."[34] In contrast, the con artist Randall Treadwell promised an unbeatable complication: investments in loans that were "zero risk" and could pay "50% interest per month and 2% interest compounded monthly."[35] These terms too attracted some investors who were sufficiently impressed by the returns to accept the zero risk promise as well.

Low risk is sometimes supported by promised collateral, such as a real estate mortgage, insurance, or government or bank obligations. In *United States v. Hayes*, investors lost more than $1 million in an offering of individual equity shares in oil and gas properties. The con artist attracted investors by assuring them that 85 percent of their investments would be used to "acquire and operate income-producing oil and gas properties" and that the investments were "*risk-free* because they were covered by insurance."[36] An offer involving promissory notes based on currency trading that guaranteed interest payments of 2 percent per month was also sufficiently enticing, along with the con artist's presentation.[37] The title of another con artist's instrument (an International Certificate of Deposit) seems to have proved convincing.[38] Similarly, the stories of con artists may include explicit assurance of low risk. For example, the story about oil fields and the like is not about *searching* for the riches, but about *having found* them. Old mines have already been discovered. The government surplus that can be bought for close to nothing is already known to the con artist. No need to search, and no risk of failing; one need merely collect the rich resource.[39]

Short-term obligations are viewed as low-risk investments. They reduce the anxiety of parting with one's money. It makes sense to assume that short-term obligations are less risky, but not entirely risk-free. In one case, the victim was aware that the con artist had been served with a court cease-and-desist order. The investor understood the implications of such an order, which prohibited the con artist from raising and receiving additional investments. Nonetheless, the con artist represented that the investment would pay 15 percent interest in a very short period and was secured by the U.S. Government. This assurance must have tempted the victim, who invested $113,000 with the con artist.[40]

B. STORIES TO SATISFY INVESTORS' CURIOSITY

An important element of the Ponzi design is the need to satisfy the investors' curiosity. A promise of unbelievably high profits does not necessarily induce all investors to hand over their money, but it makes them stop and listen attentively. Potential investors may be skeptical; they may ask questions. They may want to know, Where does all this money come from?

Con artists' stories explain the sources of the high returns that they promise. Although the schemes share the same basic structure, they come wrapped in a rich variety of investment stories. Barbara R. Rowe noted that the "range of Ponzi-type offerings is a tribute to the imagination and ingenuity of the promoters of these swindles." The offerings can describe "just about any kind of deal you might imagine, from . . . synthetic rubies to hydroponic farming, windmills, tropical islands and equipment used in outer space,"[41] constructing ambulances from automotive coachwork "shells",[42] buying and leasing bus stop shelters,[43] buying mortgages and promissory notes secured by them,[44] buying and restoring historic buildings,[45] investing in leases of telephone numbers in Canada,[46] in gold mines,[47] in oil,[48] in precious stones,[49] in telecommunication systems,[50] in Internet kiosks,[51] in an investment company,[52] in tax lien certificates,[53] in legal settlements,[54] and in a payroll services business.[55] There are investments in leasing electronic advertising banners,[56] lease of pay telephones (back in 2000),[57] a Malaysian latex glove manufacturing company,[58] and building a large processing plant,[59] as well as a grocery distribution business,[60] electronics,[61] and radio stations.[62] A proven attractive investment is a food products business that made monthly payments without sending tax forms, thus allowing investors to avoid tax payments.[63] There are also offers of investments in commodity futures,[64] and purchase of foreclosed properties that were sold at a profit.[65]

Then there are investments many people do not understand and know nothing about. "In a fast-changing financial marketplace," declares one financial fitness fact sheet, "Ponzi promoters have an increasing number of ways to dress up their schemes and shield them from ready detection."[66] These include insurance,[67] "certificates of deposit evidencing billions of dollars,"[68] foreign currency,[69] real estate investments,[70] loans "created, packaged, marketed, and sold" as a series of real estate-backed investments,"[71] bridge loans, and court settlement funds.[72] There are also offers of investments with a "trusted financial advisory firm with agents and representatives who can be trusted to give advice on insurance and financial matters," or as reliable "feeders" to another investment manager,[73] and to other global financial services.[74]

A con artist named Motilall Sudeen offered "high yield investment programs," including an arrangement in which the investors' principal payment "would remain safely in banks [with] little or no risk," with "marquee banks, including the World Bank and the [International Monetary Fund]," and "the trading programs were monitored by the federal government." Investors were periodically paid "dividends" thereby "encouraging to roll over their investments instead of seeking immediate returns."[75] Sudeen and his friends "continued to maintain the appearance of safety by issuing investors bogus 'Private Placement Agreements' and 'Joint Venture Agreements.'" He told investors that his personal wealth guaranteed their investment and that they should buy banks' certificates of deposit so that he could use the credit based on these certificates to borrow and invest.[76]

These lists are in fact far longer. The investment stories are limited only by imagination. One con artist can create more than one story. Thus a con artist told various stories to suit his potential clients' interests. His companies were investing in "the top three banks in the United States," or had "clients in twenty-nine countries," or "made investments guaranteed by the United States government," or "had invested $2 billion in a gold mine in Mexico," or "were working on a billion-dollar Columbus-era 'find' on the bottom of the ocean." In an October 2004 meeting with potential investors, he stated that his "companies were directing investments towards 'humanitarian' projects, including projects benefitting 'people that are hungry and . . . in various needs throughout the world.'"[77]

Con artists' stories can be designed to match the experiences of the environment and understanding of potential victims. For example, representatives of charitable institutions are more likely to believe a story about a secret donor who would match their investments. Charitable institutions frequently receive donations from benefactors who wish to remain anonymous, perhaps to avoid the pressure of requests for donations from others. Charitable institutions may also keep their donor lists secret, to avoid competition from other charities. Matching donations is a common practice in corporate charitable giving. So a story may be plausible, but the familiar design is fraudulent. Using a fake organization (the Foundation for New Era Philanthropy), John Bennett raised hundreds of millions of dollars by promising the investing institutions to double their money in six months.[78] He explained to them that the money would come from matching grants made by anonymous benefactors.

C. CON ARTISTS' STORIES ARE EXCEPTIONAL AND CREATIVE

Despite their enormous variety, most of the con artists' stories share important characteristic features. They present exceptional situations; they are diverse, complex, and unique. Uniqueness commands admiration. It is creative. It also breeds excitement; people admire creators and get excited over novelty. Some of the con artists' business stories are truly exceptional; tropical islands, bus stop shelters, and windmills are not run-of-the-mill investments. These con artists' stories are about investments that show breadth and complexity. Gary Dean benKeith, who operated a Ponzi scheme for a number of years, was quoted as saying: "Gold? . . . That's just a small part of it. You know what gold is? It's glitter. . . . It's neon. It gets people excited."[79]

The investment stories of con artists have the aura of a thrilling treasure hunt. A treasure hunt promises a high reward, an adventure, a risk-bound mystery. And because treasure hunting is based on personal ability, it differs from, and is more respectable than, many forms of gambling, which are based mostly on luck. Thus, discovering a treasure gives the finder a sense of personal achievement and gains the admiration of others. Owning something unique has an emotional attraction. It bestows on the owners a similar quality of uniqueness. Just as importantly, the investment is the treasure, which the investors have discovered. But because the treasure is unlimited (the con artist is always ready to issue his magic notes to new investors), it is unnecessary to keep information about the treasure secret. Instead, investors—the discoverers of the treasure—can enjoy the pride of being the *first* to discover—the pride of owning the map to the treasure. Investors can immediately offer friends and acquaintances a gift—an investment that few have heard of. Besides, a gift may bring other benefits. It bears an implicit hope of future reciprocity: "A gift is an exchange in which a transfer is not mediated by price, but is rather reciprocated at the discretion of the receiver."[80] Reciprocal giving can rise to the level of an obligation. Obtaining another person's obligation in this way is satisfying too.

C. GAINING TRUST AND CONCEALING THE TRUTH

1. Words Can Be Used to Signal Trust

A. WORDS CAN DENOTE TRUSTWORTHINESS

As we rummage through the con artists' toolbox of persuasions, we find typical signals of trustworthiness. Some words reflect institutions that signal reliability, such as *bank* and *securities exchange*. Look at how Charles Ponzi's personal notes signaled reliability and respectability. How did they induce investors by the thousands to hand him over about $15 million? Here is what they said:

> The Securities Exchange Company, for and in consideration of the sum of exactly $1000 of which receipt is hereby acknowledged, agrees to pay to the order of ———, upon presentation of

this voucher at ninety days from date, the sum of exactly $1500 at the company office, 27 School Street, Room 227, or at any bank. Signed: The Securities Exchange Company, Per Charles Ponzi.[81]

These notes are interesting. First, Ponzi's business at 27 School Street was Securities Exchange Company, presumably a trust-building name at that time.[82] It reflected business expertise and commanded respect. Second, the notes were fashioned after a usual bank note, which signaled a solid, low-risk investment. Third, presentation was required. Presentation for payment at a bank denotes sufficient funds for immediate payment (rather than payment by a check, which could delay the outlay of cash). It also denotes care on the part of the con artist; presenters must identify themselves.

One difference between Ponzi's notes and the text of a typical banknote is the word *voucher* in connection with in-person presentation. A voucher usually relates to receipt of goods and brings to mind a purchase rather than an obligation to pay. But the term *vouch* reflects a promise, a guarantee, even an oath. I speculate that the mixed form of purchase and obligation to pay may have strengthened the effect of business respectability.

Notes issued by other Ponzi schemers may include the words "certificates of deposit," in the image of bank CDs, or a combination of the con artist's business with a bank note. One con artist distributed to investors a "Deposit Agreement (Capital Funding Program)," which stated that investors' money would be put into "project funding," by investing in medium-term corporate notes.[83] Con artists' notes contained the word *guaranteed* and used phrases such as "You cannot lose," "You can only win." In response to a reporter's question, one swindling organization wrote: "The full faith and credit of BFA stands behind all investment products. This is clearly stated in all offering documents."[84] The language is telling. "Full faith and credit" are the words used in the federal government obligations. The words on nongovernment obligations seem to give the impression that the obligations are (or at least reflect the status of) government securities. A con artist used a shell bank in Nassau, named Pacific Exchanger's Bank, Limited.[85] The word *bank* is supported by the word *exchange(r)*, which triggers the image of a securities exchange or money exchange— both respectable and profitable businesses. Certificates entitled "partnership trust units" have little legal meaning but invoke feelings of both closeness (partnership) and trust.[86] Note obligations entitled "gold-backed railroad bonds" have caught investors' fancy,[87] since *gold* is the ever-enticing metal and *railroad* is associated with industry and solidity. Bonds imply safety, compared to equities. The name for this particular obligation thus combined the promise of liquidity and some glamour: the bonds "would be traded in international markets and would generate [astronomical] returns on investment."[88]

A con artist issued notes "with recourse."[89] The words are misleading, implying a promise to pay; yet legally, they are unnecessary. "Recourse" would be available even if the words were not added. However, the words *without recourse* have legal meaning: the holder of the note *cannot* resort to the seller of the note. For nonlawyers, the words "with recourse" seem to suggest an added obligor, but this is not what they actually mean.

In June 2005, in Los Angeles, John C. Jeffers was sentenced to fourteen years in federal prison and ordered to pay $26 million in restitution to more than eighty victims. Jeffers and his confederate, John Minderhout, ran what they described as a high-yield investment program, "Short Term Financing Transaction." From 1996 to 2000, they collected money from investors around the world. "[L]etters to some victims . . . falsely claimed the program had been licensed by the Federal Reserve and . . . had a relationship with the International Monetary Fund and the United States Treasury."[90] But it seems that investors did not verify the claims. Instead, they believed.

"Mumbo jumbo" contract language can confuse and help conceal the true nature of a transaction. Examples are abundant. In one real estate deal, for example, investors paid for mortgage-type instruments to finance the purchase of low-income residential property.[91] Instead of a mortgage or other security device on the property, the investors received a "money assignment," an "agreement assignment," or a "trust deed beneficial interest." As one court explained: "None of these terms had any specific meaning; and none were commonly used in the real estate business. Although the terms used in the offers resembled the terms for commonly used security devices, which do provide the sellers with liens upon the property being sold, defendant's use of the terms was quite the opposite."[92] The money assignments, agreement assignments, and trust deed beneficial interests were meaningless. Because the language of the instruments was complex, investors did not understand what they were signing or receiving.

"Units of indebtedness" sounded good for selling land in Florida (some of which was underwater). The notes promised a return of 200 percent in sixty days, to be paid in cash or land. The obligations sent meaningful signals; they seemed to imply profits from the sale of the land. At the same time, the obligations signaled to investors that the promisor was sure of this level of profit because he undertook to pay cash. Perhaps the notes suggested he reserved for himself the right to pay cash, in which case the choice signaled a belief that the land could be sold at a profit higher than 200 percent, and if that opportunity arose he would choose to pay cash.[93] "The loans," stated another organization, "are an absolute liability of [the organization]." As empty as they are, the words (especially *absolute*) imply that the organization cannot renege on its obligations.[94]

B. SIGNALS TO RAISE TRUSTWORTHINESS

Con artists use signals that encourage potential investors to identify with them. One such signal is an assurance that the salespersons have "skin in the game," meaning they themselves bought the offered investment for their own account. This assurance is followed by a story of the successful investment. Thus, in one case a con artist drew potential investors by assuring them that she doubled the money she invested personally in the same investments.[95]

Another form of assurance is behavior rather than words. First, the con artist appears to be as wealthy as the potential investors and offers the victims advice and support. After all, wealthy persons belong to the wealthy investors' class. This in itself raises trust. More importantly, the con artists masquerade as successful wealthy people, showing no inclination or desire to advise on, let alone manage, their friends' assets. But sometimes they may be convinced to do so. Joel Ross Goheen acted like a person who merely wished to do a favor for his friends.[96] Reed Slatkin went even further and served as manager of his victims' assets *free of charge*, behavior that showed friendship and his not needing the money. Waiver of the fees diverted attention from the risk of handing over to this charitable manager the far larger amounts of the investments.[97]

Some con artists' payments look like payments but are in fact merely promises. For example, con artists may send their investors statements that look like bank statements *instead* of actually paying investors the interest due. Because investors view bank "statements" as proof that their money is safe in the bank, they accept these statements as "money in the bank." Legitimate bank statements are evidence of safety and availability of the money on demand. Frequent statements showing the amounts due reflect the repeated assertion that "I have the money in a safe place, ready for you whenever you demand it." Madoff sent his victims prompt periodic reports on their holdings. As one victim testified before a congressional committee, he would check the reports listing "his investments" against the stock prices published in the newspapers and because the prices were identical he assumed that Madoff had invested the money in these securities and so Madoff's reporting was accurate.[98]

Enron Corporation adopted a similar technique.[99] Like investors who receive "statements" instead of money, Enron's public investors received "price statements" instead of cash. Unless they sold their investment notes, however, the paper profits evaporated when the Enron Ponzi scheme came to its inevitable end. In one case the con artist sent the same message orally, telling an investor that the investors could have their money anytime. That was sufficient assurance as well.[100]

C. IT DEPENDS ON HOW YOU SAY FALSE THINGS: SPECIFIC PROMISES WITH VAGUE ROLES

If con artists play vague and conflicting roles, investors can be misled. But because the different roles are not so clear, investors may simply ignore the distinctions. For example, a con artist may play the role of an agent and the role of an owner. He has the choice to appear in one capacity as representative of a corporation, or its owner, or the seller of securities to the corporation. Each role involves its own power and responsibility. The ability to change the role can induce "self-serving behavior,"[101] that is, to mislead. For example, an owner may trade his property as he wishes; an agent may trade the same property only as the owner directs. If a broker masquerades as an owner of the property, and especially if other parties seem to believe the broker is indeed the owner, the broker may be tempted to act as an owner and deal with the property in a way that benefits him (the broker) more than according to the owner's directives. He can then collect more than was due to him. However, usually investors are not inclined to ask, "Who are we dealing with? Who do you represent?" They focus more on the promises of the con artist. On promises, investors would usually concentrate on specifics.

Vague promises may be viewed differently. Investors may understand that vague promises offer opportunities for justifying nonpayment and are therefore more suspect than explicit ones. Specific promises leave promisors little wiggle room and almost no pretext to avoid payment. Specific promises are self-limiting; they show that the promisors have voluntarily closed their routes of escaping payments and obligations. Therefore, the promisors are sure about their ability to pay.

Specific promises signal both honesty and low risk. Even long-term loans that are paid in small amounts monthly, as with most mortgage loans, suggest reduced risk. Failure to make the monthly payment signals to lenders possible financial problems and a higher probability of default. These signals allow the creditors to take immediate action to reduce their losses.

D. HOW A STORY IS TOLD CAN SIGNAL TRUTHFULNESS

Con artists' stories can be quite detailed. Details increase people's trust. Like specific promises, details limit the speaker's freedom to change the story or reinterpret it, and so the greater the number of details, the more costly it is to lie. In addition, it seems that it is more difficult to remember lies than to remember the truth one has experienced. Therefore, a liar is burdened with more details to memorize and is more prone to forget them. Further, greater detail exposes a person to the risk of verification and discovery. In *An Instance of the Fingerpost*, Iain Pears described the use of details as a method of persuasion: "I told him again. Adding more details, then still more details until the smirk faded from his face, and his hands began to tremble." The listener believed the speaker.[102]

One inconsistent detail can arouse mistrust in all parts of the story, both true and false. It is not surprising that a Ponzi con artist who told venture capitalists different stories in accordance with what he believed they wanted to hear was caught earlier than usual.[103] Another con artist attempted to convince a potential investor in a real estate scam that the money earmarked for specified real estate projects was segregated for the respective projects, and that the investments were secured. The con artist told the investors that one of his employees was fired when he misapplied received funds.[104] These facts could be verified, and indeed investors attempted to verify whether the investments were secured and, on finding no verification, made no more investments.[105] Therefore, people assume that a liar would not be inclined to offer details, give the listeners an opportunity to verify, and risk discovery. Con artists take advantage of this assumption.

We should remember, however, that "[c]on artists are good liars."[106] They may fudge the truth and the lie together. One scam was described as "relatively safe certificates of deposit," but what was also mentioned was an offshore arrangement.[107] The true part could be used as an escape route.

E. REFUSING TO PROVIDE THE DETAILS OF A SCHEME NEED NOT UNDERMINE TRUST

When a con artist refuses to answer questions and disclose details about his scheme, he does not hide his refusal. To the contrary: a con artist may even *note the details that he refuses to divulge* and explain the reasons for the refusal. This posture commands trust as well, by demonstrating openness: "I have nothing to hide. If I refuse to tell you something I will not lie but say so up front." The specificity of the story is not blurred. The refusal is not ambiguous. And if the listeners tend to believe the reason for the refusal, their trust is strengthened.

When asked for details about the investments, some con artists respond: "Do you think I'm going to advertise where this goose that lays the golden egg is, so that everyone can go to it directly? And besides, if more people approach the goose, it will stop laying the golden eggs." Underlying an argument for secrecy is the posture of Ponzi con artists as *inventors*, similar to the justified claims of investors for patents and other intellectual property protections.[108]

This claim carries with it a tinge of moral justification. "I discovered the tree that grows golden fruit, and am entitled to the benefits of my discovery. I am willing to share with you these benefits, but not to relinquish them to you altogether," the con artist might say. "I may trust *you* (and personally, I do), but can we trust all the other investors? Should I just give away the source of fabulous wealth to 'strangers' who are going to exploit it? That may be not only to *my* disadvantage, but to *yours* as well."

In one instance, an investor asked an employee of the con artist for details of the many businesses that Gary, the employer and Ponzi schemer, had been "nebulous" about. The employee replied, "Gary keeps all that stuff really close to himself, because if he divulges it, he would be afraid that he would get scooped on some of the deals."[109] Bernard Madoff responded to questions about his investment strategy in precisely the same way.

> [Someone] once ran into Madoff and asked him how he delivered such consistently high returns. "He says, 'Well, I don't tell you my trading strategy; that's proprietary,' which is not unusual. He says, 'But I can tell you this: I can make money when the market goes up; I can make money when the market goes down; I cannot make money when the market stays flat,' which indicated to me that maybe he's doing some sort of day-trading."[110]

"The way it was vaguely described to us," said a person who asked Madoff the question, "was that the 'New York people' had a system whereby they placed a series of instant trades—at once with futures, currencies and stocks—and out of this magic recipe fell a tiny 1% guaranteed, no-risk profit for the group. You do that 20 times a year, take away management fees and, voilà, a steady 15% return. Man, these guys were good."[111]

2. Familiar Transaction Businesses and Forms Seem to Make Verification Superfluous

Some promises of quick and high returns may seem reasonable because the stories are commonplace. In 2010 Michael Goldberg pleaded guilty to operating a $100 million Ponzi scheme, by promising quick high returns on buying and reselling diamonds or buying foreclosed assets from JPMorgan Bank. He swindled hundreds of investors of more than $30 million during a twelve-year period.[112] As commonplace as this story is, without information and understanding the details it can be fraudulent.

In another case, according to court documents, "John A. Hickey ('Hickey') and his business partner, Mamie Tang ('Tang'), induced over 700 individuals to invest approximately $20 million in two real estate development funds. Their plan was to purchase land in Northern California, prepare the land for residential development, and then resell the properties to developers at a profit." The documents relate the outcome: "As it turned out, however, the investors were duped by false representations regarding land title, guarantees, and securitization of the funds."[113] The couple used the investors' money to pay first investors, and by the time the fraud was discovered the investors had lost about $18.5 million.[114]

Transaction forms that are familiar to investors serve con artists well. Familiar, often-used forms assure investors of what they "know" and thus reduce their level of care. These forms divert the investors' attention from disturbing aspects of the transactions ("Oh, I've done that lots of times"). When investors believe they understand the transaction, they tend to pay less attention to verifying relevant facts and inquiring about what they do not clearly understand.

In May 2002, the *Boston Globe* reported a scheme involving eight banks that lost close to $1 billion.[115] The scheme was designed as lines of credit of short duration (180 days). The lines of credit were backed by receivables due from merchants. This is a common bank transaction in a very familiar form, and it evokes memories of many low-risk transactions. The familiar form of the transaction must have reduced the lenders' attention to other defects and heightened their trust in the promoters. The crucial fact, that the receivables were due from merchants in *India*, may have faded in light of the familiar form and circumstances. It was later discovered, however, that there were no Indian merchants and no receivables.

The well-known form of "limited partnership participations" can also cause alertness to fade. Such "participations" are the traditional form of financing real estate, and oil and gas explorations. Both the giant Enron and the small First Petroleum Inc. used this legal financing form for these types of explorations.[116] However, behind the form could lurk fraudulent schemes.

3. Hiding Fraud by Actions: Prompt Payments That Spell Trustworthiness, Low Risk, and Much More

Actual payments can speak louder than words and divert attention from lack of disclosure. Lance Van Alstyne and his brokers induced investors to buy risky securities. Then they offered prospectuses that disclosed the true nature of the securities, but soon thereafter the investors received checks. Thus the truth was sandwiched between false assurances and receipt of money. The payment distracted investors from the true information. Needless to add, the checks were largely funded by the investors' own principal payments.[117]

Con artists always pay on time (until they stop paying altogether). These payments speak louder than words, and their effects feed Ponzi schemes. The payments diffuse doubts about the stories con artists tell. Prompt repayment of the invested capital also signals low risk. Like the persistent fulfillment of any promise, these payments induce trust. Timely payments at short intervals help establish a reputation for trustworthiness. Each payment brings added proof of the con artist's credibility, strengthening the influence and weight of the previous payments and allaying suspicions about the source of the payments.

When the first question, "Will this person pay?" is answered positively by actual payment of the return, the second question, "Where did he get the money to pay his obligations?" either is not asked or becomes far less important. Payment to investors on demand increases their trust. In one case, the court noted: "[I]n the initial stages of the plan, those investors who wished to withdraw their investments were promptly paid. The effect of such prompt payment, of course, was to convert every investor into a missionary spreading the word of the enormous profits which could be speedily attained with no discernible risk of loss."[118] In a recent case a con artist told one investor he could receive his money back whenever he asked for it.[119] This statement seemed to demonstrate that the con artist had no liquidity problem and that the investment was safe, like a bank demand deposit.

Generous payments received on time help trigger a "herding" effect, regardless of culture, country, or class. They worked their magic in Romania's Caritas. Katherine Verdery reported that those she met in Romania described to her "[o]ver and over" their decision to put money into Caritas. They said that even though, at the beginning, they did not have faith in Caritas, when they saw "everyone else getting money" they "decided to trust it too."[120]

Consistent payments can blur for investors the distinction between interest and capital. Taubman promised investors to return *their capital* in monthly payments and add the profits of 100 percent of their investment after the last payment. He found investors that took the bait.[121] Periodic repayment of their own investments seemed to have the same effect on the investors as payment of interest in other schemes. It appears that the promptness of the payments, and not what the payments consisted of, created trust in the con artist. He was true to his word; that is what counted: "Any story will do, as long as payments are regularly made to earlier investors to provide credibility."[122]

In addition, when checks are paid they may give investors the pleasure of receiving money, almost like an instantaneous gratification. For some investors, there seems to be more pleasure in collecting small amounts often than in receiving a large amount less often. In addition, the checks bring investors the satisfaction of "being right"—a reminder that the investors were correct in deciding to invest with the con artists and in rolling over their short-term investments. The checks provided proof.

When people try to predict the future, they may focus on the *results of a past decision*—for example, in our discussion, that an investment will bring high returns. As returns keep on coming, people predict they will continue to be paid. On the basis of promised and delivered returns, they conclude that this investment is a "sure thing." They focus on the particular evidence—payment of the profits—and view it as evidence of the reliability of the entire transaction. There are many cases in which this assumption is not true. Past performance does not signal future performance in the financial markets, and in the case of Ponzi schemes longevity is in fact a signal for an imminent end, not continued stability. And yet, many new investors who focus on what they learn about the longevity of the purported enterprises may invest toward the end of the scheme, while those who invested at the beginning of the scheme may recoup their investment or even retain some of the profits.[123]

D. HIDING THE VULNERABLE PART OF THE STORY: SECRECY AND COSTLY VERIFICATION

1. Concealing the True Nature of the Ponzi Business

Even if it is believable and enticing, the investment story is the most vulnerable part of the con artist's scheme.[124] For con artists, the danger is that the investors or government officials will attempt to verify the investment story. Some incorrigible Ponzi schemers—those known to the authorities, or those under current investigation—must hide not only their schemes but also their very involvement. Therefore, Ponzi investment stories and the structure of the enterprise contain a number of elements that can help convince those who are inclined to be convinced of the stories' truthfulness. They help hide the information that would destroy the perception of truthfulness, and trust in the people behind the schemes.

Sometimes hiding the true identity of the actors behind the legal entities through which they act can be crucial to the Ponzi schemer. In a 2008 case, a court found that an offshore bank and other entities through which the defendant operated "did not maintain any formality or distinction between the assets that belonged to one or the other because the bank was a mere pretense." The bank was a convenient entity in which to hold the defendant's money.[125] Therefore, using these entities to conceal the true actors may not always be successful when the matter comes to court. But for investors it may be harder and more expensive to uncover the true ownership and control of these entities in order to reach the con artist.

2. Use of Justified Secrecy

Justified secrecy can become part of a Ponzi scheme's attraction. Secrecy can make the con artists' stories more believable. Secrecy about the scheme also helps the con artist conceal the truth about the scheme, as illustrated in the case of Michael Calozza.[126]

Calozza was an agent for a mutual insurance company, Sons of Norway. He made up a letter purporting to be written from the Sons of Norway to himself and other members of its staff. In the letter the company offered the staff a "tax-advantaged high-yield secure investment." It was unfair, Calozza told his clients, to deprive clients of this opportunity. He suggested that the clients borrow against their insurance policies and hand the borrowed money to him in exchange for his personal high-interest promissory notes. He would then invest the money in the investment offered to staff members only, and pass the returns through to his investing clients. Because in the fake letter the Sons of Norway seemed to be limiting the (nonexistent) investment to its staff, an element of deception was involved in offering the opportunity to the clients. However, the circumstances suggested that deceiving the insurance company in this case was justifiable. Calozza advised his clients to keep secret this pass-through scheme and their participation in it. They thankfully agreed.

In fact, Calozza was operating a Ponzi scheme. He used the clients' money to pay off his gambling debts and build a $1.6 million mansion. He paid off earlier clients with the later investors' money. The scheme cost unfortunate clients about $8.8 million and benefited fortunate clients about $2.3 million. The secrecy that the investors kept up delayed discovery of the fraud.

Secrecy has other connotations. A plan that involves hiding the truth from a third party establishes a bond between the con artist and his "marks," as any sharing of secrets does. The "little wrong" that both parties commit binds them into a delicious conspiracy for gain. The arrangement also shows that the con artist trusts the marks—a gesture that invites reciprocity. If I trust you, and trust you first, you should trust me. In a scheme by Charles Braun, for example, investors were divided into clubs and told to keep their membership secret or they would be expelled and never readmitted.[127] Secrecy was crucial for Braun because in addition to fraud the clubs were unregistered investment companies, in violation of the law. Ultimately, the scheme was discovered by chance because one of the investors committed an illegal act in another venture. The discovery of the scheme, however, came too late for many investors, who lost heavily.[128]

Anyone who has received a "Nigerian letter" will recognize the same ingredients. There is usually a declaration of trust in the receiver of the letter ("I inquired and found that you are an honest person"), a proposal to do something that may not be completely "kosher," a repeated request for secrecy, and of course a promise of millions.[129]

Ponzi schemes may contain these features. A tinge of "safe illegality" adds flavor to the treasure story. In one case, Kenneth Weiner told a story about the source of profits, which was "a clandestine multinational group, a cartel of large international corporations that purportedly had the power to provide investment opportunity and returns."[130] This story smacks of an "insider" tip. It allows insider trading and capture of large profits in something that seems, at least at the time, virtually safe from detection. A clandestine cartel and large corporations are powerful, and the fact that the entire plan was to be executed abroad seemed to keep this investment safe enough. It contained the ingredients of secrecy and bonding together with safety and profits.

3. Stories That Are Costly to Verify

Con artists use techniques and features to protect their stories from exposure. They choose investment stories that are quite costly to verify. As Bradley Skolnik, Indiana's securities commissioner and president of the North American Securities Administrators Association (NASAA), commented, "The amount of homework you have to do to check one of these things out is too much."[131]

One con artist searched for an old abandoned mine in the middle of nowhere, unreachable by easy transportation. A reporter who joined the con artist told this story:

> [The con artist] insisted that I not reveal where I was, ever. He pulled out a legal document requiring me to keep secret the location of these supposed gold mines, which, he said, would yield fantastically lucrative treasure worth tens of billions of dollars.

I was told that I couldn't see the mines, not until I signed that paper. . . . [N]ow that I've seen two mine shafts, both of which appear to be abandoned, dusty relics, I am allowed only to reveal only this: We're in Mexico. . . .[132]

To be sure, a gold mine can be hard to discover. Walter Edward Scott was a prominent public figure in the Old West. He convinced many investors to back his gold mining operations. Investors eventually discovered that the mines did not exist. Scott turned to selling stolen ore instead of selling mine operations. He was sued by his creditors and ended up in jail.[133]

Stories of Ponzi con artists point to a source of income in faraway countries and places. In one scheme the profitable investment was derived from a nonexistent bank in Nauru, entitled the Greater International Bank of Nauru.[134] Enron's trading was global and costly to trace and verify, or even understand. It takes time to sort thousands of contracts, read them carefully, and evaluate their impact once it is all put together.

There is nothing new in a company's expansion abroad. A source of revenues in a faraway land might be older than Ponzi's schemes. An Australian regulator explained that "[t]ypically, the scam involves investment in the US via an English national operating out of Thailand who invites Australian investors to send money to Hong Kong. . . . [They] are complex and difficult to shut down."[135]

However, a scheme's source of income can be difficult to verify even if it is not global. The United States is large enough to impose high costs on anyone checking a con artist's story. In *United States v. Hayes*, the con artist "sold working interests in five oil and gas leases located in Louisiana to residents of Hawaii."[136] In another case, Wayne Burton, a real estate broker, managed eight offices all over California and conducted a Ponzi scheme. He sold obligations purportedly collateralized by mortgages in California.[137] Few investors could afford to verify the stories on site.

When pressed for details, con artists may produce forged financial statements and other false documents.[138] In one case the con artist forged the signatures of the officers of a reputable company in order to establish his purported affiliation with that company.[139] These documents were difficult to authenticate. In fact, what looks like evidence may not be reliable in the context of the entire picture. David Phillip Munoz and his accomplices led investors to believe that the sales agents were receiving less in commissions than they were.[140] In the Great Rings scheme, the promoters made statements that may have been difficult to verify, including a statement that the general partners would not receive commissions.[141]

Con artists may offer assurances from trusted professionals— lawyers and accountants, and regulated intermediaries such as brokers or insurance salespersons. In fact, during an IRS audit one con artist provided fabricated minutes of a board of directors meeting and misrepresented the true condition of the not-for-profit organization he managed. Consequently, this organization "received a favorable audit letter from the I.R.S."[142] Ironically, that letter was a source of comfort to investors.

Dennis L. Helliwell ran a Ponzi scheme as a bank employee, promising investors 18–20 percent annually and paying investors' claims with the proceeds of money from new investors. He used the bank's stationery to send the clients "official receipts." Investors accepted these receipts as proof that their investments were safe with the bank. After leaving the bank, Helliwell continued to use the bank's stationery. Few investors demanded their money back and were happy with the frequent income checks. The bank was unaware of the scheme, until by chance the bank received a complaint letter addressed to Helliwell's home address. An investigation followed, eleven years after the scam began.[143]

Although many items of con artists' stories are costly to verify, some are less expensive to pursue, especially if the con artists are not careful. For example, a con artist's story that he was a software designer, that his company was paying him $10,000 a month, and that the clients had contracted with him to put a certain system in place could be easily checked by asking for the documents, or just the clients' names.[144] But for many reasons, investors do not typically ask for proof. The personal relationships that con artists cultivate make it uncomfortable to show mistrust by demanding documentation, asking for details, and seeking other forms of evidence.

Investors might not *insist* on evidence, even if they do ask for it. In one case, an investor asked to view the promised secured bond: "He believed that the promised 30 percent in three months was unusual, but he was familiar with similar returns on syndications for commercial 'bridge' loans."[145] He never saw the bond. Either he forgot to insist on production or the con artist found reasons to forget. Nonetheless the inquirer invested. He was satisfied with "sketchy details." Madoff took a different approach. Unlike some con artists, who gave misleading information, Madoff refused categorically to give any information. If an investor complained or inquired about how Madoff did business, Madoff would threaten: "If you don't like what I do, we'll send your money back." The investor did not receive an answer and yet did not withdraw the money.[146] Friendly investors may have said, "So what if he didn't give you an answer? What's so terrible about that?"

A con artist may divert the investors' attention to lower risks, while hiding the greater investment risks. The diversion may also serve to show the con artists' trustworthiness when they themselves point to risk, seemingly against their own interest. For example, a con artist promised a return that at the time would be deemed usurious (10–15 percent a year) in a state that prohibited such interest. Investors in that state felt justified in receiving a higher interest rate and assumed that financing corporations would be represented as the borrowers. The investors' attention was diverted from the risk of the con artist's embezzlement to the risk posed by the law of usury.[147]

4. *Details That* Hide *the Truth by* Drowning *It*

A. DETAILS CAN HIDE THE TRUTH

Con artists' businesses are often diverse and complex. The business empire of one con artist "swelled to a network of dozens of companies and partnerships, embracing a gold mine, an oil company, a commodities brokerage and a second car dealership."[148] In the year 2000, as clients were beginning to use Internet-based technology around the world, a company named CitX partnered with Professional Resource Systems International, Inc. ("PRSI") to market its software.[149] Similarly, from 1990 through 2006, a company named Southwick used more than 150 companies to cover costs and compensate prior investors.[150] The sprawling empire drew investors.[151] The complex structure was assumed to signal reliability and honesty. But examination and proof were costly and not easily available.

Even though, as we noted previously, telling a story in detail enhances trustworthiness and gives an impression of truth, details can also hide the truth by burying it. For example, in 1992 a con artist's "business empire swelled to a network of dozens of companies and partnerships, embracing a gold mine, an oil company, a commodities brokerage and a second car dealership."[152] It was difficult to trace the receipts and expenses of the business. It was impossible to determine its net worth and find out whether it could meet its obligations in the long run.

How the worm in the Ponzi scheme's apple is hidden is well illustrated by the Enron debacle. Enron refined and modernized its Ponzi scheme. The company used complexity to hide its true financial condition and guaranteed the value of its securitized assets by using its own shares, or the promise to use its shares. In sum, it guaranteed one type of its own liabilities by another type of its own liabilities (shares). Both the legal structure and the financial instruments of these arrangements were complex and difficult to verify. Unless one viewed the entire picture, one could not uncover, through the maze of limited partnerships, the concealed losses that were masked as revenues.[153]

B. COMPLEXITY HELPS HIDE THE TRUTH AS WELL

Complexity can be used to deceive in a pyramid scheme as well. Jim Henderson described a case in which the investors, including businesspeople familiar with numbers, tried hard to figure out how the promised returns could be achieved. They were unsuccessful. The con artist attempted to explain the intricacies of his mechanisms but ended up saying: "I'm the only one who can understand it."[154] He did not explain; it seems that there was no rational explanation or basis for his claims.

There are scheme structures that make it difficult to uncover the identity of the owners of purported assets. For example, Van Alstyne, whom we met before in this chapter, created a number of companies through which he defrauded approximately 450 victims. He started in 1992 by building thirteen oil and gas limited partnerships, which he controlled. Other companies, under his ownership or control, served as the general partners for the limited partnerships. There were two other companies this con artist owned as well. These companies acted as agents with respect to oil and gas properties on behalf of the limited partnerships.[155] This structure and the division of functions were difficult to follow.

In a case involving a tax consultant turned con artist, investors not only did not understand the applicable tax laws but had reason to rely on the con artist for tax matters. The court noted: "[I]nvestors were encouraged to roll over their accounts, rather than receive taxable 'interest' at the end of the original term so that they could continue to receive 'tax free' monthly payments."[156] Focusing on the results—avoidance of taxes—they did not seek to understand what was actually done with their money. The details hid the true story.

Some investments are inherently hard to verify. It was difficult to evaluate and verify the existence of all the several thousand bus stop shelters in Metro Display Advertising, Inc. (MDA).[157] It was also difficult to find out if the advertisements were placed on the bus shelters. Yet these advertisements were to be the source of the profits from the bus shelter investments which MDA sold. The promoters sold to investors bus stop shelters for which investors paid a fee of $10,000 each. Next the investors leased back to the promoters these bus shelters for a fee of $200 per month, less a $30 maintenance fee. According to the contracts between the investors and the promoters, MDA would "repurchase the shelters from the investors after five years for $10,000. MDA was to solicit advertisers to place ads on the shelters in order to generate the necessary revenue to make the lease payments."[158]

However, bus stop shelters are unique investments for which there was no market and not many competing manufacturers. These facts rendered it hard to ascertain and compare the prices of manufacturing the shelters. In addition, the inventory of bus shelters was not easy to locate and inspect. As it turned out, during the five years that MDA was in business "it sold approximately 4,600 bus stop shelters to 1,442 investors, but installed no more than 2,600 shelters. MDA's advertising revenues were insufficient to cover the lease payments and overhead, so MDA used the capital investments from new investors to cover those expenses. In short, the shelter investment was a Ponzi scheme."[159]

Charles Ponzi's stamp arbitrage investment could not be evaluated. There was no information about such an investment or similar investments against which to compare it. Experienced skeptics view "creative investments" with reservation. For them, lack of information and experience spells risk. These were the people who examined Ponzi's scheme more closely and found it lacking.[160] But for the marks, ingenious investment stories are interesting and attractive.

They ignore the absence of information and inability to compare the scheme with other schemes; instead they rely on the con artist's assurances about the low risk involved.

A version of financial frauds that is difficult to uncover is trading in certificates of deposits that do not match, as this vignette illustrates:

> In 1986, Robert Bentley established Bentley Financial Services, Inc. ("BFS") to broker "bank-issued certificates of deposit (CDs). In 1993, Bentley formed the Entrust Group ('Entrust') . . . to act as custodian on BFS-brokered transactions. In the CD-selling industry, the broker is responsible for connecting CDs available for purchase from banks with particular investors. The custodian then collects the money from each investor, wires it to the issuing bank and holds onto the CD, while issuing a "safekeeping receipt" to the investor indicating that it has title to the CD held by the custodian.[161]

The CD seller profits from the difference between the terms of the CD purchased from the bank (e.g., 5 percent) and terms of the CD sold to the investor (e.g., 4.5 percent). "A more complex, and risky, way a CD broker can profit is by mismatching maturity dates. . . . This form of mismatching is legal as long as the mismatch is disclosed to the investor (including the fact that the investor may not be able to reclaim its principal at the maturity date stated in the investment contract)."[162] However, he operated a Ponzi scheme with respect to *part of the returns on the investments.* He received investors' money and bought CDs as promised. But because the CDs provided less than the profits that he promised investors, he paid to existing investors the difference between the returns on the CDs and the promised profits with the money paid by new investors. Complexity disguised this crucial fact.

E. CON ARTISTS' DECEPTIVE FRIENDSHIP AND SEEMING VULNERABILITY BY AGE AND NAÏVETY

1. Deceptive Friendship and Love

People believe in the friendship of their business partners or their lawyers. Deep inside, they may suspect that these friendships are linked to the lucrative business relationships. But they may refuse to think about it this way, especially if they crave friendship. For some victims, the con artist's attention and conversation fill a crucial psychological need. Lonely victims may intentionally stay home to receive phone solicitations and remain on the phone longer to hear fraudulent sales pitches. Some are homebound and need human contact. Conversations with the con artists are more than mere recreation for them.[163] Thus people who crave friendship are diverted from the business aspects of the relationship and may deceive themselves by denying the price tag, which this so-called friendship carries, in order to convert it into a *real* friendship.

In addition to gratitude and pressure to reciprocate, personal emotional relationships between con artists and their victims blur the victims' clear vision of the monetary aspect of the investment. As one sophisticated businessman who became a victim to a Ponzi scheme confessed, he was influenced to invest by a longtime friend who was raising money for the scheme. Although this victim did not believe that the friend intended to rob him, the victim "acknowledge[d] that he let friendship cloud his judgment and undermine his instincts. 'Had it not been a friend, I would have done more up-front fact checking.' . . . 'I would have found out all this about ten times sooner and probably would not have invested in this.'"[164]

Yet seeking friendship in a business relationship is not entirely unreasonable. It seems that, in contrast to a business relationship, personal friendship may offer better protection from lies.[165] It has been noted that people lie less to close friends than they do to others.

This may be one reason investors and clients seek the friendships of those who advise them.

Friendship may provide a kind of insurance against the dishonesty of the people on whom one must rely. This feeling of insurance is deep and natural. Yet it may be deceptive, which tends to convince the believers that the other person likes them for their own sake and not for the sake of monetary gain, and that it is justifiable to trust the person. Mixing friendship and business could reduce reliance. It seems that people lie more to business partners than to close friends with whom they have only personal relationships. The assumption is that people would not defraud a friend, while they might defraud a business partner. After all, business is not supposed to be guided by emotion. Con artists who engage in Ponzi schemes may exploit this belief and tendency.

Friendship may play a role in the relationship between con artists and representatives of institutional investors. Con artists offer institutional representatives a chance to bring higher income for their institution. Profits for their institution provide institutional representatives with an opportunity to show their investment acumen, as well as gain recognition, gratitude from superiors, and promotion along with a higher salary and bonuses. These benefits are linked to the representative's personal career while they divert the representatives' attention from the value and details of the transaction and investment at hand.

Con artists frequently offer individual investors nonmonetary personal relationships that are uniquely valuable to these investors. In the film *The Producers*, Bialystock, a chronically unsuccessful producer of theater shows who finances his failing shows by courting rich "little old ladies," induces a nondescript, timid bookkeeper to join him in a wild scheme that makes some sense. The producer would raise double the amount needed for production by promising lady investors a very high return. In fact, he promises 25,000 percent on the aggregate investments. Then Bialystock will produce a sure "flop," as he has done for many years. The investors will collect nothing, as the show will close (hopefully) on the first day. The producer and the accountant will pocket the excess amount that was raised.

Bialystock tries hard to produce a terrible show—so much so that it becomes a hit. The two con artists attempt to bomb the theater to close the show down. They end up in court and are found "very guilty" as the foreman of the jury declares.[166] Before sentencing, Bloom, the bookkeeper, has his say. Bialystock, he says, is a *crook, a swindler, a dishonest man* who makes others do things they never dreamt they could or would do. But, he says, Bialystock is a *wonderful man*. He called Bloom by his first name (no one did that, even at school). Bialystock made Bloom's life exciting. He gave Bloom a new personality, illusory as it might be. He made the little old ladies feel young, beautiful, and desirable. Hearing this, the little old ladies wipe their tears, stand up, and cheer![167]

Bialystock, the con artist, gave his investor ladies and Bloom a wonderful gift. He listened to them attentively, as no one did anymore (or had done before). He gave them the feeling that they had a true friend. He treated them with respect, cared for them, made them happy. The ladies had money to pay a psychiatrist to listen attentively, and to pay a gigolo to compliment them. But true friendship and true compliments must be given voluntarily as gifts, not enticed with monetary compensation. Friendship and love cannot be acquired by exchanges. Payments destroy their very essence. To be true, they must be *gifts, not bargains*. Bialystock gave the little old ladies signals that his attention and his compliments were for free— *gifts, not bargains*.

A similar sentiment was produced by Madoff in this advertisement: "In an era of faceless organizations owned by other equally faceless organizations, Bernard L. Madoff Investment Securities LLC harks back to an earlier era in the financial world: The owner's name is on the door. Clients know that Bernard Madoff has a personal interest in maintaining the unblemished record of value, fair-dealing and high ethical standards that has always been the firm's hallmark."[168] Even as he made it very difficult to reach him and gave the impression of his heading an exclusive club, he advertised the relationship with his investors as personal.

Fake love appears in many ways. In 2002, Joseph Zirkel offered much happiness to a number of women. Convicted of an investment scam in 1994, he served fifty-seven months in prison. Then he moved to New York from which he reported to his probation officer. His reports showed a meager salary backed by a weekly pay stub of $434, and modest living conditions backed by a story of his parents' small apartment. From that salary, he could make restitution of $300 a month to repay his victims the sum of $1.9 million. In fact, Zirkel was not working at all, and his paychecks were forgeries issued by a shell corporation. He was living in luxury, a familiar face in the best restaurants in town, posing as a wealthy heir to a New England family of fortune. The source of his money was wealthy women who trusted him to manage their investments. His relationship with them was close, and at least on two occasions it involved a marriage proposal. Love and marriage were mixed with investment management.[169]

2. Deceptive Weakness of Age and Seeming Naïvety

A. OLD AGE CAN DECEIVE

Just as a friendly and loving attitude can be used to mislead and gain investors' trust, so can physical feebleness mislead and gain trust, especially when the investors are physically stronger than the frail con artist. A seventy-seven-year-old man misled investors by inducing them to invest in six funds he managed over a ten-year period ending in January 2009. Prosecutors alleged that this man, Arthur Nadel, regularly lied to investors about "achieving 'consistent, positive annual returns.'"

"At an age when most people slow down and consider retirement, [his] criminal activities were just getting started," Assistant U.S. Attorney Reed Brodsky said in a court filing. "[Nadel] used his old age and frail appearance as a weapon to deceive others in believing that he was experienced, wise, kind and trustworthy. In reality, nothing could have been further from the truth. He was a con man dressed up as a kind, old soul."

Nadel pleaded guilty to a 15-count indictment in February, including charges of mail fraud, wire fraud, and securities fraud.[170]

B. NAÏVETY CAN DECEIVE

A con artist can act as a vulnerable, naïve, unsophisticated person. This impression can lower the victim's protective caution and tempt a victim to try to cheat the con artist by offering to sell property, such as stock, for more than it is worth. Once the relationship is well established, and the victim feels assured of the con artist's naïvety, the con artist makes an offer of worthless stock in which the victim becomes interested. After the victim buys this stock at great loss, the con artist disappears.[171] Thus relationships, and signals of the seeming weakness and naïvety of the con artist, can be misleading, to the advantage of the con artist.

So we have learned what kind of offers and stories con artists tell that draw their victims. Yet the puzzle remains. How do con artists meet their victims? After all, they surely cannot just call strangers and offer investments. How do con artists manage to contact the marks? Chapter 2 tells us how they do it.

Chapter 2

Selling The Stories

A. ADVERTISING

1. The Importance of Advertising

To attract investors, Ponzi schemers need a widespread reputation. Unlike the victims of thieves and burglars, the victims of Ponzi schemers offer their money to the con artists eagerly, and sometimes *beg* them to accept their money. The tools of these con artists are not force but persuasion; not breaking into homes to rob the victims, but charming their way into the victims' hearts to be offered the victims' money.

Ponzi schemers differ from the one-shot con artists who play with loaded dice or marked cards. These con artists must avoid publicity and move on quickly, or else they could be tarred and feathered and locked up by the sheriff to stand trial. Thieves, burglars, and one-shot con artists must shun the glare of publicity in order to remain free. In contrast, publicity and reputation are the lifelines of con artists of the Ponzi variety. For their scheme to work, Ponzi schemers must make their offerings and trustworthiness as public as possible and for as long as possible. Their scheme depends on incessant advertising and rising reputation to continuously attract new investors. These con artists must stand out in the crowd to develop a following.

Thieves, burglars, and one-shot con artists seek reputation among their peers and within their groups of trusted friends, which are fairly small. To hide from the authorities they must avoid repute among strangers. In contrast, Ponzi con artists must develop a double image. They must know what they are *actually doing*, and be publicly well known for what they *seem to be doing*.

2. Where to Operate and How to Build a Reputation

Con artists may choose a town that is not too small (which would attract only a few investors) and not too big (which would accommodate strong competition for reputation).[1] A more important factor is where con artists choose their homes. Living in the right neighborhood makes a huge difference; it opens many doors. The *Wall Street Journal* noted that Madoff and his family moved, in 1984, "into a sprawling duplex on Manhattan's Upper East Side." "One former resident was . . . a onetime U.S. ambassador to France. . . ."[2] "Madoff's clients had in common . . . membership at the Palm Beach Country Club. It's an exclusive club, with a beautiful golf course, ringed by palms, overlooking the Atlantic Ocean. Madoff was a member, and other members sought introductions in hopes of being allowed into an even more exclusive investment club that brought steady, double-digit returns even when the market was down."[3]

Madoff "became more involved in [NASDAQ], serving as its chairman in 1990, 1991 and 1993."[4] He became "a member of the board of directors of the Securities Industry Association" and "a founding member of the board of directors of the International Securities Clearing Corporation in London."[5] Networking and getting to know wealthy people and managers of their wealth is important for con artists in the Ponzi scheme business. Connecting to powerful politicians helps, and so does a reputation as a wealthy individual, which we noted in Chapter 1.

One of Madoff's victims described the flavor of reputation that is carried by word of mouth:

Of course, we never heard the name Madoff—which has a pecu-liarly Dickensian ring now—and had no idea how he achieved such fantastic returns over the past 40 years. All we knew was that my wife's entire family had been in the fund for decades and lived well on the returns, which ranged from 15% to 22%. It was all very secretive and tough to get into, which, looking back, was a brilliant strategy to lure suckers. Unlike the usual Ponzi me-chanics, the fund even stopped investments into accounts a few years back, at least in our network.[6]

This victim was hooked.

3. Showing Generosity

Among the many ways in which con artists draw attention is showing generosity and engaging in civic activities. Their contributions are well publicized. A Ponzi scheme operator, Cornerstone Prodigy, "attracted publicity for sponsoring a celebrity golf tournament. The event raised money to help offset the medical expenses of Justin Laird, the 16-year-old paralyzed in the Wedgwood Baptist Church shootings in September, and Chassidy Young, a 12-year-old Fort Worth girl who was born without arms and legs."[7]

The benefits that con artists bestow often extend to their commu-nity. As one court commented, "Mr. Bennett made a large number of civic, charitable and public service contributions and performed good works in the areas of substance abuse, children and youth, juve-nile justice."[8] Con artists may donate funds to a town to build a golf course[9] and represent themselves as the operators of "a thriving real estate business" whose business is to buy and refurbish run-down homes, remodel them, and sell "the newly renovated residences at a handsome profit for the company and its investors."[10] One con artist who was a chief financial officer lulled his employer's suspicions by "civic involvement in groups such as Boys to Men and the National Association of Black Accountants." Although this officer embezzled his employer's money, his position and actions did not fit the image of a person with a criminal record.[11] He could continue the fraudulent operations far longer than he might otherwise, without raising suspicion.

Charitable donations further benefit Ponzi schemers because they bring about reciprocity. Gratitude, sympathy, and enjoyment of hospitality attract civic leaders to con artists' podiums and seminars. Thus they add credibility to the con artists' stories. The donations offer opportunities for contacts with other wealthy donors and fundraisers, with their friends, business allies, and the most desirable clubs in town, thereby broadening the con artists' network. Donations can bring in the mayor on the con artists' invitation, and people who have served in official capacities, such as city treasurer, city finance director, state representative, judge.[12] Because Madoff seemed to have enormous wealth, he became a "pillar of finance and charity." He joined the board of trustees of Yeshiva University and operated with his wife the Madoff Family Foundation. In 2007, this $19 million operation contributed to "Kav Lachayim, a volunteer group that works in Israeli schools and hospitals, and to the Public Theater in New York."[13]

In addition to charities and institutions of learning, con artists donate to political parties and politicians. For example, in Romania Caritas, a Ponzi scheme of enormous proportions for that country, was supported by the Party of Romanian National Unity. Caritas negotiated to establish its headquarters in the Cluj city hall, with the mayor's consent. The location enhanced its exposure, reputation, and credibility.[14] Needless to say, the mayor of the city received Caritas with open arms.[15] Donations of Ponzi schemers oil their way into the halls of power, facilitate networking with the rich and powerful, and provide information, influence, and benefits. In the process, con artists' credibility deepens and draws more investors. Donations signal the presence of an altruistic person who cares about others. They enhance an image and reputation of trustworthiness, and leadership for the good of society.

4. Entertaining

Entertaining can help strike friendships. Con artists entertain lavishly. Spending money satisfies the con artists' need to tell their stories without telling them in full. In her book *Crooks and Squares*, Malin Akerstrom describes thieves and their similar need to spend money. Thieves, she wrote, "often display successful scores by spending freely, offering drinks, etc. to colleagues at bars known to be criminal hang-outs." They do so despite the risk that this lavish entertainment and generosity might raise the suspicion of police or informers. Because the thief's activities must remain secret, he must communicate his successes and competence in some other way, one of which is entertaining.[16]

"Unless someone shares the knowledge of his activities with others, there is no way he can get the respect, fear, or admiration which he has earned. . . ." Money is furthermore one of the few measures of status in the criminal world. People in the conventional world have more areas through which they can attain respect or status: work, family, a house, a new car, etc. The same argument can probably explain the conspicuous consumption that some criminals engage in. . . . Where persons are firmly entrenched in public statuses that are respected, trustworthy or powerful, they can afford the art of understatement, subtlety and modesty. With so many virtues it is easy to wait for someone else to point them out."[17]

Akerstrom describes the environment of Swedish thieves and burglars, who need to hide their identity, rather than the American Ponzi con artists, who need to advertise their offerings of investments.

Yet her description seems to fit both groups. Ponzi con artists too have something to hide. They too have an insatiable desire and need for recognition. If this need has no bounds, and in many cases it indeed is insatiable, then it makes no difference how much recognition they receive; they always want and need more. Spending money is one way to feed these needs. But in addition, unlike the Swedish thieves, whose generosity may raise the authorities' suspicions, generous con artists are likely to allay such suspicion and gain protection from the law. Neither their financial success nor their lavish spending would provoke wide suspicion, although, as mentioned, a watchful examination of these con artists, who spend other people's money, can raise attention and concern.

5. Attracting Attention by Engaging in Attention-Drawing Conflicts

It should be noted that creating conflict to draw attention is not necessarily the exclusive province of con artists. During the mid-1880s, P. T. Barnum, the creator of the "Greatest Show on Earth," fought with the editor of a large New York daily for years. The more offensive his opponent was to Barnum, the more offensive the delighted Barnum became. This conflict amused readers, and Barnum recognized the advertising and entertainment value of the conflict.[18] The point made here is that Ponzi con artists do not neglect this aspect of advertising; they use it well.

Con artists can become real competitors in action, not only in words. Melvin Ford, a promoter of a pyramid scheme, disparaged the banking industry and highlighted his programs as a superior alternative to traditional banking and investment. Ford was one of the defendants in the Securities and Exchange Commission's case against International Loan Network. He declared that his company's bonus program was "the most powerful financial system since banking."[19] A pyramid con artist could not explain how he would manage to pay investors up to 1,300 percent in six months.[20] Yet his claim of superiority over the established financial system served his purpose: it drew attention.

B. RECRUITING HELPERS

1. Cooperation, Competition, and Congregation Among Con Artists

Con artists connect with each other and forge friendships, in and outside prison. Many become friends.[21] Some are family members. Because con artists can hardly speak about their exploits outside the group, they strengthen their self-image by feeding each other's egos. With "their own kind," they share and reinforce their conception of the world. In the con artists' world, everyone is engaged in the conning business. The same reinforcement is evident in other groups as well, as in corporate settings, including managers of legitimate businesses in distress.

Con artists behave as legitimate competing merchants do. For example, legitimate businesses that sell the same merchandise may open their shops in the same area even though shoppers may enter their competitors' shops rather than their own. Such competitors may share marketing and advertising costs. Except for very large enterprises, the gains to each merchant from this cooperation exceed the losses from the competitors' sales. It seems that in the con artists' business, as in any other business, there are customers who are drawn to Ponzi schemes.[22] Con artists may sell to each other lists of possible victims. Many of the victims do not recognize the same elements in the new stories and fall for them. Thus con artists who must move on to another area can nonetheless sell their stories to other con artists who would draw the attention of the same victims.

Con artists form alliances to participate in each other's ventures.[23] A 2010 case revealed a scheme in the form of a venture capital arm of an enterprise that "utilized single purpose entities to obtain billions of dollars of funding, purportedly to acquire merchandise for sale to wholesalers and retailers nationwide." The con artist had several business associates "alleged to have generated more than $3 billion in fraudulent proceeds."[24]

A con artist established four fraudulent investment companies. He managed three companies all alone, and the fourth one with his colleagues.[25] His associates were aware of his criminal record and concealed his involvement in the scheme by acting as "front men." In another case, from 1996, two con artists co-owned and operated investment companies that defrauded investors.[26] A group of con artists who met in prison formed a successful scam for four years, until it ended with the suicide of its leader.[27]

Trust among con artists can pose a riddle. After all, they, more than anyone else, know that trust can be mimicked and faked. Perhaps con artists, who view themselves as businesspersons, behave as cooperating competitors would; they trust and cooperate to a limited extent. Perhaps the desire to be liked and the need to belong to an identifying group may drive con artists toward one another. Very few predators act and live alone.

This does not mean that con artists are entirely trustworthy and trusting toward each other. For example, one con artist argued that his "investment scheme was ruined by the embezzlement of the middlemen involved in the transactions." His two friends collected exorbitant commissions and spent money on personal items. In court, the friends argued that they were the victims of this con artist, and that they should not be joined with him as co-defendants. They argued that they were "duped, like the other investors."[28] Con artists who partner may end up distrusting each other. "'I don't need him,'" said a con artist of his partner, "the man with the malevolent stare who has supposedly lined up concessions to seven Mexican gold mines. 'He needs me. He's impossible.'" During this conversation the con artist was planning his escape because he no longer trusts his partner in this wild gold-mining scheme."[29]

In some respects, con artists' relationships among themselves are similar to those of criminal fraternities. For example, con artists who are defrauded by other con artists cannot seek police protection or justice in the courts. They must take care of themselves in other ways, and therefore resort to self-help. In *United States v. O'Toole*, the leader of a scheme failed to pay one of the promoters the amounts due to him.[30] The promoter took revenge. Using the same scheme, he continued to sell the "gold-backed railroad bonds" that the scheme involved. But rather than deposit investors' money in a bank account, presumably that of the group of con artists, he pocketed investors' money to the tune of $163,284. That was safe to do; the leader of the group could not complain to the police either.

A new breed of con artists who conduct fraudulent schemes in the corporate context has its own group of friends. The members exchange information and benefits and support each other. This group's members do not usually end up in prison, but if they are jailed then they rarely fraternize with the other prisoners or maintain contact with them after they complete their sentence.[31] The fraternity of these con artists, however, exists and functions like any other group members who share interests. Those in prison are the members of the family, black sheep that they are. The outside support is crucial to them, as it is to all con artists.

2. Birds of a Feather Flock Together

A 2010 case demonstrates how birds of a feather flock together. Travis Correll founded a purported investment company (Horizon), raising about $175,000 from friends and family. The money was to be

invested with a New Zealand businessman in "a high-yield international banking program."[32] The New Zealand businessman absconded
with the money. Rather than report the theft, Correll began to operate a Ponzi scheme, paying dividends to current investors from the
money he raised from new investors, whom he enticed by promising
substantial returns.[33]

Then Correll found a partner, or, more accurately, a partner found
him. Midkiff, an insurance salesman and operator of the Shiloh
Church in Forest Lake, Minnesota, contacted Correll regarding his
offerings of a "high-yield international investment opportunity."
Midkiff brought Correll members of the Shiloh Church's investments
for significant compensation[34] and recruited other investors for Correll's enterprises as well as for his own.[35] Then a theft occurred in
Midkiff's shop. True to form, he did not report it but contacted Correll instead. Correll invested $1 million on behalf of a new Midkiff
entity. When the authorities finally arrived and began an investigation, the parties agreed to cease operations in Minnesota but began
another enterprise in Nevada, which collapsed in December 2005.
"With the eighteen programs combined, 519 individuals invested
$30 million with" the companies, and "[o]n December 12, 2006,
Midkiff was indicted in the District of Minnesota on charges of mail
fraud, wire fraud, promotional money laundering, conspiracy to
commit mail fraud, and conspiracy to commit promotional money
laundering."[36]

What is interesting and informing in this story is how the
con artists "flocked together" and networked. They also acted in a
similar manner. Both Correll and Midkiff were the victims of
people who absconded with their investors' money, and rather
than seek the help of the authorities used their own self-help.
They grew the number of similar companies, and made similar
wild investments, and recruited investors until there were no more
to be found.

C. HOW DO CON ARTISTS APPROACH THEIR VICTIMS?

1. From Family and Friends to Institutions and Affinity Groups

A. INTRODUCTION

A direct approach to relatives and friends is the easiest way to start a con artist venture. Thus Kirschner induced friends to invest their money with him and operated a scheme from November 2006 to May 2009.[37] This approach is effective because the victims know and trust the con artist. However, the number of family and friends and the amounts they can invest may be relatively small. Besides, even though the con artist can devote a limited time to this sales effort, the approach may not leave time and resources for breaking new ground and reaching new potential investors. After all, not all friends and relatives continue to invest—and some may demand repayment.

Therefore, con artists use the legitimate technique of soliciting groups and spreading their message by word of mouth, websites, promotional materials, and representatives acquainted with the local residents. In the case of M25 Investments, Inc., representatives "solicited many customers after church services they attended, and at meetings at the representatives' or the customers' homes."[38] Those who are approached may spread the word about the attractive investment program and offer contact information. One court noted that "[w]hile soliciting potential customers in person, [the con artists] or their representatives obtained telephone numbers of other potential customers." Then they solicited additional potential customers by telephone.[39]

Group solicitation of potential investors is more efficient than one-to-one, although it may involve higher costs. Both con artists and legitimate sales organizations can pitch their investments to prospective investors by offering free lunches and interesting seminars in motel conference rooms.[40] If investors are wealthy, then hosting potential investors on a long trip is effective as well. Steven Ferguson offered potential investors a fully paid trip to Hawaii. The group traveled from Switzerland to Los Angeles and then to Hawaii. During this period the travelers were induced to invest hundreds of thousands of dollars in Ferguson's Ponzi scheme.[41] The wife of another con artist held shorter meetings at home and created and managed an "investment club."[42] Both long-term trips and investment clubs demonstrate methods of grouping potential investors for longer periods and more effective sales.

The next most efficient contact would be through institutions. Institutional investors provide a sales channel that is effective and less expensive than selling to individuals and to groups. One sale to a single institutional investor (a pension fund, a mutual fund, or an insurance company) can equal sales to thousands of investors. Pooling investors' money, these institutions make very large investments, usually in securities and other financial assets. In addition, because such institutions are sophisticated and regulated, their investments add credibility to the con artists. However, institutional investors pose a danger to con artists; the institution may be too close to regulators, or more accurately, the regulators may be too close to these institutions.[43]

Therefore, the more attractive targets for con artists are charitable and religious institutions, which are often one and the same. Charitable and religious institutions are not as strictly regulated, and their managers are less supervised by their members or contributors. The representatives of such institutions are often not as knowledgeable as those of regulated institutions, and their representatives may be more easily attracted by the con artists' sales talk.

In addition to offering protection from close scrutiny on the part of the authorities, religious and not-for-profit organizations can offer the con artists relief from taxation and state regulation. State agencies do not have detailed information about religious orders because they do not regulate them closely. For example, a gift program called Sovereign Ministries was founded shortly after a court ruled that a similar program, initiated by the founder's uncle, remained outside of state scrutiny and regulatory power so long as the program promised no guaranteed returns. Gifts are not subject to securities regulation.[44]

Further, because the relationship between religion and tax exemption, for example, is unclear to many people, believers invest with the con artist without asking for details. The mantle of religion and charity can serve as a means of limiting information to investors.

Similar and sometimes overlapping targets for con artists are affinity groups and their membership, such as employees in the same unit. In Sydney, Melbourne, and Brisbane, Australia, a large group of police officers invested in such a scheme. Apart from a few who managed to get their money back in time, as many as two hundred police agents (including the wife of an Australian federal police commissioner) were believed to have invested in the Ponzi scheme. The members' losses were significant. Of these participants just one couple lost $400,000.[45]

Not surprisingly, such institutions have fallen prey to con schemes with regularity. For example, Charles Blair was the promoter of three nonprofit Colorado corporations that sold securities through a "Department of Development." For more than two years, the corporations and related entities were insolvent and in desperate financial condition, with no real hope of recovery. The money the corporations raised by selling new securities was used to cover the payments on their current debt, but these facts were not disclosed to investors. Representatives of the corporations and the entities told investors that the assets exceeded liabilities by $3 million and gave assurance that the investments were safe. In fact, the corporations had a deficit of about $6 million and finally filed for reorganization in a bankruptcy court. Only then did investors discover the fate of their investments.[46]

A similar story involves the Baptist Foundation of Arizona, which was established to support good works. When its founder died, his son gained control of the foundation. He spent the foundation's income, assets, and contributions of affiliated churches for his personal use and that of his friends. He paid investors somewhat higher interest than what was being paid on government securities, and offered notes that were not secured. In 1996, for example, the foundation spent half of its total $69 million spending in salaries and administrative expenses. "In 1995 alone, [it] spent about $329,000 on staff automobiles. According to an investigation by a newspaper, the foundation made personal loans to insiders to finance their real estate deals. In contrast, the charities to which the payments should have been made received little. Those who controlled the foundation were not accountable to anyone. Government oversight was negligible, supervision by the foundation's directors was very lax, and the donors did not control the foundation's use of their contributions.[47]

B. ETHNIC AND RELIGIOUS AFFINITY GROUPS
Members of affinity groups may be bound by purpose and belief. The members of these groups are more vulnerable to a herding effect, tending to follow others even if the actions conflict with the members' personal information. Investors buy and sell securities on the assumption that the aggregate of many people's judgment is better than their own.[48] "The markets" speak.

Pyramid schemes suggest similar results. As more people engage profitably in pyramid sales, more people will join, until the pool of future salespersons dries up. In another type of herding people follow others, driven by a desire to maintain or enhance their own reputation. Information plays a lesser role among such followers than does perception. But belonging to the club or to the organization in which other important people are members is the drawing card. The followers strive to maintain their own reputation, or to curry favor with group members, saying in private what they are not likely to utter in public or repeat in front of the group members. This is one way in which social culture is fashioned. People follow the crowd and mediate this following with their own convictions.

Members of affinity groups share beliefs and interests. They meet often, support one another, and trade influence. Members of pyramid schemes are similar. These organizations fuel a tendency to follow others rather than rely on one's own information and judgment. However, people can be influenced by the behavior of others even if they do not belong to a group.

In one experiment, the subject was told he should come to an office to be interviewed. He entered a small room and found other people there. The others then stood up and took off their clothes. The interviewee looked on in amazement, but after a few minutes he did the same and stood naked, waiting to see what was to come. This illustrates one aspect of following a group unthinkingly. The flip side of this behavior is the joy of mastering and directing what other members of the group will do.[49] It seems that this is what con artists feel when they lead and implicitly dictate what the members of the target group are doing. Or a member of an ethnic group may draw investors from that group, individuals who trust "one of us." If the con artist is a successful and respected leader, the members of the group bask in his warmth. Identity draws trust. Proliferating warnings and enforcement actions against con artists who are members of cultural, ethnic and affinity groups appear to be less than fully effective.[50]

Because they share faith and values, members of religious organizations offer attractive victims to con artists. These groups are almost as cohesive as institutional investors, the con artist enjoys lower costs of advertising the scheme and establishing personal contacts with potential investors. Within the groups, information spreads quickly. The number of investors that each person must personally recruit is relatively small because group members are likely to follow the recommendations of brother and sister worshippers and their leaders. In addition, group members may be more vulnerable and amenable to influence if they are older retirees, living a more secluded life and not as informed as active investors might be, or worshippers who simply follow their leaders.

Member of such groups tend to influence one another even in matters outside their faith. Therefore, the business sense and independent judgment of congregation members is dulled by their mutual reliance. If a scheme is introduced by a fellow member, other members tend not to investigate it closely.[51]

In one case, "Alice Faye, as everyone called her, had been operating a pyramid scheme for nine years, wheedling an estimated $10 million from fellow church members, many of them elderly."[52] Another con artist solicited investments by invoking his position in the congregation and announcing: "I consider it a real honor and a privilege to be able to be an elder of this church . . . and when we finally get this facility, were [sic] gonna be able to minister to so much [sic] more people."[53] The church reciprocated by building up his reputation; he "was constantly being praised from the pulpit as an 'anointed Christian businessman.'"[54] A victim of this same con artist described how he took advantage of her faith: "Luca [the con artist] skillfully manipulated my faith in God to his advantage, looking me in the eye while praying to God to bless the investment."[55] One victim testified that Luca would pray with her "just before he showed her fraudulent layouts for his purported developments."[56] This victim added: "Normally I could spot someone like Luca a mile away, but believing [the church's] active promotion of him, I turned off my internal alarms."[57]

Investors who belong to a religious group tend to believe, rather than to question. When an accountant questioned the reliability of an investment in the Baptist Foundation of Arizona, his client who was investing in the foundation answered: "I'm not worried about it.

It's for the glory of the Lord. I have faith in the organization and especially in the Good Lord. To me it's as safe as if it's Bank One."[58]

Con artists' religious cover is effective in creating credibility and in blocking information to investors even if they seek details. A con artist defendant who refused to comply with a court order to refund investors' "gifts" explained that "to do so, I would have to deny my faith in God."[59] His supporters "crammed into [the] courtroom, murmuring 'amens' when [the ministries' attorney] asserted that the state's actions violated [the constitutional protection of religion]." The ministries subsequently issued a statement announcing that "overall the hearing was very successful. Our position regarding the Lordship of Jesus Christ was made very clear and established for the record. We are ready and willing to 'stand and fight' by taking this case all the way to the United States Supreme Court."[60]

A similar scene was described in another case, where the con artist "was like a pastor to them [the investors, and] as a business guru." When the government sought to shut down the con artist's operation, "nearly 150 of them, some making 15-hour drives, attended the hearing. They huddled in groups to pray. They hugged [the con artist] and expressed support for him. They assailed the government for interfering in their business. Since then, they have bombarded the U.S. attorney's offices with faxes and praise for [the con artist] and have contributed to a legal defense fund for him." One of the investors said: "Most of us are Christian people. . . . My source is God almighty. He will see me through this."[61] This investor did not lose money in her dealings with the con artist, but she was disappointed nonetheless. She was counting on more to come in order to support her son and finance her grandson's college education.[62] Though recognizing that more money was not forthcoming, she accepted the con artist as a fellow believer.

Rabbi Marc Gellman noted that people called Madoff "their brother, their best friend," and "used to talk about getting in with Bernie.

He was a member of a club and clubs that defined who is in and who is out, maybe that is what this is all really about, who is in and who is out."[63] Bette Greenfield, a retired event planner for Merrill Lynch, noted:

> My father was told that this is the man that really knew how to keep his money safe. He never met Bernie Madoff, but . . . he kept telling us: "This man has a stellar reputation. He's brilliant." [Although] he couldn't figure out how Madoff made such consistent returns, he wasn't suspicious. My father—an accountant, and a very smart man—was dumbfounded, amazed, and had just such admiration [for him].[64]

Whether the admiration was related fully to religious affiliation is unclear. However, it certainly seems that identity of religion made the victim proud.[65]

C. RELIGIOUS INSTITUTIONS

Con artists target not only church members' money but also the churches' coffers. Most churches are investors, raising funds to maintain their assets and serve good causes. Serving as a church official can help expand the Ponzi scheme. Con artists have acted as ministers,[66] managers of church plans,[67] and members of other charities.[68] One con artist was a nun, recruited by con artists one of whom had served time in prison. Soon after their release, one of the recruiters pleaded guilty to helping operate a Ponzi scheme.[69] The nun continued the project and later left the religious order.[70]

Creating a church can help a con artist's scheme. In early 1977 a man named Hakeem Abdul Rasheed founded the Church of Hakeem Rasheed and preached "about the importance of a positive self-image through belief in one's self."[71]

He taught that one could achieve one's desires by focusing and concentrating on those desires. The central tenet of [Rasheed's] Church was the belief in "the God within you." One of the aspects of the Church's beliefs was the "law of increase, or the law of cosmic abundance," which provided that if one gave freely one would receive returns greater than the initial gift.

Shortly after founding the church, Rasheed established the "Dare to be Rich" program. Rasheed preached that this program was consistent with the law of cosmic abundance: He taught that if one donated money to the Church, one would receive an "increase of God" of four times that amount within a particular period of time. . . . These time periods were based on "psychic birth cycles," which Rasheed claimed had a basis in scripture.[72]

To combine benevolence and faith with personal benefits, a church might offer investors special tax-exempt deals.[73] It is not surprising that unrecognized churches are among the institutions that attract con artists. In 1994, wealthy film stars and their friends were attracted to the Church of Scientology. There they met Reed Slatkin: charming and giving, with an excellent taste in cars, a passion for flying, and the lifestyle of the very rich. He prayed with members of the community, listened to their problems, and magnanimously offered them free advisory management of their assets with fabulous results. They rewarded him with valuable gifts and unlimited trust. In fact, he made no investments. Instead, he used the assets of new investors to pay these great profits to earlier investors. With each new recruited investor his obligations increased, and inevitably the bubble burst. Investors suffered great losses.[74] In Great Britain, a multimillionaire commodities dealer "claim[ed] that he and his family and friends have lost [£35 million]in such a scheme. . . . [H]e invested not only his money but that of his wife, children, and parents."[75]

D. HYBRID INSTITUTIONS AND OVERTONES

Some schemes enable charitable investors to have their cake and eat it too. In the case of the Greater Ministries International Church, the church offered "gifters" (that is, investors) a "double your money" investment plan. The gifting ministry asserted the ability to double the gifters' investments in seventeen months. The source of the profits was alleged to be gold and diamond mines in Liberia and international trading in commodities.[76] The word *gifter* reflects a feeling of charity and benevolence. Doubling the money is satisfying as well.

Another scheme sliced the pie differently. It allowed the victims to retain the principal but donate the excess profits they would receive "to help build God's kingdom."[77] Members were promised the same rate of return that they were currently receiving: "A brochure printed by the church invited parishioners to invest with [the con artist], announcing that 'in almost every case, our plan will be able to at least match or out perform your current yields, and at the same time earn dividends for our church and its future.'"[78]

Religious overtones help draw investors to an investment scheme, even if the investment is not directly involved with any particular church. On one website, a con artist raised money from investors for the purpose of producing a motion picture called "Messiah, The Coming."[79] Another schemer claimed to be a "Messianic Jew" by virtue of his wife's father, who was a Jew. This con artist sometimes used a biblical sounding name, Gary Dean benKeith, who "had worn out several bibles just by reading them so much" and declared that "his business answers to a higher authority: God, not the SEC."[80] A report in another case described how, after they bought into a pyramid business, the "owners are encouraged to participate in conference calls three nights a week—some lasting two or three hours" to pray with the con artist who "reads Scriptures." He told investors "that the idea for the business was a gift from God and large numbers of his network members came from fundamentalist church environments."[81]

One Arizona-based pyramid scheme, marketed on the Internet, requested donations to charities and offered the contributors earnings as well. Another called "GIFT" (given in freedom), sponsored by humanitarian philanthropists, recruits recruiters. Anyone who recruited three people was "gifted" tax-free returns that could amount to $20,000 annually deposited in an offshore trust account.[82] In fact, this was a classic pyramid scheme.

The Romanian Ponzi scheme Caritas benefited from the support of religion as well as patriotism. The leader of Caritas was described as "a saint," the "Pope," "a messiah," the "prophet." Said one believer: "God sent him to take care of us." "Thus saturated with divine symbolism, Stoica, the leader of Caritas, and Caritas became matters of *faith, of trust.* . . . With faith came also hope. People referred to Caritas money as their 'hope money' . . . without which they would have absolutely nothing, and declared that their only hope was Caritas. . . ." Faith did not require an explanation. Therefore "[a]nyone who could not . . . explain how it [Caritas] worked could assign it to the sphere of the divine." "Some people were not sure whether Caritas gave money from heaven or from hell. And some believed that the devil was at play here." "The money was no good." "It came too easily."[83]

2. Technology Has a Growing Impact on the Growth of Ponzi Schemes

An Australian regulator remarked that "investment scams are not a new phenomenon and will never disappear—they just re-emerge in a different guise." "However, investors today are more vulnerable," he said, in part "because technology has given scam artists a greater range of vehicles and opportunities to perpetrate a scam, to add to the traditional door-to-door method. 'The telephone and Internet have opened up whole new avenues for scamsters.'"[84]

Financial frauds have mushroomed in recent decades with the high-technology revolution. As millions of baby boomers move into retirement age, the problem could grow into an epidemic.[85] It is estimated that in 2000 telemarketers in the United States defrauded victims of about $40 billion. Not all frauds are classic Ponzi schemes; a con artist may simply sell a product, and fail to deliver. But some frauds are close to financial schemes, for example soliciting donations for charities that do not exist.[86] An unemployed single father, who faced rising debts, started a dot.com fund—EE-Biz Ventures— promising 40 percent to 100 percent in seven to ten days. EE-Biz claimed to be a Christian-based humanitarian organization and received about $50 million from thousands of people. A number of investors collected the promised returns, but others lost their investments. The plan lasted less than a year as investors' interest in the fund flared quickly and then died.[87]

Technology can help con artists in a number of ways. First, it reduces the cost of establishing personal face-to-face relationships, or the need to finance a large sales force to spread the word. One can send hundreds of thousands of letters and reap gains even if only a small percentage respond. Second, through the Internet con artists are better shielded from detection. Third, technology can help con artists avoid paying their obligations (the high return) by collecting investments and disappearing. Unless victims belong to an affinity group, news of failure to pay one investor does not travel so quickly to the other investors. Fourth, a change of name and style of the con artist's message can restart the game with little cost. Fifth, impersonal relationships have an emotional benefit for con artists. It may reduce any empathy for their victims; it is easier to hurt those you do not see or hear. Many con artists lack such empathy even in personal contact. But avoiding personal contact may produce more con artists today than there were in the past. A fascinating "blog" discussion that lasted at least four years relates to pyramid schemes.[88] It is worth reading because it demonstrates the enticing power of the scheme as well as its corruption. Some participants just aim at the money, while others point to the developing pressures they must exert over friends and family. Some encourage joining a plan and others recommend avoiding it in capital letters: DON'T.

A story of a fifteen-year-old and his loving and supportive father demonstrates this tendency. The father allowed the son to use his brokerage account for stock trading. The son bought penny stocks and used investment sites on the Internet to spread misleading information about these penny stocks. As interest in the stocks rose, the price of the stocks rose. The boy immediately sold the stocks at a huge profit, while the investors lost as the price fell to its former level. It may well be that this pair, the con artists, son and father, would have found an outlet for their tendencies without technology. But technology helped![89]

D. THE SALES FORCE

1. Collecting and Distributing Information

Because Ponzi schemes require an ever-growing number of investors to survive, their longevity depends on an effective securities distribution system. Investors can be recruited by advertising, mass mailing, or in this new age through the Internet.[90]

Information is important to con artists, especially if they deal in securities transactions. They are interested in investors' moods, and investment opportunities and new ways to reach more investors. Con artists use information networks, including people with access to information sources who can remain unnoticed.[91].For example, messengers can access large firms and glean information, yet they rarely draw any attention. These messengers are "so lowly and absurd in their pretensions to gentility and education that few ever take them seriously."[92]

Investors can serve as a sales force. The first sales force for Charles Ponzi consisted of his initial investors: family members, friends, long-term acquaintances.[93] This is still the case today, as low-income immigrants from the con artist's country serve to spread the word.[94] In November 2005, Edmundo Rubi pleaded guilty to operating a "scam that bilked hundreds of middle and low-income investors out of more than $24 million" from 1999 to 2001. Most of his investors were members of the Filipino community in the San Diego area.[95]

As noted, once a few are convinced, affinity group members are prone to invest together. But they are also the "songbirds," the ones to publicize the offering of unique investments. After the first-tier investors are paid high returns, these investors are likely to roll over their short-term investment, or increase it. When they are convinced, they serve as an unpaid sales force, by helping to establish the con artist's trustworthiness with friends and friends' friends. They spread the word as a favor to *their recruits*—perhaps in the hope of reciprocal treatment, and in order to demonstrate their own wisdom by showing their find. As one court explained: "[I]n the initial stages of the plan, those investors who wished to withdraw their investments were promptly paid. The effect of such prompt payment, of course, was to convert every investor into a missionary spreading the word of the enormous profits which could be speedily attained with no discernible risk of loss."[96] In Australia as anywhere else, "[a] scam is spread through word-of-mouth and initial investors, enthused by their returns, encourage others to join."[97] The "herding" phenomenon is enhanced by the investors themselves, many of whom are the victims.

2. Paid Sales Force

Even though the original investors can serve as a sales force, in the past the most effective form of distribution was by paid salespersons.[98] This conclusion may hold true today as well. In the 1920s Ponzi used paid salespersons.[99] Until 2008, Madoff used highly paid "feeder organizations." They were often the investment advisers and money managers for investors.

Salespersons and feeder funds are attracted to Ponzi schemes by the promise of generous commissions. In the case of Madoff, "Fund managers everywhere wanted in on it—Latin America, Asia and Europe—and they went to major banks looking for clients. . . ." It is rumored that even in Switzerland, which is known for a culture of discretion and secrecy in finance, financial institutions accepted payments from Madoff for recruiting investors: "By 2008, one third of all Geneva fund managers had invested with Madoff to the tune of $14 billion."[100]

Van Alstyne operated a scheme "by selling interests in . . . limited partnerships to elderly and retired investors." He recruited broker-dealers registered with the National Association of Securities Dealers (NASD). Van Alstyne tightly controlled his sales force, requiring "the brokers to adhere to a script that described a safe investment with a more than ten percent annual return, backed by AAA-rated government bonds" instead of the risky securities that they actually were.[101] Being paid well, some brokers became willing partners to this con artist.

In addition, Ponzi schemers may recruit salespersons who have clients of their own, such as insurance brokers. They may influence their clients to borrow on the cash value of policies and invest the cash in short-term promissory notes bearing a high interest rate.[102] The notes might be issued by risky start-up companies, yet represented as safe investments. The clients know and trust their insurance salespersons; after all, clients may have known the agents for some time.[103] Besides, the agents have offered policies from reliable insurance companies, so clients are likely to assume that any other offering from their agent should be just as reliable. Consequently, the agents turned Ponzi schemers exert less effort in gaining the clients' trust.

Usually, all distributors, be they investors, volunteers, or paid salespeople, are effective in spreading the con artists' reputation for success and trustworthiness. Those who discover the scheme but do not wish to get involved are likely to leave quietly without a fuss. Their motivation for keeping quiet seems similar to the motivation of investors and professionals who discover the real schemes and wish to disengage and forget they ever knew about it.[104] Rarely does anyone want to expose fraud within one's own group or profession. Nor would anyone wish to admit to friends and acquaintances or clients who have suffered a loss that he or she was a participant in such a fraud.

3. A Pure Sales Structure: Pyramid Schemes

Close cousins to Ponzi schemes are pyramid distribution schemes. The basis of these schemes is *sales of the right to sell a product that is generally not sellable*. One court defined a pyramid scheme as "any plan, program, device, scheme, or other process characterized by the payment by participants of money to the company in return for which they receive the right to sell a product and the right to receive in return for recruiting other participants into the program rewards which are unrelated to the sale of the product to ultimate users."[105]

A pyramid scheme combines two usual transactions to create an unusual sales organization. For example, a familiar transaction is the sale of gold and a down payment of part of the price. Paying commission is another ordinary form of compensating salespersons. In a pyramid scheme, the two are combined. The buyers of the gold pay for it partly in cash. The buyers pay the rest of the price by recruiting others to sell the gold. The recruits pay those who recruited them part of the money paid by their recruits, creating a hierarchical sales force with a strong incentive to sell not the gold but *the selling* of the gold. No wonder the scheme is named after this feature: "pyramid."

The genius of this scheme is that the victims *pay* the con artists for a story and for the privilege of selling a story to others, and pay not once but continuously, so long as they are paid by their recruits. The victims become to some extent con artists. This arrangement looks like a franchise, but it is not. In a franchise arrangement,

SELLING THE STORIES

investors pay for the franchisor's name, reputation, and services (e.g., a franchise to operate a Holiday Inn hotel). Investors-franchisees then build and operate their hotel as their own business under the franchised name. They continue to pay part of their hotel business profits to the franchisor for its ongoing services. The similarity of a pyramid scheme to franchising is that investors pay for a sales program, and continue to pay that person a percentage from the sales they made. But unlike a franchise, the so-called investors' income is derived not from any business or sale of products but from selling the same idea to others who pay for the plan to further sell to others.

An example of a pyramid scheme is the "Fulfillment Center." It promised investors $50 for each new recruited investor plus 20 percent of the new recruit's earnings from the fund. The promoter receives 10 percent from the earnings of recruits, raising about $6.5 million.[106] Another con artist allegedly raised more than $10 million through such a scheme based on the sale of cell phones. However, the business brought negligible returns. Most of the profits came from selling the same idea to others.[107] To draw investors into a pyramid scheme, some con artists place a newspaper advertisement in the "help wanted" section, implying a paid job. The people who respond are then pressed into buying "participations" in the scheme.[108] There is something enticing and challenging in the image of the pyramid: "Oh! To climb to the top of the pyramid!" And there is a very supportive group to boost the morale of the participants.[109]

From 1995 to 1996 the wife of a police captain in Sacramento operated such a club. The club involved at least sixty-seven employees of the police force. Some police personnel reportedly received tens of thousands of dollars for the $500 they invested. Others lost their investment of $500 or more. Police involvement added a special dimension to this scheme, for it provided legitimacy, trust, and authority to the recruitment. Needless to say, once the scheme was discovered it undermined the legitimacy, trust, and authority of the police department itself.[110] In the United States, high returns and low risk are sufficient to draw the marks. In other countries, additional allure may be clothed in associating with the upper class. In England, "Upper School Charm" has been added in the form of "The Oxford Savings Club [with] business addresses in Amsterdam and Antigua, West Indies."[111]

Fraudulent schemes of this kind share one prominent feature: in all cases, the victims contribute to the distribution of the schemes. And yet, the victims' involvement, and the methods employed are very similar to legitimate and reasonable forms of nonfraudulent distribution of investments. It makes sense for investors to rely on friends and people they know, instead of suspecting foul play. It makes sense to be drawn to leaders of a group to which they belong. And it makes sense for those who look for a source of income to be drawn to pyramid schemes.

To distinguish a pyramid system from a legitimate "multilevel" distribution system, one needs only to find out *who is buying.* If the buyers are consumers, the system is a multilevel distribution system. If most buyers are future distributors, and if they are paying for the privilege of selling, the system is likely to be an illegal pyramid scheme.[112]

How can con artists be so successful, especially when they must act in the limelight of publicity rather than hide? Why is it so difficult to distinguish honest persons from con artists? What is it that tempts the victims to sell fraudulent plans? Chapter 3 deals with these questions. We will find out how close the behavior of con artists is to the behavior of humans generally—including children. We discuss how similar Ponzi and pyramid schemes are to legitimate businesses and behavior, and how difficult it can be to distinguish between them.

Chapter 3

Con Artists' Behavior Seems a "Normal Usual Behavior"

This chapter demonstrates how difficult it is to distinguish most con artists from truthful and trustworthy people, and most Ponzi schemes from legitimate investment activities. The cons' behavior and enterprises are often quite similar to reliable promises and real business. In many respects, con artists' behavior and their enterprises are like those of everyone else, but in addition, we discover that con artists actually view their activities as business. They believe in these businesses. Their belief can make them believable.

A. HUMANS HAVE A NATURAL ABILITY TO PRETEND, LIE, AND INFLUENCE OTHERS

Con artists influence investors and induce them to invest by way of both true and imaginary statements and made-up signals. So do many people, in their everyday interactions. We send fake and false signals by actions, words, and expressions in order to induce others to act or react in a certain way. How many times have we given a fake compliment? How often have we laughed at a joke that we did not find funny? How frequently do we apologize for being late to a meeting by telling a story that is not entirely true? To smooth relationships and cause desired behavior, we often do not tell the entire truth or behave truthfully.

1. Humans—and Even Primates—Have the Innate Ability to Lie Convincingly

It has been suggested by Sanjida O'Connell in *Mindreading*, that "genes for lying play a crucial role in propagating this species." The ability to lie is embedded in our DNA, and some people are better at lying than others. According to O'Connell, some people excel at falsehood. These natural liars are usually quite aware of their talent, since they have deluded parents and teachers to escape punishment since early youth. They are confident and feel no fear or guilt about getting caught. Yet they are not sociopaths; they don't use their skills to hurt other people. In fact, they score the same as other people on psychological profiles. "But they seem to do better in certain careers, like sales, diplomacy, politics, acting, and negotiating."[1]

Pretending is a gift humans possess from a very early age. A child may put a banana to her ear as a telephone, even before she understands fully the falsity of the situation or distinguishes among mistakes, and separates pretense from false beliefs.[2] We smile indulgently when a toddler manipulates her parents into buying a toy. With his limited experience, he instinctively knows how to do that.

Deception by manipulation is practiced not only by humans but also by primates. Chimps and other animals are "artful liars."[3] A gorilla hid fruit that she found and walked nonchalantly away only to return three hours later to retrieve the fruit when no one was around. A chimp whose mother rejected his attempt to suckle pestered a male until the male hollered at the young chimp in exasperation; the infant shrieked and the mother ran over and offered him her nipple. The sign-language-using chimpanzee Lucy offered another chimp a plastic flower, which he took to be a gesture of friendship, only to be bitten by Lucy when he reached for the flower. A pair of baboons acted precisely like con artists in cooperating to deceive a third baboon. They watched that baboon hide the bananas he had found, and then one of the baboons diverted his attention while the other retrieved the bananas, only to enjoy the loot with the other conspirator later.[4]

2. Signs of Misleading Signals

It seems that along with the human ability to send misleading facial signals there exist ways for uncovering such signals. The science of discovering lies has been used for many years, especially in questioning criminals and suspicious persons. Methods of finding out intentional lies have been developed to determine the trustworthiness of money managers. The methods are not foolproof, but they help.[5] Although it is not easy to expose the true underlying feelings and intentions of other people, we do have some means of finding them out.

Facial impressions tell us much. In his book *The Face*, Daniel McNeill describes how facial expressions signal truth and hide lies. He classifies facial deceit into three basic types. One is opacity—revealing *nothing*, wearing a mask to hide thoughts and feelings. Joseph Stalin's stony face represented opacity. Successful poker players know how to control their facial expressions to avoid sending information about their reactions. Another form of facial deceit is used to show something that may not be entirely true. For example, the "Japanese smile" can be explained as a rule of etiquette designed to show politeness. This smile is important and acceptable, even when it does not express the feelings of the smiling person.[6] Third, facial expressions can signify active untrue messages, as with crying sadly even though one does not feel sad, or happily laughing when one does not feel happy.

A professional investigator can discern a lie by looking in the liar's eyes. A liar blinks more often, and his pupils are more dilated compared to a person who tells the truth. His expressions are more asymmetrical than that of a truth teller. Physical movements can provide signals as well. When a liar is focused on the words he speaks, his legs may be shaking; he might wring his hands or turn his feet inward. In addition, truth is usually told directly and forcefully: "I didn't do it"; a hidden lie may be told with formal grammar: "I did not take the money." Words like "honest to God" or a resort to religion may also raise concern as to veracity.[7]

Perhaps because the ability to manipulate is innate, humans have acquired protective mechanisms against manipulation. It seems that we are born with an ability to recognize other people's emotions and the nature of false signals and beliefs.[8] Children younger than three seem to "have an implicit understanding of false beliefs, even though they cannot verbally answer questions about a person's false beliefs until they are nearly five."[9] They seem to understand that there is a distinction between something that is real and something that seems real. Further, "'[h]uman communication is not just a transfer of information like two fax machines connected by a wire; it is a series of alternating displays of behavior by sensitive, scheming, second-guessing social animals.' Genuine communication where symbols, words or vocalizations have a meaning only occurs when the speaker intends listeners to understand the meaning of the word as the speaker understands it."[10] Yet even then, mistaken receptions may occur, especially when the speaker intends the listeners to understand the meaning of the words differently than he understands them.

The same techniques of fraudulent signals and the same protective responses are practiced all over the globe, regardless of race or culture. One explanation for this phenomenon is that the ability to manipulate and defraud, and the vulnerability to fall victim to such manipulation, as well as the capacity to protect ourselves from fraud, are all built into our experiences and brain. There is a certain maturation that enables people to play both roles of fraudulent and defrauded, relating to our retrieving mental images and comparing them to the present. With experience we can make comparisons and draw conclusions in an attempt to distinguish the real from the manufactured.[11]

3. Legitimate Lying

Lying and manipulation can be a respected profession or entertainment, as in acting, and a source of amusement, as with practical jokes. An interesting study of theater and movie actors, related to understanding con artists, suggested that actors can put on different personalities very quickly, but in order to do so they must feel *nothing*. Then they can "counterfeit all feelings," because "[t]rue feeling was an obstacle." Actors do not act *their own feelings* or the *feelings of the subjects* whom they mimic. This is why actors improve over time; they do not continue to exercise and experience feelings that might wane and be depleted with repetition.[12]

Not everyone agrees with this study, but it does resonate with respect to con artists and manipulators. As we shall see in Chapter 4, most con artists are unable to empathize with others. In fact, they may have little ability to feel anything at all. This may be the link to acting. Actors *think*; they do not *feel*.

Another study explains how actors can be so convincing without feeling. The actors *think* their characters' thoughts, and make these thoughts their own, acting the part and becoming the part.[13] It may well be that con artists act the character they have long been dreaming of. Therefore, the character comes naturally to them. They may not be able to act any other part, except to be the rich and powerful and famous that they crave and dream to be. This enables them to act naturally and be as convincing as good actors are.

Masks have been used in the theater for centuries. Perhaps one of the purposes of using masks is to make it easier for spectators to identify and understand the characters in the plays, and to interpret what the characters say and do in the context the plays. There are "universal faces," prototypes we accept, at least in our particular cultures. Hence, one can generalize, and create a mask or a prototype of con artists. The problem is that too many honest people have the characteristics of good actors, and the distinction between true and fake remains difficult. But one difference is obvious: theater actors tell the truth about their lying. The context—the stage or film or the circus—puts spectators on notice that they are witnessing mimics, and not real, active persons. Con artists send the opposite message: the spectators are witnessing not mimics but real people. This is the lie.

Practical jokes and hoaxes, some cruel, some pure fun, some fraudulent, some innocent, have been around for decades in the United States. Americans are willing to laugh at themselves, and some feel quite good about making fun of others. Jokes and hoaxes can be very profitable. Some are wholesome entertainment, and some are downright illegal. P. T. Barnum was a practical joker and a great American entertainer. His family and the village in which he grew up relished a good practical joke, and the inhabitants of the village retold the joke for years. Barnum is reputed to have authored the saying "There is a sucker born every minute," which his biographer disputes, probably quite rightly. Barnum was not about to humiliate and offend his vast audiences. But he did play jokes on them, and they loved him for it nonetheless. They loved his museum, his fake mermaid, and later his circus. In fact, until it became illegal, he ran a lottery, which served as a significant source of income for him and fun for the visitors. Barnum was first and foremost an advertiser, a master of "herding." He knew how to draw attention, build expectations, and whip up curiosity to a frenzied pitch. This was a significant part of the pleasure he gave.[14]

In a special double issue of *U.S. News & World Report* of August 26, 2002, the magazine presents "The Art of the Hoax." It does not mention P. T. Barnum. However, it reminds us of Charles Ponzi's saga. The magazine suggests that ours "is the golden age of hoaxes" and proceeds to name and describe dozens of such hoaxes. They include a hoax by the Allies on Hitler during the Second World War, an anti-Semitic fraud, a lie about the Freemasons, stories about hidden treasures of pirate captains, life on the moon and other science fiction tales, fake medicines, psychics' connection to the dead, and so on. People believed, and more often wanted to believe. The "age" covers more than one hundred years, and it includes today's frauds.

So what drives a magazine to call this day and age the golden age of hoaxes? The choice of the frauds in the article may signal the answer. They are not entertainment material; they are materials of serious deception. They end not in innocent fun but in severe losses by the believers. Some, like Charles Ponzi's story, are downright financial fraud. The difference between the types of deceptions has been blurred. This is therefore the age of "mixed hoaxes" that combine truth and falsity and slipping toward the fraudulent.

4. Exploiting the Weakness of the Social System

Con artists may exploit not only the weakness of individuals but also the weakness of a social system. In "Portrait of a Con Artist as a Soviet Man," Golfo Alexopoulos describes Vladimir Gromov, an impostor who has taken on so many roles that it is hard to know who he really is. An interesting aspect of the story, however, is that the man was a product of the culture of communist Russia during the 1930s. He did not succumb to the coercive system of the Soviet Union; instead, he exploited its weaknesses. The system was clogged with requirements for documentation, everywhere and for everything. Yet the system had no mechanism for discovering forgery. Therefore Golfo accumulated documents for every occasion and used them skillfully. This Soviet man was amazingly similar to con artists described both in the

United States and in Sweden. Capable, intelligent, and a risk taker, who knows how to manipulate not only people but the system, he uses correct dress, and manner of speech to project, and emulate Comrade Stalin and the power elite.[15]

The Soviet man recognized that the enforcers of the rules were slow to discover fraud. He evaluated correctly the cost of imposing the law that prohibited frauds and recognized the system's inability to enforce the prohibition on forgeries.

American con artists seem to manipulate the system in a similar way. Just as the Soviet man emulated the glut of documentation in Russia, American con artists emulate the powerful and identify the system's weakness in America.

The Soviet man was finally caught, one could argue, because of his obsessive risk taking. Most American con artists meet the same fate, except for one difference: they are treated far more leniently.

5. The Slippery Slope: From Honesty to Fraud

Honest people can succumb to temptation and secretly cross the fairness line, if the payoff is high. For example, through the Internet con artists may send an e-mail that *seems* to have been intended for someone else and sent in great confidence. The message contains a recommendation of an investment, which the recipients are led to believe is a real "tip." Some recipients of the message will rush to buy the stock. But after more and more recipients buy, and the price of the stock rises, the con artist (who held the stock before sending the message) sells the stock at a profit. The tempted investors lose.[16] They used information that was not addressed to them, and in fact they misappropriated it if they bought the securities on the assumption that no one knew about this secret information.

Honest mechanisms can enhance the ability to cheat. Dale Carnegie's book *How to Win Friends and Influence People* has spawned a teaching center advertising the book as "the most influential business book of the twentieth century."[17] The teaching at the Center is based on the book's principles. There is nothing wrong in attempting to influence and convince other people. The court system is based on influencing judge and jury. Congressional arguments and presentations seek to convince the other parties and the voters. However, the skills of influencing people may be used for teaching good arguments or for evil, misleading cheating. Just as sales organizations can help salespersons sell goods, fraudulent pyramid schemes can produce not sales but salespersons. The form and teaching of both organizations are similar.

How much can be gained by the wrongful act may make a difference. In one experiment, a bus driver gave passengers the "wrong amount of change." Most people returned the difference if the "mistaken" amount was small; fewer people returned the difference if the amount was higher. There were always justifications to accept the "mistake"; after all, the bus company is wealthy and the passenger may be in need of money. Besides, the bus driver should be more careful handling change, and it is his fault that the passenger received more than was due. The circumstances corrupted fundamentally honest people.

Ponzi schemes have many components that, standing alone, reflect legitimate business practices. For example, although people can have very good ideas, they may lack the persistence and ability to put these ideas into practice, to plan their projects carefully, and bring them to fruition. They may have little patience for tending to the details and no endurance to wait for eventual rewards. Thus they lose the opportunity to create a legitimate business, even when this opportunity exists. Therefore when they launch their enterprise they may be truthful, but as it develops and begins to falter, some business operators turn to fraudulent solutions. Precisely where and when they change course is sometimes hard to detect, except in retrospect.

To demonstrate the ineptitude of some con artists in their business attempts, consider a businessperson named John Aptt, who operated Financial Instruments Corporation from 1994 to 1997. The company raised about $14 million from investors, promising high interest rates and periodic "Double Your Money." The payments to earlier investors brought in new investors: ability of the company to pay these returns was explained by the "exemplary" business acumen and technical creativity of its founder. When in early 1995 Aptt's promotional materials were noticed by an attorney in the Enforcement Division of the Securities and Exchange Commission, Aptt assured the attorney (untruthfully) that he did not raise any money from investors and was thinking of abandoning the project. Instead, Aptt continued to solicit investments in an empty corporation.

Aptt and Douglas Murphy, whom he enlisted, concluded that they had to go on or else default. They had to solicit additional investments, although this was not a permanent solution. Therefore, in early 1996 Murphy and his brother Bruce, a disbarred attorney, transferred the current business to a new corporate shell and used it to raise long-term low-interest debt. Using another lawyer, who was not aware of the corporation's problems, Murphy sought to make an unregistered securities offering as the original company invested in "promising investments" that failed. Then in early 1997, the Securities and Exchange Commission received an anonymous tip that the company was operating a Ponzi scheme; the SEC brought an action against the company. Of the $13.5 million due to investors, the company had $1.8 million. Aptt was sentenced to nine years in prison and Murphy to about eight years.[18]

A con artist who offered enormous returns did not seem to understand how his own Ponzi schemes worked. He wrote that the "way it is set up is really cool and we will make plenty and pay everyone, too." But when asked how he would achieve this "cool way," he seemed to struggle for the next several minutes to understand how the scheme could receive $300 and pay back $600 a few days later. He "solved the problem by suggesting he would invest money in other people's Ponzi schemes."[19]

Some businesses start as lawful businesses and have a Ponzi ending. There seems to be little difference in the way legal businesses and Ponzi schemes operate and in how they end. After all, a business that is lawfully conducted can fail just as a Ponzi scheme does. But the circumstances which lead to the failure differ. For example, in 1998 a money manager, who invested clients' money in a friend's company, faced tremendous losses as that company was on the brink of bankruptcy. His choices: he could try to save the investment, he could disclose the losses to the clients, or he could "try to stave off the clients' wrath" and the regulators' examination. He chose the third option. When the regulators caught on, they accused the manager of operating a Ponzi-like scheme to cover the loss of $200 million by diverting the money of new investors to pay interest to current investors.

The manager and his partner started very young and were known for risk taking. The manager had legal problems before, in 1982, 1992, and 1995. But even though his business flourished, there were persistent signals of problems. A newspaper reported that from 1996 to 1998 his company "helped finance expensive hunting and fishing trips for at least nine trustees from five different union trust funds."[20] The company financed a moose and caribou hunt in Alaska to the tune of $22,000. There was a consulting contract worth $950,000 to the co-chairperson of investing trust funds.

Then, as a large investment was going to default, the manager began hiding the losses, according to the government's accusation. To the clients, the manager described his actions as a "heroic" attempt to save their investments. He told the clients that an "unknown company had promised to pay them $160 million for their future stake in the nearly dead" investment. They did not question the statement, and their interest payments continued to arrive. In fact, the government argued, the clients' money was lent to the company so that it could pay them the interest, and the maneuver failed. The manager described the efforts differently: "We had legal opinions every which way to make sure we did it right. It just amazes me it's gotten so much attention." He continued to be optimistic and defend his efforts.[21]

Similarly, a hedge fund manager who controlled about $450 million of investors' money incurred significant losses and in attempting to recoup the losses he paid investors with the money of new investors. Most of them were abroad and had little control over his activities.[22]

In a 2009 case, an Ohio con artist controlled a number of entities that purported to be in various business ventures. In reality, he operated, between November 1997 and December 2001 a Ponzi scheme

in which he solicited investments in businesses that were either unprofitable or unable to pay interest on the promissory notes [the con artist] gave to investors as security. Instead, [he] used his investors' money for other purposes and solicited additional investments in order to pay interest to earlier investors and prolong the scheme. He also provided guarantees from a number of entities claiming to be insurance companies. But . . . these insurance companies did not have the capacity, ability, or intent to repay the notes if the corporations defaulted.[23]

In this case, some of the businesses were failing enterprises that slipped to a Ponzi scheme instead of declaring bankruptcy.

Another owner of three failing companies had his conviction upheld in 2000 of embezzling from the employees' profit sharing plans, which the owner controlled. He used the money to pay operating expenses of the companies.[24] In the last analysis, there is little difference between these failing businesses and the beginning of

Ponzi stories except in how their owners (and the controlling persons) chose to solve their difficulties.

Borrowing with good intentions to repay the loans can slip into a Ponzi scheme. Thus a travel agent, who had many clients, solicited short-term loans (usually thirty days) from these clients and in return promised to "give them free travel benefits, such as cruises and first-class airline tickets." But then the scheme expanded and the agent sought loans to repay previous loans or buy airline tickets for previous lenders. Eventually, the agent "used clients' personal information and credit card numbers to open new lines of credit or to purchase tickets." One thing led to another, as the agent "left vendors or cooperating travel agents with unpaid bills and 'repaid' some lenders with bad checks." Complaining clients received one-way international tickets as round-trip tickets, leaving them (including one person who was a minor) "stranded in foreign countries."[25] These activities, which may have started as small-scale borrowing with a sincere intention to repay, ended up in Ponzi criminal activities.

6. Ponzi Scheme "Businesses" Mirror Respectability

A. LEGITIMATE BUSINESSES: BANKING AND FINANCIAL INSTITUTIONS

The structure and image of many Ponzi schemes can be legitimate, respectable, and familiar. Many Ponzi schemes mirror banking and other financial institutions. The con artists receive money from investor-depositors and are expected to transfer the money to borrowers who promise to repay the money with interest. Ponzi schemes are very similar to refinancing, which is what many legally operating enterprises do. That is, they borrow from Peter to pay Paul, for example when interest rates fall and they can get financing cheaper elsewhere. If the chances for a successful enterprise are low, and if the entrepreneurs recognize this fact but continue to borrow and repay former

creditors, they may end up backing into a Ponzi scheme.[26] The difference between banking and Ponzi schemes is not necessarily in the
structure of the institution, or in the nature of the transactions, but
mainly in the truthfulness of the information about the borrowers,
and the reliability of the guarantees that the investors receive from
the con artists.

B. STOCK MARKET TRADING: FOLLOWING THE TRENDS
To some extent, it is hard to distinguish the victims of Ponzi schemes
from stock market traders. Robert Shiller, a Yale economist, "has likened the entire stock market to a 'naturally occurring Ponzi process,'
where the prosperity of later investors depends on the willingness of
the earlier generation to put its money down."[27] Most investors are
"free riders" following the herd. Free riders seek to benefit from the
research and information that others have accumulated; the free
riders wait to see how others act before they make their investment
decision. Their inclination to rely on others' efforts is rational, and
not necessarily unfair. After all, others may rely on the traders' actions
in the belief that they have done their homework.

But free riding does not work well in stock market trading. As the
herd of investors grows and more investors buy more shares, the price
of the shares rises. Therefore, slow, more cautious, or lazier investors
end up buying the same shares at a higher price. If some investors lead
the herd to sell, then the trend reverses. Investors who bought at a
high price are often reluctant to sell their shares; they are loath to
sustain losses. Again, they may be waiting to see what many other
investors will do. After these cautious investors finally sell their shares,
prices have plummeted and they suffer significant losses. Following
the herd, they pay attention to what other purchasers and sellers are
doing and less attention to rising and falling market prices and evalu-
ation of the securities. Therefore such free riders, as cautious or lazy
investors, lose the most.[28]

Ponzi schemes produce a similar result, although the investors' intentions do not enter the picture. Those who are first to invest in the schemes seem to be taking the highest risk, but in fact they are likely to be winners. Those who are more cautious and wait longer before they invest are likely to be losers. In Ponzi schemes and in the securities markets, investors who follow the actions of others and do not rely on their own information or their own research and independent decisions are likely to be losers.

To be sure, there are differences between Ponzi schemes and market games. In the markets, early investors do not always gain at the expense of later investors. The chances of gain are hard to calculate because markets are mostly chaotic and unpredictable. In a Ponzi scheme, earlier investors are far more likely to gain at the expense of latecomers. The market *system* and the laws supporting it give every player a similar chance of securing information, and no one is allowed to rig the prices. In Ponzi schemes the rules are set in advance; the game is not truthful and therefore is unfair to those who are in the dark. The price is unreal, rigged. What seems fair and real is in truth unfair and unreal.

C. SALESPERSONS AND TRADERS

It is difficult to distinguish con artists from legitimate salespersons and traders. After all, con artists engage in selling, just as many honest salespersons do. In fact, some con artists started their careers in sales.[29] Salespersons often talk customers into buying what they would not otherwise buy.[30] They may "puff" and exaggerate the virtues of the offered merchandise and services. They may use the pressure of reciprocity by offering gifts such as free lunches. The gifts can press buyers to reciprocate by buying, and in the process return the value of the gifts manyfold.[31] Reciprocity is sometimes effective even after the sale. A small gift after a sale of a horrendously overpriced item may reduce the probability of cancellation of the sale.[32] Generally, salespeople attempt to forge friendships with customers and gain their trust.

At the same time, salespersons can have a sense of entitlement, driven by a strong desire for results. I remember one salesperson telling me, "When I speak to a customer, I feel that part of the money in his pocket belongs to me." This statement, made in earnest by a person who considers himself honest, is revealing. If some of the money in a potential buyer's pocket belongs to the salesperson, then actions that might otherwise be questionable are permissible. The sense of entitlement may be the reason salespeople offer information that is not entirely accurate, and why in many cases they are allowed to do so. The assumption is that the buyers understand the salespersons' state of mind, and therefore are more skeptical about persuasive techniques. However, not all buyers are protected from the persuasive attractions. When this assumption is wrong, the buyers can be defrauded.

Buyers can send sellers misleading signals as well. In the bazaar, buyers often divert the seller's attention from the buyer's interest in a particular object. When there are no fixed prices, the parties bargain. In this environment, a shopper interested in a particular item will show an interest in *another item*, and only casually ask for, or offer, a price on the desired item, usually together with an item in which he or she has no interest.

Animals can trade and bargain as well. They can evaluate the "market demand" of an item. If an object falls into the chimpanzees' cage and their keeper motions to have it returned, the chimpanzee may demand (and receive) a reward of food. If the item is valuable (or if it is an item that is dangerous to the animals, which the zoo keeper wishes to retrieve quickly), the chimpanzees may demand not juice, which is their commonplace drink, but grapes, which they receive only seldom.[33] They can tell the value of the service they are asked to perform and the rewards that they can bargain for. Furthermore, some animals develop rules on how much cheating they will tolerate. They pay less attention to the alarms of females than to the alarms of the male members of the group.[34] They have developed simple rules on limiting interaction with strangers, and reciprocating in kind. Therefore, it seems that trading, reciprocity, tolerating some deception in the interactive process, and drawing a line on how much deception is acceptable is innate in some animals as well as humans. It is not surprising that investors cannot easily distinguish between similar products that carry different prices, so long as the price difference is not glaring.

D. ENTREPRENEURS

Many con artists behave like entrepreneurs. Entrepreneurs are creative, and their offerings are usually unique. This is also true of con artists operating Ponzi schemes. Entrepreneurs are optimistic, and sometimes overoptimistic. The managers of newly established companies are more optimistic than the managers of old and diversified companies. So are con artists.

Studies suggest that competitors win not because they are more fit before they enter the arena to compete, but because they are more optimistic: "Optimistic people are inclined to take more and higher risks, and are less affected by failures. As they try more often, they have a better chance of succeeding than those who do not try."[35] Further, in business "people exhibit significant overconfidence in the validity of their predictions."[36] Like entrepreneurs, con artists show a remarkable inclination to be optimistic.

An example of optimistic behavior is the case of the con artist Terry Spirk, who started his career in insurance and became the owner in 1991 of an annuity service business. He operated the business profitably for several years. Then he decided to found American Senior Alliance, Inc. (ASA). He created a holding company that held two subsidiaries: the insurance business and the new business offering health and travel programs for members. Because he found it more difficult to recruit members to the new business, by 1996 the new subsidiary could not stay in operation. To sustain the new business, he drew financial assistance by "selling convertible notes in its profitable sibling," the insurance company. Investors in the notes were assured that their investments were safe by pledging Spirk life insurance policies as additional security. The notes were not registered with state or federal securities regulators. In 1998 the Illinois Securities Department told Spirk to either register the notes or stop selling them. He promised to comply but continued to sell unregistered notes, telling investors that the state "had authorized the notes' sale." One might speculate that optimism played a major role: tomorrow the problems will "go away." But when the insurance company's problems grew worse he resolved them by selling more notes faster and defrauding more investors. The fact that "Spirk did not live the high life while the money rolled in" seems to verify his optimism and belief that he could revive his business. He plowed the cash he received back into the two subsidiaries and reduced his own salary so that he could pay the staff's wages.[37] He seems to have truly wanted the real business to succeed. But when it did not, he resorted to a Ponzi scheme. A similar process and tenacity is demonstrated in the 1999 Ponzi scheme by Martin Armstrong that allegedly cost investors approximately $3 billion.[38]

Like legitimate entrepreneurs, con artists take risks. If entrepreneurs fail, they usually try again. So do con artists. Entrepreneurs are "project-oriented," stimulated by starting something new. This may be the reason failures daunt them less—beginnings excite them more. So do beginnings for con artists. Most, if not all, entrepreneurs borrow. In fact, even most legitimate businesses borrow. It makes economic sense to borrow a percentage of the operating capital. Businesses pay dividends while borrowing. Financial institutions such as mutual funds redeem their securities with borrowed money, under certain conditions. Individual investors buy securities on margin—borrow a portion of the price of securities in which they invest. Hedging is legitimate, justifiable, and sometimes even encouraged by tax law. Ponzi schemers operate the same way. Thus con artists are similar to entrepreneurs.

However, there are two fundamental differences between legitimate entrepreneurs and Ponzi schemes. First, legitimate businesses, however risky, reward investors and benefit society by providing incentives to finance productive and creative efforts. Ponzi schemes do not. They transfer money from one group of investors to another group and to the con artists. No additional wealth is created from an earmarked enterprise. Second, investors in legitimate schemes are not deceived. They receive true information that allows them to make informed investment decisions, and they take the risks they know about. Investors in Ponzi schemes are not told the truth, even if some may guess at the truth. They make an uninformed decision. Nevertheless, these two differences are hard to identify because the form and many features of Ponzi schemes resemble and actually constitute legitimate business practices.

E. CON ARTISTS ARE BELIEVABLE: THEY BELIEVE IN THEIR ACTIVITIES AND VIEW THEM AS BUSINESSES

Con artists are believable perhaps because they view their activities and present their activities as "businesses." But so do many honest people who start a business and seek financing. In bankruptcy cases, many con artists argue that they are businesspersons who failed. Con artists may have grandiose dreams of making a fortune, of gaining recognition and respect, and they may act on their dreams. Dreams may make their appearance real and their behavior natural and believable. Grandiose dreams are not the exclusive province of Ponzi con artists; people engaged in legitimate activities—business, academic, and military leaders—share such dreams and act them out. So it is possible that con artists may be dreamers who could not rise to the height of their dreams. Yet even this trait is not unique to them. Investors and managers may start out or find themselves on a losing route. But they might continue to follow it, and sometime escalate their commitment to it in the hope of recouping losses. The psychological explanation for such behavior is the "need to justify previous investments and reduce the dissonance provoked by high investments and little or no returns."[39]

Charles Ponzi had an unshakable faith in a magical idea that would come to him and materialize. He had no doubt about it, and this made him a formidable persuader.[40] Believing that this magical idea would come, if one idea did not work out, he erased it from his thoughts and went on to try another. After a fiasco in promoting a publication venture, he wrote: "I dismissed The Trader's Guide from my mind. Another house of cards had collapsed. That did not matter. I was getting accustomed to chasing rainbows. As one would fade away, I would pursue another. For a dreamer, I certainly was persevering. I never was a quitter. Undaunted by failure, I transferred my attention . . . to international reply coupons."[41] He hoped to acquire banks. That would enable him to reduce the returns he would promise investors, and manage a legitimate business.[42] Unshakable belief in his destiny and its success was catching and persuasive.

When con artists speak of their enterprise enthusiastically, they speak the truth—*their truth*, as they see it and feel it and want it to be. People who truly believe are convincing, regardless of whether they are telling the truth as others see it. The self-representation of con artists does not conflict with their dreams. Con artists may be like those who believe they have experienced a miracle. Studies have shown that recent events affect people's long-term predictions.[43] Con artists who live the fairyland life of the rich while being poor get trapped in their own fantasy. In fact, they may get so used to the roles they play that their businesses and their lifestyle, friends and connections become real to them: "Many first-time perpetrators of this crime become so accustomed to the lifestyle it generates that they themselves are in disbelief when it crumbles, convinced over time by their own lies."[44]

People may believe that their activities constitute their business, while in reality their business differ from their activities. The Ponzi business has two main components. One is producing a story about a business. The other is selling the story together with worthless obligations. That is, the con artist may think long and hard about a story that would appeal to marks and then build a distribution system to market the story. Nonetheless, the activities and the stories are very similar to real activities and businesses.

A journalist's description of a certain con man is revealing. The con artist and a potential partner were traveling to a remote area to examine an abandoned gold mine, to which access was very difficult. The con artist kept repeating that he was looking, so far in vain, for "added value" in the mine.[45] Other investments, he said, offered added value. This term is puzzling—that is, if we focus on the *mine as an investment*. To the con man, however, the mine must produce another kind of added value, that is, added to the story that he intended to market. Now we understand: if his business was simply selling a story, then the existence of the mine could not attract investors, or could be too easily discovered for what it was.[46]

This con artist refused to give the journalist details about the mine. The journalist retorted that this refusal made the con artist look suspicious. "'Suspicious?' [the con artist countered.] 'I have projects to protect. I have no use to publicize a project that's in development.'"[47] The con artist viewed the mine as a "project in development" that could not be publicized until he was ready to *sell the story* about the mine, and so he had to make sure that the location of the project would remain difficult to reach.

We have noted that during the life span of a Ponzi scheme, con artists rarely let their investors become unsatisfied. Dissatisfied investors, wrote Charles Ponzi, "might have wrecked the whole structure."[48] What structure was he writing about? A plausible answer is that he was referring to the structure on which his business was founded, that is, paying prior investors with the money paid by later investors. He considered himself a successful businessman and a financier, drawing evidence from how adoring investors treated him.

Con artists attempt to draw out their projects as long as possible. But they are not discouraged by the ultimate and inevitable failure of a project. When one project terminates, they start another. As a scheme comes to an end in one place, they move the scheme to another place. Stories do not require a manufacturing facility; they cost little and are easily transported. The investment is in finding marks.[49] Thus their persistence and their innovative new businesses are similar to those of entrepreneurs.

F. LONGEVITY OF THE BUSINESSES BREEDS RESPECTABILITY

One reason for the difficulty in distinguishing Ponzi schemes from legitimate business is that the schemes can last for a number of years and generally played with the same marks. Ponzi schemes last far longer than crooked poker games, for example. In cards the marks can be hit only a few times until they figure out the game. In addition, they quickly lose all the money they put at risk and the con artist must disappear. But rarely do Ponzi schemers embezzle and escape with all the money that the first "marks" entrusted to them.

Long-term businesses seem, and are often assumed to be, more reliable than beginning businesses and point to the businesses' future prosperity. After all, their lasting existence could demonstrate a solid market for their products, their ability to adjust to changes, and perhaps the leadership of innovative and reliable management. These assumptions are generally accepted even though there is evidence to the contrary that casts doubt about their conclusions. Needless to say, belief in the reliability of long-term businesses supports and feeds the longevity of con artists' imaginary "businesses."

Con artists do not abscond with the money they are handed at first, for both personal and business reasons. At the outset, investors do not rush to offer their money to con artists; they must be persuaded to do so. To induce investors to hand over their money, Ponzi con artists must gain investors' trust. To gain their trust, these con artists must exert far more effort than con artists require in, say, enticing marks to join a rigged poker game. At the same time, the nature of the con artists' efforts in sending these signals differs from seeking financing by real businesses. To start their token business, con artists do not need capital, of which they have little; nor do they need to produce products, of which they have none. They need to produce more investors. For this production, they need an idea and their own labor, of which they have a lot. Con artists do not always succeed on the first try and must try again using other ideas in other places. All these efforts must be performed before the investors hand over their money.

A one-shot deal is not likely to cover the con artists' initial investment. Even if it does, an investment that is successful could produce more than the money embezzled from the first group of investors. A growing reputation could bring more profits. Besides, like any "herding" phenomenon, the first pressure, the first movement of the herd, is the hardest to achieve. Once investors have become enthusiastic about the investment, they bring more marks to the game and offer more money of their own.

The con artists' costs of producing trust fall in proportion to increasing success. To gain investors' trust and create a reputation, con artists invest in costly signals. The more costly the signals are to the con artists, the more genuine and trustworthy they appear. The more trustworthy the con artists appear, the less attention is paid to the scheme that they offer, the harder it is to uncover the true nature of their scheme, and the longer the scheme will last.

To recoup their seed money and use the reputation they establish, it is rational for Ponzi con artists to continue the game. To continue, they must keep on acting in a trustworthy manner, and pay investors the promised profits. Thus the very nature of the scheme induces con artists to deviate from short-term trustworthy behavior and continue to behave in a trustworthy manner long-term. Such behavior serves their interests.

In addition, acting in a (partially) trustworthy manner does not mean deprivation for Ponzi schemers. It means refraining from embezzling *all* the money that they collect. For them, the fruits of trustworthiness are sweet because they do embezzle part of the money, and enjoy signaling trustworthiness. Donations, entertainment, and social activities are not only beneficial but also pleasing and satisfying.

Con artists continue to savor substantial profits, luxury, self-worth, prestige, rubbing shoulders with the rich and famous, and even achieving political power. The monetary and emotional rewards for acting in a trustworthy manner and for not embezzling *all, but only part,* of the entrusted money exceed the benefit from a one-time embezzlement of the entire amount entrusted to them.[50]

Many con artists, especially those addicted to their opulent way of life, cannot do anything else but continue to operate their schemes. "Byron Keith Brown was sentenced to a 15-year prison term . . . for stealing $17 million from investors through an internet Ponzi scheme." He accumulated an extensive car collection, including BMW, Bentley, Mercedes-Benz, Lamborghini, and Land Rover models, "as well as a decent replica of a 1936 Auburn Speedster."[51] Thus, compared to any alternative, the schemes bring enormous monetary and ego rewards and excitements. They help con artists' meteoric rise to the ranks of the rich and powerful; they feed their self-worth and gain their investors' admiration. Acting trustworthy, rich, powerful, and smart comes naturally, often with the support of education and practice. This way of acting is their tool of the trade, rather than a wrongful act. For these schemers, the benefits of creating a reputation for trustworthiness are far greater than they are for hit-and-run con artists. They may hope to enjoy the good life of the rich as long as they can, to "do the honorable thing" or to "go legitimate." The probability of spending time in prison is remote, and a prison term is likely to be shorter than the good life during the existence of the scheme. Besides, prison does not seem daunting to some (if not all) con artists. Therefore, it is not surprising that Ponzi schemers are rational, repeat offenders. Most con artists continue playing the game to the bitter end.[52]

Ponzi schemes are risky for con artists, even if they share the risk with some of their marks. Yet con artists have an advantage over the marks because they know that no real business will bring the promised profits, although the con artists do not know how many investors will join the game and when investors will cease coming on their own—or as a result of government intervention. Most importantly, as noted, most con artists do not view their particular scheme as a stand-alone, one-time venture. A scheme is but one project in their business. Therefore, they attempt to maximize their benefits from every project they operate, recognizing, however, that some projects will last a shorter period than others. They are likely to wait until they are caught, settle their fines or prison sentences, and then leave to start their projects in another place.

And yet, what about the danger of prison sentencing? What about the risk of being discovered and shamed? As we will note in the next chapter, con artists are risk takers. Tempting the authorities is part of their fun. Fear of prison does not cloud their enthusiasm; indeed, it may increase it. In order to understand them and their investors, we turn to Chapter 4.

Chapter 4

A Profile of The Con Artists and Their Victims

In Chapter 3, we examined the con artists' activities and behavior, which seem "normal," reflecting the way many people behave. This chapter analyzes the unique character features of con artists and their victims. These features are different from those of many other people and can explain some of the causes of deviant behavior. We start by observing the tendency of con artists and some of their victims to become addicted to the game. We view the slippery slope from speculation to addictive investments, both legal and illegal. This characteristic, which both con artists and some of their victims may share, can help explain the survival of Ponzi schemes around the globe over so many years.

Following that, we highlight and explore the dark side of con artists—their narcissistic character (which some psychiatrists consider a disorder), their lack of empathy, their "barren creativity," and the way they protect their ego. We then move on to examine the character traits and behavior of the con artists' victims—their tendency toward gullibility (irrational trusting), "risk tolerance," a strong need to feel exclusive and special, and their predictable reactions upon discovering they have been had.

A. THE DARK SIDE OF CON ARTISTS (AND SOME OF THEIR INVESTORS)

1. Con Artists Are Different from Most People

The story of the con artist's personality includes not only charm, ability, and similarity to honest persons. It includes addiction to unrealistic dreams and overwhelming ambitions. Behind the façade of Dr. Jekyll (the benign physician and healer) lies a psychological makeup of Mr. Hyde (the killer). Con artists are likely to have a narcissistic character. Such people are consumed by an insatiable appetite for money, prestige, and the need for other people's attention and adoration. With this disorder comes lack of empathy for others, including the people they have ruined. They may not be able to feel anyone else's pain. Perhaps they are unable to experience any deep feelings at all.

The word *narcissism* is derived from Greek mythology. Narcissus was a handsome lad who paid no attention to a nymph that was in love with him. For this attitude, which the gods considered a wrong, they punished Narcissus by making him fall in love with his own reflection. It was an appropriate and very painful punishment, indeed, because he could never grasp or reach and touch his image as it was reflected in the waters of a pool. His prize was himself, but his image dissolves on touch.

Andrew Twardon, the director of New York's St. Luke's-Roosevelt Hospital's Center for Intensive Treatment of Personality Disorders, noted "that [Bernard] Madoff may be a narcissist, a personality disorder that differs significantly from the antisocial pattern. 'Whereas in the antisocial personality, the primary problem is disregard for norms and laws and the need to inflict suffering on others for personal satisfaction, the narcissistic personality is about self-aggrandizement— what you would call, in popular psychology, denial.'"[1] Although few people are entirely free of all narcissistic traits, if a number of these traits are combined some psychiatrists conclude that they can result in a character disorder.[2]

Individualism does not mean self-interest and self-love to the exclusion of others and society. We have the ability to combine self-love with love and sacrifice for others. In fact, a total negation of the self is not healthy, and perhaps impossible so long as life is valuable. But the other extreme of feeling nothing for others is both unhealthy and antisocial. Therefore, healthy people view themselves as special and worthy of friendship and love. Yet they possess a relatively realistic internal picture of who they are and what they are capable of doing, even as they may engage in daydreaming. Narcissists are fundamentally different. They have a deep feeling of inferiority that must be denied.

There are examples of famous narcissists, such as Louis XIV, who declared, *"L'etat, c'est moi"* (I am the State). He viewed everyone else as an incarnation of himself. Marie Antoinette wondered why the starving people begging for bread did not eat cake; she could not perceive of starvation unless she experienced it.[3] Both could imagine no other feelings but their own.

This character was noted as a disorder and described in the DSM-11 (*The Diagnostic and Statistical Manual of Mental Disorders, 11th ed.*) as

an inflated sense of self-importance; fantasies of unlimited success, fame, power, beauty, and perfect love (uncritical adoration); exhibitionism (a need to be looked at and admired); a tendency to feel rage with little objective cause; a readiness to treat people with cool indifference as punishment for hurtful treatment, or as an indication of the fact they have no current use for the person; a tendency toward severe feelings of inferiority, shame, and emptiness; a sense of entitlement accompanied by the tendency to exploit; a tendency to over-idealize or devalue people based largely on a narrow focus; an inability to empathize.[4]

Disorder or not, the description seems to fit a certain personality. In this book the discussion is entirely descriptive rather than prescriptive. There is no suggestion on whether or how narcissists' tendencies should be, or are, cured.

Elan Golomb explained: a narcissist withdraws from other people in order to protect himself from feeling inferior. He feeds on, and needs, continuous admiration and assurance. Yet he cannot admit the need. Therefore, he lives in a "one-person world." Either he exists and others do not or others exist, but then he does not. To continue to exist, he views others as shadows or things that help feed him; "He remains aloof from people in his automat world."[5]

Narcissists can be charming and show gratitude for gifts even while not *feeling* gratitude.[6] Yet they are easily offended.[7] Whether narcissism should be considered a serious illness depends on the degree to which the narcissists can imagine other people's feelings, that is, empathize, and be "truly productive and loving."[8] Thus, con artists do not necessarily have a character disorder. But many of them do.

Con artists may include psychopaths of various other types. Perhaps they act the character they have long been dreaming of, such that the character comes naturally to them. As noted, they may not be able to act any other part except this one: the rich, powerful and famous that they crave and dream to be. But some con artists can pose as different people. In Toronto, for example, George Croft, a con artist, entered prison as a corporate executive and emerged as a law professor. He managed to convince at least some people of his new role, until it was uncovered. A psychologist described Croft as a psychopath[9]; nonprofessionals might not detect this trait. He certainly was convincing.

2. On Very Rare Occasions a Con Artist Might Resort to Murder

Under pressure, a con artist may be driven to murder. Here is a chilling example.[10] In July 1998 a body was discovered on a trawler; "All traces of identification had been removed from the body—except the victim's Rolex watch."[11] The registration number of the watch led to the identity of the dead man and the story of his murder. "The victim had sold his identity to his killer—a Canadian who had been on the run for five years from charges in Ontario of stealing millions of Canadian dollars from the clients of his financial services company. At one time, he was number four on Interpol's list of the world's most wanted men."[12]

The truth about this Canadian con man began to emerge. A son of a truck driver with six children, he was considered dumb. Having failed his basic exams he left school at sixteen and attended college for six years without graduating. Yet even in the 1960s he looked and dressed conservatively, and he dreamed of retiring to Scotland as a gentleman. In college he met and married the daughter of well-to-do parents in a small, wealthy, and close-knit society. With the help of his wife and family, he developed a financial services business. He became a Sunday school teacher and a chruch elder and was considered respectable, stylish, and dynamic—a happy-go-lucky guy, a pleasant, easygoing, and well-liked man. His advisory investment company did well. However, his success was based on "creative accounting." Though investors paid large sums for the promissory notes he issued and the insurance policies he offered for a term of five years (with an option to recall the principal), he often banked the investors' money through a Cayman Islands company and conducted a classic Ponzi scheme.

Members of the community bought the con man's personal notes because he was a member of a prominent family, charming and nice, and because, not surprisingly, the notes paid higher-than-usual returns. Investors trusted him fully, but complaints began to trickle in. About three years after the first complaint against him, the Canadian police secured an indictment for fraud, theft, and money laundering. He fled just before the frauds were discovered, and investors began to demand their money. His marriage collapsed and ended in a messy divorce. The liberal congregation where they had lived felt betrayed. The reaction of the community members was not unusual; they felt "a lot of pain" and wanted "to forget about it."

The con man started to prepare for his disappearance in 1990. On a trip that year he deposited altogether over £1.5 million. When he fled, he took with him one of his daughters. They moved to London, Harrogate, and Devon, and they settled in Essex. First, they posed as David and Noelle Davis, father and daughter; then they became Ronald and Noelle Platt, husband and wife. (Platt was the name of a friend whose identity the con man had stolen and later killed.) Platt had offered his driving license and birth certificate, which the con man used.[13]

Platt (the real one) was a TV repairman, who lived in Harrogate and dreamed of returning to Canada, where he had lived as a young man. When the con man met Platt, he seized on the opportunity to acquire another identity and offered Platt money, including an air ticket to Canada. Platt left a birth certificate and driver's license with the con man. But in 1995 Platt returned to live near the con man whom he knew as Mr. Davis—who was now known as Mr. Platt. The con man realized that his new identity was in danger. He killed Platt, telling Platt's family that he had left the country; the family believed him and did not report Platt missing.

When Platt's body was discovered, the authorities were not particularly eager to begin a murder investigation. But a coroner's officer decided to investigate, and followed the Rolex watch—the only thing found on the body. As mentioned, the registration number helped the office to trace an agent, who named the owner of the watch as Platt and offered his address. The coroner notified Platt's family, who then notified the police about Platt's friend, Davis, the con man. The con man told inquiring police that he loaned Platt £2,500, whereupon Platt left for Paris. But by chance the police discovered that the man to whom they spoke was called Platt. Upon his arrest in 1996, the police found in his cottage a part of the fortune that he had stolen.[14]

Not all contemplated murders are successful. One con artist was accused of operating an $18 million Ponzi scheme involving promises of sham currency trades and real estate investments. This man tried unsuccessfully to have four witnesses who invested with him killed. He finally pleaded guilty to charges of fraud in order to avoid a charge of attempted murder.[15]

3. On Very Rare Occasions a Group of Con Artists Can Be Deadly as Well

A deadly group of con artists is described by a court as a "group of young men known as the 'BBC,' which has been popularized in the media and in film as the 'Billionaire Boys Club.' The group was formed in Los Angeles in 1982 by a youthful and charismatic accountant and commodities trader named Joe Hunt and several of his friends. . . . BBC was bound together by a theory of Hunt's known as the 'paradox philosophy,' which sanctioned lying, cheating and stealing as necessary and acceptable means to achieve personal and professional goals. Acting on that philosophy, BBC set out to generate income through various business ventures and investments. Start-up funding was obtained by soliciting the members' various wealthy friends and relatives, and a portion was used to obtain elegant townhomes and imported cars for members' use. An early BBC investor was Ron Levin, a southern California resident, who promised in July 1983 to advance several million dollars, to be invested by Hunt. However, a few months later, Levin admitted that his business dealings with BBC were fraudulent and the millions illusory. Hunt reacted to this news by devising an elaborate scheme to extort money from and kill Levin. In June, 1984, Hunt and another BBC member . . . killed Levin and disposed of his body in a remote area north of Los Angeles. [Another member] was aware of the plot to kill Levin, and provided Hunt with an alibi for the night of the murder."[16]

Thus a slippery slope may start with the philosophy of "a little bit of" fraud and end with desperate or philosophically justified murder.

4. Con Artists Lack Empathy

A. WHAT DOES EMPATHY MEAN?

One explanation of con artists' behavior and internal driving forces is that they feel no compassion or emotional sympathy for anyone.[17] That is, they lack the tendency or ability to identify with others. Other people then become objects. On the other hand, "When people observe someone in distress they imagine how they would feel in the same situation. If they can do this vividly enough, they may experience some of the same affect experienced by the victim."[18] The power to imagine that we are someone else does not necessarily relate to suffering. We can empathize with someone who is happy, and that may make us feel happy too. Nor is empathy exercised to the same degree with respect to all people under all circumstances.[19] During the 1940s, the commandants of extermination camps sent millions of people to the gas chambers and threw children into fires. Yet at the same time they could be loving fathers and devoted husbands. They could act this way because they "dehumanized" the victims and erased any empathy for them.

Empathy has been linked to moral principles of caring for those with whom one empathizes; it is related to principles of justice.[20] When people can imagine themselves as victims, their empathy with victims triggers their demand for justice, to right a wrong. Empathy induces people to contribute to just solutions. Empathic persons not only feel others' pangs of hunger but also indignation for injustice toward the hungry.

Con artists cannot identify with, or view, their marks as human beings like themselves. This does not mean most con artists cannot feel deeply for some people or animals. But in the context of their "business," such empathy seems to be lacking. The focus of many con artists is not on how their victims feel but on how they behave, watching carefully for actions that signal weakness or vulnerability. Then con artists zero in on the points of exposure, like predators aiming at the least protected spot in the body of the prey.[21]

B. LACKING EMPATHY CAN BRING REPEAT FRAUDS

Experience has shown that those who lack empathy and commit antisocial acts, whether criminal or not, are likely to repeat these acts. Therefore, lack of empathy for victims, especially victims of rape or violent crime, is considered a deviation, signaling repeat offenders.[22] The law in the United States considers empathy important for a civil society. Criminals' empathy for their victims is considered in sentencing offenders.[23] A convict's parole was revoked because he took great pains to avoid paying a judgment compensating one of the victims of his crime; he did not "indicate any concern or empathy for the victim."[24] Thus the law condemns lack of empathy, especially for the people whom one harms. The law condemns the inability to exercise self-control over the desire to harm others, and a drive to repeatedly injure others. People who lack such empathy present a danger to society. For example, in upholding the sentencing decision of the District Court the Court of Appeals noted:

The district court considered defendant's conduct to be more reprehensible than the typical fraud scheme because of whom defendant chose to defraud (his family and friends), not merely because the resulting losses were extensive. Also, the fact that the district court weighed defendant's "history and characteristics" against him rather than for him was no reason to overturn the district court's sentence. Additionally, the district court did not abuse its discretion in concluding that the likelihood of someone with defendant's employment history actually paying back a million dollars was negligible.[25]

In considering the sentencing of another con artist, the court noted that this man "preyed on vulnerable individuals, people in crisis, in difficult spots in their lives; the victims' statements indicated that defendant preyed on those who were disabled and in physical pain, or were emotionally vulnerable due to a child's hospitalization." The court may consider the fact of the defendant's use of religion to lure investors into his Ponzi scheme; the crime reflected a moral failure, not a spiritual failure, and that sort of inquiry into the degree of defendant's blameworthiness was appropriate to the court's selection of a sentence.[26]

In contrast, repentance or fear may bring a voluntary confession. For example:

[I]n early 2009, Shawn Merriman approached an otherwise unsuspecting U.S. Attorney's Office and disclosed he had engaged in a long-running Ponzi scheme that defrauded investors of over twenty-million dollars. . . . [He] offered several million dollars of assets to the government so that it could liquidate the assets and eventually remit the proceeds to Mr. Merriman's victims. He cooperated with authorities throughout the proceedings and ultimately pled guilty to one count each of mail fraud and forfeiture.[27]

C. LACKING EMPATHY CAN RENDER CON ARTISTS EFFECTIVE

Lack of feelings for the victims makes con artists effective in hiding their fraud. A researcher of nonviolent psychopaths noted that con artists who do not or cannot empathize are "intelligent psychopaths." In his opinion, most high-functioning psychopaths are not murderers: "'Many of them are quite charming and appear to be extremely sincere, which may account for their success.... A good part of charm is an absence of social anxiety, and because psychopaths do not feel guilt, anxiety or empathy, they can look someone straight in the eye and tell the most egregious lie.'"[28] Jane Kusic, "a victims' advocate and expert on the psychology of the con artist," described con artists as "manipulative predators who practice mind control over victims and derive a sadistic pleasure out of 'psychological rape.'"[29]

Usually people empathize more strongly with those they know, such as family and friends, less with people they do not know, and even less with people they cannot see or hear. Most con artists, however, lack empathy with the victims they know and befriend. Absence of empathy toward dependents who are not family and friends can be just as heartless, for example, in the case of trustees who control beneficiaries' money. (A newspaper reported the story of a widow who was a beneficiary of a trust fund established by her husband. She needed $20,000 for dental work. Since the income from the trust fund was insufficient, she asked the bank trustee to "invade the capital" for that sum. After the bank trustee told her to have her teeth pulled, the court refused her request to remove the trustee.[30] As a business matter, the trustee may have made a defensible judgment, but it seems that empathy was entirely lacking. It is doubtful whether the deceased husband expected the trustee to treat his widow this way in such a case.) Corporate con artists can be devoid of empathy toward shareholders whom they do not know.[31] Thus, regardless of intelligence, people might be unable to imagine any feelings except their own, or imagine and identify with other people's feelings.[32]

Fraudulent telemarketers are likely to lack empathy, guilt, or remorse.[33] One such telemarketer considered his victims to be idiots: "'I had it so perfected that I could get these customers to buy again. . . . I made sure they were happy so I could sell them again,' the telemarketer told the researchers. 'I wanted to sell these people 10 times.'"[34] He did not target old people because they were old. He merely sought vulnerable victims, and because older people happened to be more vulnerable they were more likely to become his victims. But any other type of vulnerable person would have been just as attractive.

5. How Do Con Artists Present Themselves?

A. PROTECTING THE WEAK EGO: WE ARE SPECIAL!

How do narcissists protect their ego? Con artists act with tremendous self-confidence, while their inner self is too weak for them to acknowledge any weakness. They cannot help but deny categorically that they have done anything wrong. They justify their behavior by blaming the law, the government, and the victims. Some con artists argue that their deception was necessary as "self-defense"; their victims would have deceived them—the con artists. Therefore, the con artists had the right to protect themselves by deceiving their victims *first*. Hence, con artists are unrepentant offenders. Let us explore these traits.

To survive, narcissists' egos use defensive mechanisms that *require self-deception and feed on deception of others*. The narcissist's "life is organized to deny negative feelings about himself and to maintain an illusion of superiority."[35] Narcissists use their superior view of themselves as a defense. They imagine themselves to be larger than life. They "construct an elaborate persona (a social mask which is presented to the world). This persona needs an appreciative audience to applaud it. If enough people do so, the narcissist is relieved; no one can see through his disguise. Behind the grandiose parading, the narcissist feels empty and devoid of value."

True to character, con artists present themselves as special, superior, risk takers. After all, this "dare to" attitude draws attention, strengthens reputation, and feeds the ego.[36] Con artists can be viewed as the Evel Knievels of the financial world, just as thieves and burglars enjoy being chased by the police. Taking risks makes them feel alive. Success makes them feel superior. As we shall see later, a study of Ponzi scheme victims suggests they too have a relatively high inclination to take risks. However, the two groups differ. Con artists initiate risks; their victims are enticed to take risks. Con artists initiate risks for themselves and for others. The victims are enticed to take risks that only they bear.

A con artist named Sam Antar, who called himself a crook, explained the nature of con artists in a revealing way. He emphasized two important points in answer to the question, Why do "Ponzi operators and fraudsters steal money by taking advantage of 'nice people' for years, only to be arrested after their schemes collapse and lives are wrecked"? One explanation is the con artists' disdain for the "squares." "'Criminals like me consider your humanity a weakness to be exploited in the execution of our crimes,' Antar told participants at a recent conference at the John Jay College of Criminal Justice." The other explanation for the behavior of con artists is pride. "'We can steal more money with a smile than we can steal with a gun.'"[37] This is pride in ability and superiority.

Colorful con artist behavior attract attention and sometimes admiration. Ponzi schemers, like other white-collar criminals, exhibit outwardly a very high level of self-esteem. They work hard at maintaining this image.[38] Research in the psychology of self-serving behavior points out other characteristics common to con artists. The explanation for this behavior is similar to that of narcissistic behavior. Self-serving behavior is used as a person's defense against a threat to his identity.[39] Paradoxically, because their ego is so frail, con artists cannot afford to act but with a high level of self-esteem. They sometimes cannot live having lost self-esteem. For example, one con artist

boasted of being a child prodigy who was not only playing steel guitar at 9, but [also taught] others who have been playing for years. By 19, he owned a chain of music schools . . . and also performed on radio and television. . . . At 23, he went to work for [an instrument company and his innovation enabled them] "to triple the employees' wages, quadruple the production, cut costs by 40 percent and make a profit [where they had lost before]."[40]

Another con artist told his investors that he was a financial genius, "who made his first million by the age of 21." He declared time and again to his employees: "I do not seek to be a common man."[41] And indeed he was not. Thus, most Ponzi schemers are characters, standing out in the crowd.

This behavior may reduce admiration of prudent people who take prudent risks. But such behavior often draws admiration from people who would like to take unbounded risks but do not dare to do so, people who would like to be noticed but fear criticism or ridicule (or who have sufficient self-knowledge and a good picture of who they are).

Like their magnetic stories that draw attention, con artists may present the mystery that some people cannot resist: "Few have seen the likes of someone as beguiling as [Luigi] DiFonzo. The man depicted in dozens of interviews, court records and personal letters seemed to have lived five or six lives . . . who adopted a more fantastic persona with each incarnation." His impact on investors is telling. Since the collapse of his empire "investors have become obsessed with unraveling the mysteries of its alleged mastermind." One woman who lost $75,000 in her investment "knew she'd been had the moment she finished DiFonzo's biographical work, 'St. Peter's Banker.'

But the revelation that the same man behind the book and DFJ also had worked with the FBI to investigate organized crime left her angry and grimly determined." She did not expect to get her money back, "but I need to know the truth' she said. 'Were the FBI protecting him instead of the people he was ripping off?" The mystery, attraction, and attention remained after his death.[42] Of such mysteries, reputations are built. Luigi DiFonzo, the self-styled Don, was most hurt when police led him away shackled for questioning. Although he was also ill and wrote that he "lost everything," this incident may have contributed to his decision to commit suicide.[43] Thus the presentation of such a con artist has a singular effect in creating followers.

Similarly, in *Crooks and Squares* Malin Akerstrom describes the condescending view that con artist criminals have toward "squares." This attitude, and a feeling of superiority,[44] fuel con artists who conduct Ponzi schemes. Not surprisingly, con artists are sensitive to slights. Charles Ponzi wrote: "when somebody tries to put on airs and make me feel like thirty cents, I am off on a rampage." He remembered the slight he received from a small bank that required him to furnish references before opening an account. When Ponzi was done, he had acquired that bank.[45] White collar criminals in general "have a high sense of self-esteem."[46]

Consumers may be proud of buying bargains. Thieves find bargaining "demeaning." They are proud of being able to handle "big money," which the marks do not seem to be able to do. The thieves are not willing to accept budgets and restrictions, which are "the opium for the middle classes."[47] Said one thief: "You know, for you money is probably worth a lot, but for me one thousand is like one hundred for you ... I can always go out and buy me a Bacco chisel and steal my money again."[48] Yet at the same time these criminals are driven to get more money. As one con artist said, "It gets to the point where you spend money just to have the motivation to continue, because without that motivation you might as well quit."[49]

6. Con Artists' Mechanisms of Ego Protection and Justification

A. DENIAL

Denial is an ego-supporting tool. Typically, white-collar criminals continuously deny having done anything wrong.[50] These criminals share a "strong culture of denial," and this culture persists—even in prison. They have "imagined superiority over other inmates," an attitude that also helps them maintain their dignity and their coping with prison life.[51]

A study of forty-seven fraudulent telemarketers conducted by University of Tennessee researchers who interviewed their subjects at various locations across the United States found symptoms identical to the con artists of Ponzi schemes. These telemarketers refused to admit they were criminals even though they were convicted. "Five of the 47 convicted telemarketers admitted they knew they were involved in criminal activity. But the rest," like many other white collar criminals, "rejected the words 'criminal' and 'crime' as being applicable to them and their activities."[52] Con artists act the same way. In addition, the telemarketers "had absolutely no sympathy for their victims, many of whom were elderly."[53] It is not their fault that the victims were hurt, they argue. It is someone else's fault—the victims, the police, the government, the law. Armed with this deep conviction, they avoid the internal conflicts and feelings of guilt and shame that would accompany recognition of their actions as wrong. They convince others all the more easily because they show little hesitation and much assurance.

A recent example of ego protection through proclaiming superiority is the case of William W. Lilly, nicknamed "Condo King." The King was convicted of real estate and banking crimes and spent almost five years in a federal prison. During these years he seems to have created a "real estate empire" acquiring "hundreds of condominiums, commercial buildings and raw land from Massachusetts to Florida." Joe Clements reported in *Banker & Tradesman* that "the prosecutor has wrested approximately half of the $5.1 million restitution order imparted upon Lilly for these frauds." Lilly was required to pay the $5 million, or his assets would be seized. But when Lilly lost the legal battle he did not concede. On the contrary. He parked a large yacht at Rowes Wharf in Boston, about 100 yards from the U.S. attorney's courthouse office. Painted in large letters on the yacht were the words "We Won." As an anonymous official has remarked, "The audacity is astounding."[54] More impressively: Lilly refused to recognize reality. Probably, his ego could not withstand and survive such recognition.

Ponzi con artists and white-collar con artists deny that they have done anything wrong. A study conducted in 1988 found that white-collar offenders are "highly resistant to negative interpretation of their actions, [and] they rationalize their crimes even after conviction and display a remarkable inability to accept the moral implications of their conviction. . . . In rejecting negative labeling [sic], they also reject or manage the accompanying emotions." Shame and guilt depend on whether an individual accepts how others define a situation. White-collar offenders reject the definitions constructed by others.[55]

Beliefs, signals, and following a losing route are not unique to con artists. Leaders might strongly believe in their message, mission, and destiny. When success seems to fade, refusal to admit possible failure may lead to a slippery slope of fraud, from which there is no return. One psychological explanation for such behavior is the "need to justify previous investments and reduce the dissonance provoked by high investments and little or no returns."[56] The cons, their victims, and many honest people might share the same psychological drive.

Natural moral behavior requires the capacity for self-condemnation, and mature moral behavior requires cognitive capabilities, that is, responsibility, which makes one feel guilty. The standard evokes an emotional response. It is different from a convention, for example, of driving on one side of the road. Rational analysis is not without value, but those who believe in rational behavior do not give enough weight to the emotional aspect of behavior.[57] It seems that con artists lack the capacity for self-condemnation or feelings of guilt.

The similarities and the differences between two groups of white-collar criminals are interesting. One group consists of the con artists who seek the luxurious lifestyle and success of the rich and powerful, and achieves it only by fraud. These are the mimics. The other group consists of those who have achieved the desired status but resorted to fraud mostly in order to increase or to maintain what has been achieved. These are the elite. Both have strong egos, high self-esteem, and less sensitivity to the law. Both are likely to be little affected by empathy for the victims or self-condemnation. Con artists may have vitality and sustenance even after serving a prison sentence. A Canadian who defrauded a number of banks and perhaps other sophisticated individuals in a Ponzi scheme involving leases was sentenced to fourteen months in prison. What is interesting is his view of the future: "When I walk out of here I'll probably be seen as the biggest son of a bitch," he said. As to his long-term future he said: "I'm going to start all over again. I've got all the energy in the world." In addition: "I'm going to play golf four months out of every 12."[58] Perhaps this was the view he wanted to present himself. Perhaps this was how he truly felt. The words, however, are true to character.

B. BLAMING THE GOVERNMENT

One of the arguments made by many con artists is that, given more time, their enterprises would have become successful legitimate businesses. Therefore, when their scheme is terminated by government actions, many con artists blame the government for its failure.[59] If they had been given *just a little more time*, everything would have turned out fine. As one of the Australian con artists said: "The ASC's

[Australian Securities Commission] press release said they shut us down because we were destined to fail. Well, they ensured we failed. They wouldn't have a commercial bone in their bodies."[60]

In bankruptcy court, Ponzi con artists often pose as businessmen who failed. They failed, their arguments go, like other businessmen and entrepreneurs whose vision was too creative and too great for reality. The government is one of the reasons for their failure. When caught, a con artist argued that the government framed him. He said in his bulletin: "The SEC over the past three years had deliberately contrived and implemented a violently hostile, Mafia-oriented type of combative posture versus the ABT exchange and marketplace and against me [Arthur N. Economou], personally."[61]

Another con artist who insisted that he had done no wrong[62] blamed the government for the victim's plight: "The twenty-one executives in the Equity Funding insurance fraud, the largest business crime in history, even while sitting in their prison cells ... rationalized that if the government had held off in the prosecution and let them continue a short while longer, they would have solved their company's financial problems, ended their illicit activities, and saved the thousands of stockholders from financial ruin."[63] In some respects, the con artists are right. Had the government not interfered, the scheme could have continued longer. In one respect, they are definitely wrong. A longer period would not have helped convert their scheme into a legitimate business. In such an event, the legitimated scheme would lose its attraction and would have to compete with other lawful businesses. On this level playing field, con artists may not have the upper hand.

C. BLAMING THE LAWS

Con artists justify their actions by attacking the legitimacy of the laws and the regulators. The regulators are responsible for the losses of the con artists' investors. Laws hinder legitimate business, undermine free enterprise, and hurt the shareholder-owners of the corporations. These laws are unnecessary, deal in trivia, and are unjust. They are, costly, complex, and implemented by a slow-moving bureaucracy. Government enforcement is ineffective, anyway. And there are many good business reasons to violate particular laws.[64]

These arguments are supported by theoretical studies and logical arguments based on the belief that the markets will take care of most problems that may arise. Although the year 2008 raised doubts about the ability of the markets to control serious dangers to the financial system, regulation can indeed stifle creative businesses. The line between law that prohibits fraud and law that inhibits legitimate business is sometimes hard to draw. Thus when con artists berate the government, and when the victims—especially those who benefit from the scheme—parade in protest of government interference, in support of the con artists, their words and actions resonate, mimic legitimacy, and sustain their denial of having done anything wrong.

D. BLAMING THE VICTIMS

To add insult to injury, con artists sometimes blame the victims. These people are not merely stupid; they are greedy. Otherwise they would not fall for the scheme ("How could they believe a scam like mine?"). One con artist said he felt innocent because the scheme would not have "defrauded a reasonable investor."[65] It seems that most con artists do not feel remorse at the losses they cause. For them this view is important in supporting their own ego and the conviction that they are superior to their marks. Joseph "Yellow Kid" Weil was a prominent con man in his time, the late 1800s. He worked with other con men to swindle his victims and was quoted as saying, "Each of my victims had larceny in his heart."[66] Madoff joined the same crowd from jail. He blamed large investors for having been complicit in his scheme.[67]

In addition, some con artists note that the victims were warned! One person with a bankruptcy and a prison record claimed that he cautioned potential investors about the risks involved in his investments: "I and the people who worked for me asked two simple questions of investors: (a) can you afford to lose this money and; (b) if you do lose it, will it affect your lifestyle? If the answer was yes to either of those questions, we didn't want their money." He knew how to send legal warnings to investors and use these warnings well as protection. The problem, however, was not the warning, but the fact that behind these warnings there was no business at all, neither risky nor safe. Behind it was a Ponzi scheme. Denying this, he said: "Ponzi or pyramid schemes are based on a non-accumulation of assets. We have bought businesses and entered into joint ventures. Due to cash-flow problems, we sometimes used money from new investors to pay interest owing to existing ones but there is no law against that."[68] Yet, these justifications are manipulative in and of themselves. "Cash flow problems" are in fact a description of the scheme. They highlight the similarity to legal businesses: the legal language of risk warning and the form of refinancing. Cash flow was not a problem. Absence of any true, potentially profitable business was the problem.

Besides, the victims have agreed. After all, no one forced them to part with their money. One person convicted of fraudulent telemarketing said: "They know what they're doing. They're bargaining for something, and when they lose, they realize that they were at fault." Yet another said: "They're dumb enough not to read, dumb enough to send me the money. I really don't care, you know. And, you know what I used to say: 'They're gonna blow their money in Vegas. They're gonna spend it somewhere. I want to be the one to get it.'"[69]

Con artists view their victims with contempt. White-collar criminals, as well as thieves, view themselves as hard-working: "Earning one's income by illegal means demands a lot of individual initiative and creativity. . . . The skills and time used in making necessary connections and so on can be seen as an investment by the criminals as in any other types of work." You need skills, ability to make connections, and nerve to keep cool in the face of danger and difficulties.[70] Their disdain of the victims is based on a comparison. Even the victims who are public shareholders can be viewed as parasites who do not deserve the money they claim from hard-working white-collar criminals.

E. BLAMING OTHERS, BUT AVOIDING A SHOW OF WEAKNESS

In interviews with Swedish thieves and burglars, researchers found that these criminals took full responsibility for their choice of lifestyle and their imprisonment. In their view, blaming others for their problems was a sign of weakness, a sign of "not being a man."[71] It is unclear whether these studies are applicable to con artists in the United States. In addition, perhaps the culture of thieves and burglars does not correspond to the culture of Ponzi con artists. Yet members of both groups aim at enhancing their prestige and reputation. Con artists and the Swedish thieves adopt similar attitudes, for example, spending money to show off. Therefore, perhaps the "manliness" of taking responsibility rather than blaming others is just one deviation between the two groups. Or perhaps the deviation from this posture occurs only in the courts, where it might be more useful.

F. OUR ACTIONS ARE JUSTIFIED AS PROTECTION AGAINST OTHERS WHO ARE FRAUDSTERS

Besides, everyone does it. A related form of justification that con artists use attributes wrongful and bad intentions to their opponents and accusers. These bad intentions justify unethical behavior as a defensive measure. The attitude fits research results reporting that when negotiators were encouraged to act unethically, they tended to view their *opponents* as less ethical. Untrustworthy people sometimes view others as untrustworthy and thereby justify their own behavior.[72]

Iain Pears wrote a perceptive description of this feeling: "I walked away slightly discomforted, which now I understand. I was deceiving her, and she gave kindness in return. It made me very confused, until I later learned how much greater her trickery was than mine."[73] Deceiving can make a person feel uncomfortable. But believing that the others are deceitful, even more so than the person who has deceived, helps overcome the discomfort and justifies unethical actions as a defense. Defensive action can be taken before the harm is inflicted. If a treacherous act is initiated before the other party has done anything, the act can be justified by the assumption that the other party would be faithless. Then taking a faithless act first is a justified *defense* against anticipated harm.

A similar protective justification is the argument that "everyone does it." If everyone does it, then one must protect oneself by doing it too—and doing it first. Otherwise, the competitors will win.[74] If the con artist associates with others of the same view, then in their world everybody indeed does it. Subordinates, who do not usually disagree, also follow along doing it.

G. OUR GOOD WORKS TESTIFY TO THE LEGITIMACY OF OUR ACTIONS

Con artists base the legitimacy of their actions on good works in supporting their communities and donations to charities. Even Al Capone used this approach. To gain support, affection, and respectability, he distributed money among the needy and acquired a strong and loyal following. The head of the huge Romanian Ponzi scheme Caritas was called by some victims "Jesus," for he lavished money on those who sought his help, and like Capone he gave tenfold the amount requested.

Some con artists believe they were acting for the benefit of others. For example, the executives and many employees of Equity Funding were engaged in mass production of forged insurance certificates. At that time, Equity Funding was the darling of Wall Street.

The executives "believed that they were not engaged in fraud just for their own benefit but for the benefit of the company to which they had intense loyalty and dedication."[75] Thus, con artists sometimes assert not only that the government is doing evil, but that they are doing good.

Con artists attempt to prove their innocence: after all, they did not abscond with the investors' money even though they could have done so. An Australian con artist who operated a Ponzi scheme made this argument in 1988: "He said he could have decamped with $10–12 million 'if I was that way inclined.'"[76] Yet, coming from people who are repeat offenders, the claim sounds hollow. As discussed, con artists view each of their schemes as just one "project." It therefore makes sense to exploit the project fully, until it is no longer productive, from their point of view. Corporate con artists can hardly make this argument. Before their company goes under, they usually distribute what money they can among the members of their group. Before Enron was publicly announced insolvent, millions were distributed among its top management.[77]

B. THE PROFILE OF THE VICTIMS: WHAT KIND OF PEOPLE ARE THE SOPHISTICATED VICTIMS? WHAT MAKES SOME MORE VULNERABLE TO PONZI SCHEMES THAN OTHERS?

1. The Dark Side of Some Investors: Lacking Empathy Toward Other Investors and Shared Greed

There are allegations that some of the money managers who invested their clients' money with Madoff may have realized that something was amiss. Yet so long as they were paid, they did not inquire about or examine the secretive Madoff, notwithstanding some red flag. In fact, one money manager requested Madoff to make sure that none of the *manager's clients' accounts* would report even a single losing trade.[78] What does this request imply? How could the manager make such a request without suspecting that the investment results depended on Madoff's decisions and reporting and did not reflect real investments? In another case, the SEC alleged that three senior executives at a small brokerage firm, co-founded with Madoff, "knowingly helped finance the Ponzi scheme and conceal it from regulators for years."[79] Therefore, these trusted representatives of some investors cared little about other investors from whom the money was derived.

2. Investors in Ponzi Schemes Who Suspect or Know the Nature of the "Investment" Yet Invest

Investors who sense a Ponzi scheme but hope to gain from other people's investments may even recruit more investors, suspecting or knowing that the new recruits' money will flow to the current investors. Unless they do not suspect that their recruits are more likely to be the losers, these investors mimic the con artists. To gain other people's money, they exercise persuasive techniques, learned or innate. If the recruits are family, friends, or acquaintances, these investors' lack of empathy is even more pronounced.

Similarly, when initial public offerings (IPOs) are in great demand, investors stand to gain much if they receive such IPO shares at the initial offering price and sell them within a few days—"flip" them over, as it is called—for a far higher price. Within these few days, the price of the shares could rocket, and then they can "download" the shares on other investors, who would hope to do the same to still others. Investors anticipate that the price of the shares will fall within a short period but they expect to sell the shares before that occurs.

For example, the first major American social media company to go public had profits of about $16 million in 2011, and its shares were offered at $45 a share. The share price rose very quickly to $94.25. Yet the number of shares that were offered doubled on the first trading day. This suggests that many shares were handed to the underwriters' favorite investors, most of whom may have "sold the stock during the morning run-up. It's the easiest money you can make on Wall Street."[80] After a short period, some shareholders were left holding shares for which they paid far more than the current price, and perhaps more than what the price would be for a long time to come. Whether the favored shareholders who reaped large amounts from the flipovers and the underwriters who favored them committed actionable fraud is not the issue here. What is important is that the favored shareholders seem unconcerned about other shareholders to whom they sell such shares at a much higher price. Perhaps they believe that this is the way markets should work. Yet in this case the markets act like a Ponzi scheme. Losing investors can sue for the payments other investors were paid as "non-existent principal and fictitious profits." This was the claim in the case of Bayou Hedge Funds.[81] To the extent that the investors who benefited had a suspicion about the source of their profits, there is a question about the level of their empathy.

3. The Element of Greed

It seems that con artists, and perhaps some of their victims, are beset by greed.[82] They are driven by a *desire that is never satisfied*. In fact, greedy people seek to obtain for themselves more than what is good for them and more than is their due. They desire to take without boundaries and without giving. They violate the social rule of reciprocity, take more than is due to them, and do not give back anything (or do not give back enough).

What makes people so constantly hungry? One explanation for greed is envy and low self-esteem. Some people need to get what others have just because the others have it. The greedy believe that by having these things they will become different people, like those they envy. But then they find that having these things does not make any difference; it does not satisfy their self-esteem. This is why when they get the things they crave greedy people still want more. Con artists as well as some of their victims may have the psychological makeup of such people. For them, there is never enough. Therefore, we may find not only greedy con artists but also greedy victims. Although con artists' greed may drive them to fraud, investors who suspect such fraud may be driven to invest even when they have an inkling that their profits consist of other people's money.

Greedy people may desire to maintain their status or advance within their organization.[83] They may seek to avoid losing what they have acquired, rather than acquire more. Perhaps this happens when a company's financial fortunes are deteriorating, and its managers fear losing income, prestige, and self-worth. They might believe that the company will turn around soon. Therefore, they push the envelope and slowly cross over to the illegal side. Hiding a small loss by using accounting tricks or misstatements in vouchers leads to keeping two sets of books and forging signatures. As it is hard to extricate from the results of this behavior, they sink further into the quicksand of criminal actions until exposed. But some white-collar criminals simply are not willing to wait for the changing fortunes of the organization. Like con artists, they want the benefits of great wealth, power, and prestige in the present and not in the future. The greed they experience is the need to have it *now*. And once they acquire wealth and prestige by illegal means, there is no reason to stop—and perhaps no way to stop, especially if the hunger is all-consuming.

4. What Drives the Victims?

Victims are victims, even if they are at fault. They all deserve deeply felt sympathy. Yet in order to understand and learn from experience, painful and horrendous as it is, a review of some of the studies that were conducted in this area may be useful. The discussion here draws on two comprehensive studies, performed in somewhat different ways, and on a few added sources. The first is a recent 2010 survey, of 402 investors in Jamaican Ponzi schemes, that produced a model of investor types and their circumstances. Researchers built a profile of persons most likely to be drawn to Ponzi schemes, and they listed the factors that explained the popularity of these schemes.[84] The second is a 2006 study, far broader, that was commissioned by the National Association of Securities Dealers regarding consumer securities fraud, and other sources of research.[85] The "raw materials" in this book closely support the conclusions of both studies.

Who can predict the reliability of others? How difficult is it to detect fraud?[86] Researchers have analyzed "experimental evidence on whether untrained subjects can predict how trustworthy an individual is." The 2010 researchers concluded that "naive subjects are able to distinguish" between trustworthy and not-trustworthy persons.

You need not be an expert or well educated to sense whether someone else is trustworthy. The ability depends on other attributes, as the examples described in this book suggest as well. This research on the attitudes of Ponzi scheme victims suggests that they are driven by two strong tendencies, which render them more vulnerable to the lure of the schemes.[87] One powerful tendency is the drive to trust; it is a tendency that borders on gullibility. The other tendency is "heightened risk tolerance." Additional factors may increase the weight of these basic tendencies, among them irrational exuberance, social pressures, and education. Each of these factors is discussed below.

The 2006 NASD study found that, compared to nonvictims, victims are more likely to listen to a sales talk and to have experienced more "difficulties from negative life events." The study also found that men victims constitute a larger group than women victims (although this difference may be due to cultural conditions whereby men deal with financial matters). Both studies found that victims tend to be optimistic and rely on their own experience and knowledge. One study noted that in the aggregate these victims underreport the frauds. Additionally, both studies found that compared to nonvictims these victims are more educated. The NASD study also compared the victims of lottery frauds to nonvictims and found the two groups very different. It is interesting that women are more likely to be victims of a lottery fraud, to have had more negative life events, to be more religious, and to read materials or listen to sales agents whom they do not know.

The two studies differ in that the 2010 survey focused on the character of the Ponzi scam victims while the NASD study compared the victims with nonvictims and focused on lottery frauds as well. Nonetheless, these studies as well as the materials in this book are quite similar in their conclusions, perhaps not surprisingly.

A. GULLIBILITY

Gullibility means unbound and unreasonable trust. Trusting is desirable in a society that thrives on investments and reliance on experts. Gullibility and trust are very close and sometimes hard to distinguish. But they differ in degree. Gullibility is unreasonable trusting— believing fully in others and their stories. But especially in business transactions, trusting people base their belief on reasonably sufficient evidence; gullible people believe on insufficient evidence. The trusting are drawn by rational considerations and sufficient relevant information that they can gather; the gullible may be drawn by emotion, hope, or fancy.[88]

Those who accept an offer that is too good to be true could be viewed as gullible.[89] After all, if *on its face* an offer suggests that it cannot be true (because it is too good) then the offer itself sends the message, "Do not trust me because I am very likely to be false."

A person who ignores this message is not a trusting person but a gullible one. In addition, the gullible are internally more dependent and therefore weaker than skeptical and suspecting people, who depend more on themselves than on others. As between the two personalities, con artists put on a front of invincible, never wrong, strong individuals. Compared to these indestructible and supreme persons, victims feel inadequate. They have more doubts and are not as assured and strong as the con artists. They feel less smart or insufficiently sophisticated. Above all, when victims cannot deny their inferiority, they wish to hide it. To some extent, the victims seem to adopt values and behavior that are similar to those of the con artists. They too hide their feeling of being weak.

Foreigners may be more gullible than local residents merely because they have less information. The con artist George Parker targeted immigrants and tourists in New York City and sold them popular landmarks. He preyed on unsuspecting foreigners who believed that America was the land of opportunity, assuring them they could buy as an investment the right to charge tolls or fees for access to the landmarks.[90]

There are examples of high-level gullibility among investors. Con artists' stories can be "a fairytale world" of "fantasy money, imaginary banks and bogus $US1000 billion government certificates." One scheme offered enormous returns from "1934 US government gold bond certificates, which Euro Credit is about to purchase from a Dominican company and that have a total value of as much as $US600 trillion."[91] Another supposedly obtained the bonds he offered "from a woman who is said to be in short-wave radio communication with Hatton, 'a 9ft 6in [2.8 meter tall] extraterrestrial.'" And yet another "claim[ed] to be acquiring old US government bonds worth as much as $US600 trillion." The schemes "are so wacky it is hard to understand how any half-sane person could believe them."[92] But some people are caught nonetheless.

As the cost of verification rises, the criticism of gullibility falls. One court noted: "While . . . the [investor] could have investigated the [story of a promoter], the means of knowledge were not readily available to him"; therefore, his reliance was justified.[93]

However, gullibility alone does not mark the type of Ponzi scheme victims. The other strong tendency of such a victim is risk tolerance. Gullibility and risk tolerance may combine to create a strong tendency. Such people are inclined to take more risk not only in financial matters but in other contexts as well (as an example, they might be mountain climbers). Thus people who take high risks in other situations are more likely to do so when exposed to offers of Ponzi schemes.[94]

B. TOLERANCE TO THE RISK OF BEING CAUGHT FOR ILLEGAL ACTIVITIES

The degree of risk taking may be manifested by the patterns of people's investments. Risk takers act out their tendencies by rolling over their interest in Ponzi schemes and investing larger amounts in these schemes. Another example of risk taking was noted before: we found that some Ponzi schemes suggest a "whiff" of illegality. Researchers likened acceptance of legal risk to the desire for exclusivity as well as risk tolerance. In this case, exclusivity may provide some protection from this risk through lower likelihood of being found out. It is hard to determine, let alone measure, the balancing forces that make us move in one direction rather than another. Yet it is a possible explanation that the suspicion of illegality raises the attractiveness of the scheme, while the lessened risk of discovery reduces the concern of being caught and makes the scheme less attractive.

Various factors influence risk tolerance. These include, for example, a person's "outlook on their present personal economic condition."[95] Some researchers suggest that, at least in the United States, wealthy people are more risk-tolerant than poorer ones. However, even though wealthy people were ready to experiment and take some risks, they were not ready to put their life savings at high risk. In contrast, those investors who viewed their financial condition as average or poor were willing to take greater risks and overexpose themselves to Ponzi schemes.[96] The poor have less to lose and more to gain.

C. AN OPTIMISTIC NATURE AND OUTLOOK ON LIFE AFFECTS RISK TOLERANCE

Investors in Ponzi schemes "tend to be generally optimistic, with the large majority of investors expecting better personal economic conditions in the future, and just over half expecting better national economic conditions."[97] The risk exposure of these investors may represent their desire "not to be left behind in a period of expected widespread prosperity. Being dissatisfied with their current economic status, such investors are willing to take significant risks in an effort to share in the expected national prosperity. . . . Persons who received higher returns from such schemes were willing to invest larger sums of money in proportion to their income."[98] Scott Halford noted that the optimists make more money, provided they take risks with a measure of realism.

In contrast, pessimists may be more accurate. Yet they are more prone to depression. Halford suggests that the balance is to avoid viewing a bad occurrence as permanent and a good thing as temporary. Thus the tendency of both optimism and pessimism depends on the effect that events have on future expectations.[99] Optimists will view a failure as temporary and will try to do the same thing again. Pessimists will not try.

Risk tolerance may be traced to personal circumstances. It has been shown "that single people in managerial and supervisory positions are more likely to be highly risk tolerant."[100]

One reason for taking investment risk that has not been emphasized in this discussion is the expectation of returns. Returns draw people who value and crave more money. Money represents many other gratifications: feeling strong, immortal, special, admired; being powerful enough to do what we want to do when we want to do it; and being able to tell others to do our bidding. These are the ingredients risk taking is made of. These are the payoffs for taking risks. Investors in Ponzi schemes may be driven to take the investment risks in these schemes for any of these payoffs. The investors who value these returns are ready to take greater risks.

D. SOCIAL STATUS

Pressure to belong and feel special, and risk reduction while taking risk, all play a role in the victims' behavior. We noted in prior chapters that Ponzi schemes generate excitement in potential investors, and that affinity group members can influence each other in encouraging investment in these schemes. David Tennant's study found that when many "close friends are getting rich by investing in Ponzi schemes the temptation to invest larger proportions of income becomes harder to resist." Yet here is a puzzle: the study found that if potential investors discover that *more* people are invested in the scheme, the investment becomes *less attractive* and potential investors are *less likely to invest.* If potential investors know that *only a few of their friends are investing* in the scheme, they are more likely to invest in it.[101]

This "twist" suggests another influencing factor that we noticed before as well. As discussed previously, Ponzi schemes often promise exclusivity.[102] Exclusivity makes some investors feel special. Not all investors crave this feeling, but those who need it or enjoy it are more susceptible to the allures of the scheme and are more likely to invest if the number of their investor friends is relatively small. Similar conclusions were reached in another study concluding that there is a universal need for people to feel unique.[103] We need a sense of identity and self-validation; our unique traits help define and enforce our sense of a stable identity. Being somewhat different from others, we *need* the difference. We will resist changes in how we perceive our-selves. Group identity serves as a source of uniqueness as well, distin-guishing members of the group from outsiders.[104] Greed, too, may be linked to the need to be unique.[105]

Therefore, people experience conflicting drives. They need to be part of a group. In fact, they are dependent on others. Yet they also need a sense of being unique, and this drives them to search for a balance. People want to be unique but avoid social rejection.[106] They try to act according to social norms and receive social approval, but they desire to be special and therefore different.[107] A small, special group may provide both the feeling of belonging and the recognition of being special.

E. THE ROLE OF EDUCATION IN RISK
TOLERANCE IS UNCLEAR

On the one hand, people with higher education can evaluate risks better than people who are less educated. Yet higher education does not shield investors, especially those who have a taste for experi-menting. For example, education does not seem to undermine or erase popular beliefs completely. A small percentage of victims exam-ined in one study invested in a Ponzi scheme believing that the in-vestments were safe because of the long past record of the scheme: "The longer Ponzis are allowed to operate, the greater the perception that they have an established track record, and greater the likelihood that people will place their trust and their money with them."[108] As noted before, this belief is mistaken because in Ponzi schemes the first investors might gain, while the later investors are sure to lose. The probability of retrieving their capital and gaining the promised profits will depend on the chance of being wrong, the probable number of new investors, the length of the period in which these new investors will join the scheme, and how much money the new investors are likely to invest.

Intelligent and knowledgeable professionals can fall victim to con artists for a number of reasons. A 2006 study by NASD (now FINRA) found that "investment fraud victims scored higher than non-victims on eight financial literacy questions."[109] Some may be sure that their own intelligence, and expertise in their area, can assure them of expertise in other areas as well. They might believe that intelligence could protect them from fraud, even if they have no information on the investments.[110] Some may suspect a Ponzi scheme, but rely on the assumption that they can withdraw their money in time.

However, this attitude has serious pitfalls. Financial investments require more than a choice between two possibilities. It has been shown that our brain is efficient in making a choice between two possibilities but is far less adept in choosing among many alternatives. Therefore, regardless of how smart people might be, they do not process many possibilities quickly. Instead, they tend to rely on their general wisdom. This may be the reason for their reliance on others as well, as the discussion on affinity groups demonstrates. This human tendency is the basis for the legal requirement that permits investors who choose certain complex investments, such as variable annuities, to rescind their purchase within a few days. This time period allows them to withdraw from a signed obligation. The permission may also be based on the recognition of strong, effective salesmanship.

Added to belief in one's own brain power is the optimism that many fairly successful persons carry. In his book *Wealth of Nations*, Adam Smith noted:

> The over-weening conceit which the greater part of men have of their own abilities, is an ancient evil remarked by the philosophers and moralists of all ages. Their absurd presumption in their own good fortune has been less taken notice of. It is, however, if possible still more universal. There is no man living who, when in tolerable health and spirits, has not some share of it.

The chance of gain is by every man more or less over-valued, and the chance of loss is by most men under-valued, and scarce by any man, who is in tolerable health and spirits, valued more than it is worth.[111]

F. A REMINDER OF THE STORIES IN CHAPTER 1: THE WAYS CON ARTISTS MAKE THEIR OFFERS

The conclusions of the NASD Study reflect the stories outlined in Chapter 1. The conclusion is that "investment fraud pitches" are extremely varied, "tailored to match the psychological needs of the victim."[112]

Another source suggests techniques that affect victims of frauds, as were itemized in Chapter 1. Robert Prentice notes that "sellers can influence people to believe that they want or need things that, absent the persuasive effort, they would not buy," including tobacco and securities. He lists the basic categories of influence techniques proposed by Robert Cialdini, noting that even educated intelligent investors can be influenced by these techniques, most of the time.

First, people are pressed to reciprocate. An offer of something "free" is enticing, but it induces pressure to reciprocate (for example, buy). Second, people approve of consistency. Once a step is taken (e.g., buying from a broker) there is pressure to continue and be consistent and commit to the seller. Even when sophisticated investors choose a stockbroker, they have a strong desire to trust that broker, notwithstanding warning signs to the contrary. Third, social approval is important (following the crowd). This is generally sensible to do; after all, if everyone does it, it must be the right way. This is one reason testimonials are esteemed, especially by people similar to the followers. Fourth, people have a tendency is to say yes rather than no, especially to those whom they like, or who are usually attractive or similar, who make them feel good (for example, by flattery). This tendency may be the reason for successful selling to affinity groups.

Fifth, people pay attention to and follow others in a position of authority. And last, as we noted, scarce things are valuable.[113]

G. HOW DO SOPHISTICATED VICTIMS OF PONZI SCHEMES VIEW THEMSELVES?

In contrast to con artists, and perhaps under the pressure of social condemnation, many victims of Ponzi schemes agree with the general verdict against them. A study by the U.S. Department of Justice in the late 1990s listed the emotional consequences of fraud for victims as self-blame, shame, and guilt. Victims fear the "societal condemnation and indifferences (the attitude that victims of fraud deserve what they get as a result of their own greed and stupidity) and isolation (when victims suffer their losses in silence rather than risking alienation and blame from family members, friends, and colleagues)." A relative of a Madoff fraud victim noted: "My uncle pulled on the heart strings of Bernie Madoff and said please my niece is floundering, she is having a very hard time, she's had a terrible tragedy with the loss of her husband, will you take her on as an investor?"[114] Another person said: "I involved all my kids in it and all my grandkids." And another investors noted: "I guess the shame is shame on me, for trusting somebody that has been holding my families [sic] money for 45 years."[115] The victims' shame is often exacerbated by lack of a support group. They expect their family and friends to condemn them just as the con artists do: "How could you be so stupid?" They expect no sympathy, and no fury directed at the con artists. They feel alone. A con artist who practiced swindles all his life and specialized in the sale of fake stocks noted in his autobiography that the victims seldom complained: "They preferred to take their losses rather than let the world know that they have been so gullible."[116] Thus the public seems to send a general message that, regardless of the fraud, some victims could have protected themselves from con artist fraud, and *should* have. For their lack of vigilance, they are condemned.

Sophisticated victims blame themselves for their weaknesses and seek to hide their losses, rather than complain to the police. These victims' attitude and behavior support the view that they could indeed have avoided losses. Their behavior after the discovery of the fraud further helps the con artists, since many would rather just forget it, from embarrassment at having been "taken for a ride."[117] This attitude is true in the United States and in other countries.[118] As a former well-known sports star, who declined to discuss the Ponzi case in which he was a victim, revealed, "It was a chapter in his life he would rather forget."[119] This attitude may have changed in recent years, with frauds surfacing in large numbers and affecting quite a variety of victims. For example, one case represented "a collection of claims brought by many individual pharmacies, pharmacists, veterinarians and veterinary clinics."[120] These victims too, for all their professional prominence, fear guilt, and shame,[121] societal condemnation, indifference and social isolation.[122] For these many reasons, victims tend to remain silent. By their silence, they may produce an unintended consequence of helping con artists prolong their game.

As one court explained, "When the circumstances would suggest to an investor of ordinary intelligence the probability that she has been defrauded, a duty of inquiry arises, and knowledge will be imputed to the investor who does not make such an inquiry. Such circumstances are often analogized to 'storm warnings.'"[123] The "storm warnings" doctrine has been used to evaluate inquiry notice in cases involving claims for violations of the securities acts.[124] The victims "simply swallowed the losses to avoid the public humiliation of a lawsuit."[125] Large corporations that were caught and lost in a Ponzi scheme have a business reason to avoid publicity. They may fear losing customers. Careless in managing their assets, they might be thought to be careless in other activities as well.[126] They remain silent.

5. How Do Some Victims React to the Discovery of Con Artists by the Government?

A. THE VICTIMS' ATTITUDE TOWARD THE GOVERNMENT

One would assume that, like victims of violent crimes, the marks of Ponzi schemes would seek government help, or at least heed the government's warnings. Not always. Charles Ponzi's followers blamed government interference for the demise of his business.[127] This attitude may prevail in connection with other Ponzi schemes, and it may contribute to the victims' reluctance to approach the government or help prosecute the con artists. The deeply religious may tend to question any other authority, including the government. Terry Greene Sterling noted that there are always certain groups of people who "abhor big government": "With 16 million believers, the nation's largest Protestant denomination is staunchly independent . . . [and encourages] each individual to build his or her own relationship with God. . . . This explains why in Arizona, Southern Baptists chose to entrust BFA solely to a board. . . ."[128] There was no supervisory oversight in the church's structure.[129] It was trusted, while the government was not. Faithful supporters of con artists berate the government. In the Cornerstone case, supporters of the con artist agreed with the founder of the organization "that they are all victims of a government conspiracy."[130]

Similarly, when a con artist's dot com failed, investors continued to believe in him. They demanded his release from jail so that he would continue to produce profits or at least repay them. One investor wrote to the Securities and Exchange Commission that keeping this man in prison was "disgraceful." The writer "did not understand how American laws could suppress a man like this."[131]

High returns to a community may create strong antigovernment sentiment. One Ponzi scheme contributed to the temporary prosperity of the victims, and as a result the population of the small Canadian town fiercely supported the con artists who had robbed it, while vehemently opposing and even obstructing the government investigators. This community attributed its financial success to the con artists and blamed the government for ending its prosperity.

> On May 10, about 500 of the 6,000 residents [of the town], . . . a forestry-dependent community 1,000 kilometers north of Vancouver, gathered to proclaim their support of Glenn Anderson—a.k.a. Uncle Glenn—and their disdain for the big-city bureaucrats who had shut down his little bank a week earlier. They carried placards declaring "God sent Uncle Glenn Anderson to help people in Burns Lake and the Lakes District" and "Glenn Rocks, Government Sucks." One by one, they stepped up to a microphone outside Anderson's tiny office on the main drag, where he conducted most of his firm's business under its original incorporation name, 439288 BC Ltd. "If we can get Glenn back up and help him out, we'll see him back in his office helping us out," said resident Jack Sebastian, to rousing cheers.

Government officials had a different view of the bank. Investigators who "dropped unannounced" into the bank's office and examined the books

> were amazed by what they found. The numbered company, offering 12 percent interest rates, had taken in about $40 million from 400 to 500 "investors" in amounts ranging from $190 to $2 million—and had lent most of that money, at rates of 17 percent and 18 percent, to about 1,400 borrowers for everything from weekend spending money to heavy equipment financing. . . . By recycling vast amounts of money through the

community over the past 10 years, Anderson and Montaldi had kept the Burns Lake economy vibrant despite severe cutbacks in the forest industry. What the local CIBC and Royal Bank branches could not or would not provide, the numbered company did.[132]

What the investigators discovered was a Ponzi scheme in the form of a bank. Large loans were made to the bank's directors. "Bank 439288"— which was its registered name—was insolvent. Yet the residents of this small town were passionately supportive. In fact, one of them said: "If they did commit a crime, then the people in this community are willing accomplices. If they are found guilty, the people are guilty, too." In the view of the community, the government spoiled the business. The victims' attitude is similar to that of the players in a prohibited game of chance who hope to win the jackpot. They are hostile to the authorities attempting to protect them for their own good by shutting down the game. These investors believe that, but for the government's prohibitions, the scheme would have continued to produce large profits for them.

B. THE NATURE OF A PONZI SCHEME JUSTIFIES THIS VIEW OF SOME INVESTORS

At the very least, the earlier investors will continue to benefit from the scheme so long as new investors are recruited. The victims may be either the winners, who have already recouped their capital and continue to receive profits from the money of later investors, or those who believe they will be enriched if the con artist is allowed to continue his activities. In *United States v. Gragg*, a victim invested in the scheme despite his knowledge that the con artist had been served with a cease-and-desist court order.[133] Trust in the con artist and the desire to gamble and win was stronger than trust in the government and its wisdom.

C. THE ISSUE OF ADDICTION

Ponzi schemes are addictive for con artists, and for some of their victims. Arguably, a Ponzi scheme suggests that con artists engage in mathematical calculations. A schemer would compute the maximum dividend payout rate, given a certain investment growth rate, and estimate the surviving years of the scheme. In other words, the con artist would adopt a system and a strategy. And yet the wild variety of the schemes, the enormous range of promised returns, and the diverse approaches that the con artists adopt, on the one hand, along with the more stable psychological tendencies of the players, on the other hand, suggest that mathematical and rational calculations are not on the mind of either player. In fact, it seems that a feature shared by con artists and many of their victims is addiction to the game.

1. What Is Addiction?

Addiction is an irresistible impulse that a person/actor cannot control. It is a compulsion, dependence, obsession, or craving that mature into a habit.[134] Addicts may not recognize or admit their addiction; they "live in a fantasy world and deny reality."[135] Even though the activities could ruin their lives, addicts cannot stop.[136] For example, one con artist cashed the insurance policies of fellow church members, forged checks, sold bogus guaranteed investment certificates, and took money from his church. He also took the "money that his daughter's quarter horse riding association had raised by selling chocolate bars."[137] It seems that this con artist lacked the internal controls that would deter most people from behaving this way.

Speculative activities are not addictive in and of themselves, even if they result in losses. Derived from the Latin word for "to see," *speculation* entails analysis and thinking about a decision in advance of acting; it denotes planning. Therefore, long-term investors are less inclined to become addicts than day traders, who rely mostly on market movements and tend to believe in the luck of the draw. Addiction depends on whether the actor controls the speculation or the speculation controls the actor. Speculative activities can become addictive when their main objective is to gain, when the chances of achieving the objective cannot be rationally calculated, *and when the actors are unable to stop playing,* regardless of possible gain or loss.[138]

For example, gambling is not necessarily addictive. Addiction to gambling may depend on the type of gratification that the activities produce. Thus, gambling for amusement is not likely to be addictive (after all, paying for pleasure is not considered a loss); gambling can be a harmless entertainment.[139] As one writer suggested, the "gambler knows nothing about the event on which his gambling outcome depends, because" gambling deals with the unknown. The gambler plays for excitement.[140] So long as these activities are designed to amuse and are paid from people's internal "entertainment budget," they are not addictive. Similarly, con artists' addiction is not limited to money. They may be drawn to the excitement of "conning" and the success they feel at being smarter than those considered the smartest in society. But when they crave the emotional satisfaction and cannot control the craving, they are addicted.

Speculation need not be illegal, either. The very act of taking a risk does not necessarily make it an illegal activity.[141] But the law imposes limits. Lotteries are legal when operated by the state, and gambling and betting are legal when approved and licensed.[142] Yet the acts of buying lottery tickets, gambling, and speculating in the stock market are similar to Ponzi scheme investments. Even addiction need not be illegal, or necessarily the exclusive province of fraud. After all, lotteries, gambling, and trading in securities can involve addictive speculation.

A *lottery* is "a drawing of lots in which prizes are distributed to the winners among persons buying a chance," and "an event or affair whose outcome is or seems to be determined by chance."[143]

Gambling is placing a "bet on an uncertain outcome."[144] And trading securities in the stock market is based on predicting the future performance of the issuing company and the market price of its securities. All these activities are based on predicting a profitable outcome, and *putting money that is owned at the risk of loss.* Investors in Ponzi schemes are similar to market speculators. They bet that the alleged business will produce enormous profits or, in the case of investors who suspect the scheme, that many additional investors will join later, will finance the high returns for earlier investors. How different are they from any other investor?

However, legal and illegal speculative activities share similar features that can become addictive.[145] Speculative activities aim at a chance for quick and gratifying results. Like addictive gambling, lottery tickets often provide the betting results on the spot, or within a short period. Stock speculation, as in trading securities on the Internet, can produce gains or losses almost instantaneously. The monthly or quarterly receipt of an anticipated large check in a Ponzi scheme can produce a similar pleasure. A legal and legitimate activity can become addictive if it is treated as a gamble, for example if the choice of securities for investment is determined by the throw of the dice.[146]

2. What Causes an Insatiable Craving for More, and Loss of Self-Control?

It seems that people can become addicted if being right about a bet gives them a high, while the memory of being wrong about the bet is suppressed. Instantaneous gratification, that is, the excitement of winning, may cause some people to continue to speculate without being able to stop.[147] Addiction to securities investing and speculating can be created by the "excitement of the markets, the thrills of the trade. Millions gained and lost daily" and the "You can do it!" atmosphere of brokerage advertisements and the financial media.[148] Market volatility, the ease of trading by the click of a mouse, and the excitement of winning large sums of money can induce addiction.[149] This compulsion can grow as people play the markets for the wrong reasons.[150]

Addiction grows with the speed of the addictive activities, such as trading or Ponzi scheme playing. Its power increases not merely by the chance of becoming rich but through the chance of becoming rich *quickly*. The fact that the trader or gambler or con artist or investor controls the *timing* of the game helps create addiction. If no outside controls limit the pleasure of the activity, addiction is likely to grow. The pleasure is enhanced until the craving cannot be reined in. For this reason, some activities can become addictive very quickly, such as video poker and daily playing of the stock market.

Addiction can grow by degrees. This may depend on the extent to which people have, or can obtain, information, and to what extent they are masters of the outcome. The more active and controlling people are over all aspects of the speculative activity, the less likely they are to become addicts. For example, buying a lottery ticket can become addictive because the buyer can only choose the ticket number, and sometimes not even that. The outcome depends entirely on the luck of the draw. In contrast, some card games may involve skill such as memorizing the cards that were dealt or reading the facial expressions and other signals of the other players. Poker and blackjack games involve more skills than roulette does. This is why these games may be less addictive than playing roulette. We assume that stock trading, even when it is speculative, involves a high level of skill and judgment. Presumably the most informed trader is likely to make the most gainful decision.[151]

3. What Are Con Artists (and Perhaps Their Victims) Usually Addicted To?

Charles Ponzi's obsessive addiction was to money: *getting it, spending it, and using it to exercise and experience power*.[152] He confessed having developed "an awful appetite" to buy everything in sight, and this appetite increased with buying.[153] Ponzi believed that money talks everywhere. It is difficult to fault him as one reads of the number of officials who helped him.[154] Many con artists are similarly addicted, and so are thieves. Money seems to have a different meaning for them than for most people outside the criminal circle. Criminals assert that they do not want money to control them, and yet they are not prepared to live without having plenty of it.[155]

White-collar criminals such as fraudulent telemarketers are similarly addicted to money. According to journalist Don Jacobs, their background does not indicate low income and poverty environment. Rather, many telemarketers come from upper-middle-class families. As with many crimes, telemarketing offered them quick cash and a lifestyle that included parties, alcohol, and drugs.[156]

It seems that addicted people *love* the game. Unlike other white-collar criminals, con artists accept the law as a hindrance that is part of their lives. It does not prevent them from continuing their adventure. In fact, the danger of being caught and taking the risk of illegality may be a feature of addiction. One study found that 13 percent of shoplifters have admitted to shoplifting every day, and more than half admit to stealing every month.[157] It may be that the excitement and benefits of financial fraud satisfy the needs of con artists, and they cannot stop from engaging in their special kind of fraud.

Con artists are "manipulative," that is, they exploit and maneuver others to attain their own objectives. Yet they are less calculating in the sense of precisely and logically figuring out the results of their activities and plans, although they may be calculating in the sense of coldly scheming or conniving, or being shrewd and crafty.[158] Thus one can fit con artists into the "rational" model as well as into the model of the irrational compulsive personality. Though they are masters of manipulating others, they are the subject of their own internal self-manipulation as well. They lie to others; they may lie to themselves as well. A similar analysis may fit the victims.

4. Con Artists Are Repeat Offenders

A 1990 study found that a significant number of white-collar criminals are repeat offenders.[159] "Many white-collar criminals evidence multiple prior arrests. In the case of credit fraud, false claims, and mail fraud violators, about 4 in 10 offenders had two or more prior arrests, and about 3 in 10 had four or more prior arrests," and 46 percent of the credit fraud offenders have been convicted. More than one in seven securities fraud violators had prior felony convictions, as is true of more than a quarter of those convicted of credit fraud, false claims, and mail fraud. The authors state that "evidence of criminal careers can be found even within a highly restricted population of elite white-collar offenders."[160]

Barry Minkow served seven years in prison for "bilking investors out of tens of millions of dollars through a phony carpet-cleaning company called ZZZZ Best." He then spent ten years as a stock fraud investigator. Yet he did it again! In April of 2011 he pleaded guilty to a stock fraud conspiracy.[161]

Let us follow the story of David and Martha Crowe at length because the couple demonstrate the nature of repeat offenders so well. For more than sixteen years, this couple operated pyramid schemes involving the purchase of gold coins. Securities regulators in North Dakota and South Dakota and Massachusetts issued cease-and-desist orders against the pair. In early cases, the Crowes agreed to pay a fine and cease conducting a business in Massachusetts. Then they moved to North Carolina and resumed their operation. Their activities attracted regulators' attention in that state and "the State's Attorney General suggested that the [Crowe's] company prove its validity by paying off existing obligations before soliciting more recruits." The company failed, for unclear reasons, even before the attorney general took action. The gold vendors ceased to deliver gold, and not surprisingly investors were furious and complained daily by the hundreds. The Crowes moved to Kentucky without reimbursing the roughly five hundred victims, who claimed losses of $370,000.

On January 22, 1992, the Crowes incorporated a Delaware company based in Kentucky. Its operations lasted four years. The company offered investors a plan similar to the Dakotas and Massachusetts investment plans. In April 1992, the Crowes received another cease-and-desist order. The court found that the program "emphasized recruitment of clients, not sales of products, and thus constituted an illegal pyramid scheme." In October 1993, the couple settled with the state, agreed to pay restitution to the corporation's participants, and submitted to a permanent injunction. Then they pleaded guilty to charges of false advertising in another criminal case and received a suspended sentence.

Injunctions and a suspended sentence mattered little; the Crowes were back in business, offering investors a similar plan. A lawyer whom they consulted warned them that their plan was illegal. David Crowe responded that this was none of the lawyer's business. At this point the story becomes tediously repetitious. In February 1995 came another cease-and-desist order from North Dakota and a $40,000 civil penalty. Montana, Minnesota, and the federal government entered the enforcement arena. The Crowes' company records were seized and the offices were finally closed. As of March 1995, ninety-six thousand participants had paid $43 million to the company. The company paid participants $5 million in commissions. Its profits from the sales of 12,628 coins produced $552,620.

On July 12, 1995, the Crowes and their company were sued, among other things, for operating illegal pyramid and Ponzi schemes, substantially as they had done over the entire period. The Crowes' argument that they ran a legitimate multilevel marketing system (like Amway) was rejected. They were convicted. The district court sentenced Martha Crowe to 121 months in prison and David Crowe to 135 months in prison, and the corporation was fined $3,000. The couple were allowed to remain free until their sentence began. The Crowes opted not to report to prison on January 21, 1997; instead they fled, and presumably are still at large. They may be outside the country.[162]

Speaking about another con artist who ran a pyramid scheme, the head of a Better Business Bureau office said: "He doesn't seem to get it. . . . We've had him in our files since 1995. He had one pyramid scheme after another." Clearly this man was an addict. By now the authorities must understand that as well.[163] In Australia, Craig John McKim was convicted of a Ponzi scheme. Out of prison, he continued to entice investors with promised returns of 5 percent a week. He "invested" in gambling debts and was convicted again.[164] Con artists are addicted to their schemes and the joys of success in persuading potential investors to part with their money. The behavior of Ponzi victims after their losses, and their reluctance to complain about the scheme, fit this profile as well.

Compared to other perpetrators of large-scale financial frauds, con artists of the Ponzi variety are not as successful financially. Not surprisingly, Madoff, the "prince of the Ponzi schemers," fits in this category. For many years he and his family lived in unbelievable luxury. They *used* great wealth during this long Ponzi career. But Madoff did not seem to have *accumulated and saved* sufficient wealth. It seems that the need to spend was greater than the need to save or even think about the future. Other types of offenders accumulate sufficient resources to live in luxury ever after, provided they are not caught or if they disappear while awaiting sentence. Con artists who operate Ponzi schemes and are caught seem to have few resources left. This may be one reason they continue the game,[165] although it does not seem to be the only one. The love of the game, peppered with risk and sprinkled with optimism, may suppress all thought of planning, or even concern for the future.

Public opinion and attitude plays an important role in the lives of most individuals. Therefore, exploring the players in Ponzi schemes is incomplete without examining how the public views the con artists and their victims. This subject leads us to the next chapter.

Chapter 5

How Does The Public View the Con Artists and the Victims?

A. AMERICA IS AMBIVALENT ABOUT ITS CON ARTISTS

Some people may admire the con artists' talents; many con artists are indeed gifted people. Yet Americans condemn wasted talent. They may pay attention to the challenge that the cons pose to society, but as their danger is recognized, the charm of con artists palls and concern, or even fear, for the welfare of society's survival emerges. The harm done by their schemes to the integrity and existence of the markets becomes clearer. The dark side comes into view; the cruelty and lack of empathy of the con artists surface. The difficulties of uncovering the schemes and the great losses they cause to individuals and institutions stand out for all to see.

In addition, the public seems to distinguish between two groups of con artists. The first includes those who started as con artists; the other group includes those who resolved their problems by resorting to a Ponzi scheme. The "professional" con artist (illustrating the former group) rarely enjoys the benefit of the public's doubt as to crookedness. Everyone agrees that this con artist is a crook; nonetheless this person often is admired for his cleverness.

In contrast, the legitimate businessperson who turned to becoming a con artist should enjoy more benefit of the doubt as to bad intentions. There may be uncertainty as to whether this person intended to defraud others; perhaps the person deserves sympathy. After all, desperate circumstances could have driven him or her to fraud.

Yet this con artist invokes far less public affection and admiration. It is as if people are saying, "We expected better of you." It may well be that people feel more betrayed by honest persons gone wrong than by those who are incorrigibly bad. People might not identify with genuine fraudsters, but they may sense more affinity to legitimate businesspersons. If these businesspersons go astray, people may feel betrayed by their own kind. This sense of betrayal reflects the disappointed trust that we *want to feel* toward legitimate businesses, and it may explain why we are far angrier at Ponzi schemes that affect numerous people through public distribution of shares than at those schemes affecting fewer people in face-to-face relationships between the con artists and their marks. This may be the reason Bernard Madoff, wrapped in and hiding behind a legitimate brokerage and advisory service business, is not viewed with the same ambivalent admiration we bestow on other con artists. Our anger may reflect concern, or even fear, for our own well-being, and for the system on which the safety of our life savings may depend.

Yet even Madoff, who robbed many who trusted him with their life savings and who stole from not-for-profit-organizations money destined for good social causes, has not received the kind of hatred and fear with which those who use physical force or violence are viewed. Madoff might indirectly publish a book that people will buy without feeling revulsion in touching it, and the money they pay might bring him a softer life in prison, even though this is not the buyers' intention.

1. Con Artists Who Defrauded Small Investors Are Viewed Somewhat Differently

Though the public views con artists with indulgence for defrauding wealthy and sophisticated victims, this indulgence turns to rage when the victims are small and unsophisticated investors. Small investors are not blamed for falling prey to con artists. They had no chance; the match was uneven and unfair. Small investors are true victims who could not fend for themselves. Nonetheless, even with respect to small and unsophisticated investors, the public view of such con artists is somewhat ambivalent. After all, those victims could ask and consult others. The attitude of the public in this case is an expectation of self-protection. This may be the attitude in the United States, but not necessarily in other countries. Although in the United States independence, self-protection, and a strong belief in competition (and let the best person win) are exalted personal features, there are countries in which a prohibition of taking unfair advantage of the weaker and the duty of fair dealing are far stronger. In the United States the freedom to invest is coupled with responsibility to do one's homework and make reasonable decisions. If one does not understand the deal, one should not make the deal. In other countries the duty of people to deal fairly with others is heavier.

Whether America's public reactions to con artists and their victims have changed, in light of the financial scandals of 2002 and 2008, is unclear. The suggestions outlined above are not the product of meticulous research; they are topics for reflection and inquiry. Too many victims were unrealistic and gullible in the years of the market bubble. For example: one Ponzi scheme drew $8 million of investments that were described as safe. The court held that the investors had a duty to investigate, "given the suspicious circumstances and the plaintiffs' [investors'] savvy."[1] Could the "rational" view be that we should not condemn con artists who take advantage of market euphoria to benefit at some risk to themselves?

2. When Con Artists Mimic the Wealthy Power Elite, They Live Like the Wealthy Power Elite

The view of corporate managers as Ponzi scheme con artists has varied over the years. In 1980, for example, Clinard and Yeager wrote: "Corporate crime is indicative of the distribution of power in our society . . . . Corporations are seldom referred to as lawbreakers and rarely as criminals in enforcement proceedings. Even if violations of the criminal law, as well as other laws are involved, enforcement attorneys and corporation counsels often refer to the corporation as 'having a problem': one does not speak of the robber or the burglar as having a problem."[2] Since the 1980s, this attitude changed somewhat but was later revived. After the debacle of 2008, the attitude changed somewhat again.

The danger of viewing con artists as reflecting the power elite is still strong. Generally people do not identify with burglars, robbers, and violent criminals; nor do they identify with petty thieves. But white-collar criminals of the con artist variety are far more easily identified both with and by the power elite they associate with and in whose ranks they appear. As with the black sheep of the family who has gone astray, they are family nonetheless. The ambivalent condemnation of con artists is reflected by their associates. Those who are committed to financial leadership recoil from condemning even mimics of this leadership. The mimics' violations are ignored, forgiven, and viewed with "understanding." One example concerns the leaders of large and prestigious financial institutions, and the development of networks for acquiring insider information.[3]

The number of cases that have been—and are still being—brought against corporate management and money managers since

2008 has again marked how the power elite are viewed. Madoff is an example because he shamed many leaders of charitable and nonprofit organizations, perhaps because of the extraordinary amounts involved and perhaps because his fraud brought to the bankruptcy court conflicts among the victims themselves. These conflicts involved those investors who lost their investments (or expected returns) and those who managed to benefit from the fraud and retrieve not only their investments but also returns on these investments (which in truth constituted stolen money).[4]

3. The "Barren and Destructive Creators": The Benefits of Creative Harm

Con artists, and perhaps some of the suspecting investors, feeder organizations, and others who help them, are creative and innovative. Lewis Hyde wrote that people can shape the world, but with "shapeliness comes a set of rules meant to preserve the design. 'Do not steal. Do not lie. Do not blaspheme . . . Behave yourself. You should be ashamed. . . .' Whoever has the wit to break these rules, whoever puts the guards to sleep, slips across the threshold and floods the sacred meadows with contingency, whoever steals the boundary stones of clear distinction, that person strips design of its protective glamour."[5] Hyde notes that con artists are barren creators. They are creative, but not productive. Like mythological tricksters, they "are ridden by lust, but their hyperactive sexuality almost never results in any offspring."[6] The mythological trickster is described as self-contradictory, as a "creative idiot" and "wise fool."

Yet tricksters do not only break barriers; as they cross existing boundaries, they invent new boundaries as well.[7] Though they fraudulently implement new ideas, these ideas can then be selectively chosen to benefit society. For example, Michael Milken manipulated the securities markets and violated the prohibition on insider trading. Yet he left a legacy of "junk bonds," which became an acceptable means of financing. When all was said and done, he helped break the shackles of familiar forms of financing. Before his time, issuance of high-risk bonds was not an acceptable form of financing. He showed that they worked, and he made them acceptable. His disdain for the law may not have been necessary to introduce his invention. Moreover, after he served a two-year prison sentence for racketeering and fraud, he "helped broker a $1.35 billion investment in Rupert Murdoch's News Corp. and advised MCI in other ways, earning himself $42 million."[8] In addition he "launched the Milken Institute Global Conference, 'where ideas are born, markets analyzed and networks created.'"[9] No doubt about it, he is a very able man. He may not have been barren.

However, even though con artists put the existing order under sufficient and continuous pressure for reevaluation, they endanger society as well. Like cancer cells that do not follow the structural rules of the body, con artists do not follow the social rules of the body politic. A body can tolerate some abnormal growths, but if cancer cells continue to spread and play havoc with the structural rules, the body will die.[10] If con artists spread over the population, the health of the social body is endangered.

4. Con Artists Can Be Corrupting Teachers

In addition, some con artists are inclined, and have the ability, to teach others how to defraud. Through their efficient communication they reach not only a vast number of victims; they also reach potential con artists. Jerome Schneider was able to communicate effectively in writing, so he published a number of books. One is entitled *Hiding Your Money: Everything You Need to Know About Keeping Your Money and Valuables Safe from Predators and Greedy Creditors*. The title of another book is *The Complete Guide to Offshore Money Havens, Revised and Updated 3rd Edition: How to Make Millions, Protect Your Privacy, and Legally Avoid Taxes.* Another variation on the same theme is *Using an Offshore Bank for Profit, Privacy and Tax Protection.*[11] Schneider was indicted by a grand jury for conspiracy to defraud the United States, wire fraud, and mail fraud.[12] His co-conspirator, Eric Witmeyer, pleaded guilty to tax evasion conspiracy, having promised to cooperate with the prosecutors.[13] Schneider has had interested readers. As Christopher Albert of the U.S. Attorney's office in Boston mentioned in his talk "Techniques to Detect and Recover Hidden Assets," one of Schneider's books was found on the bookshelf of a lawyer, Morris Goldings, who was convicted of money laundering.[14] These people create a following.

The destructive consequences of pyramid schemes are social as well as financial. One English publication noted that "[o]n the Isle of Wight, family member has turned against family member, and neighbour against neighbour in the quest for a magic formula which can turn £3,000 into £24,000. Banks have had cash shortages."[15] The operator of the scheme required all payments to be made in banknotes that cannot be traced. The publication continued:

. . . Women Empowering Women (WEW) scheme. Far from being an act of gender advancement, it is a classic pyramid which purports to enrich everyone even though these plans always take cash from the many to give to the astute few. It is not even confined to women—men have taken some leading roles and hoovered up much of the cash.... [These schemes have appeared] in Glasgow, south Wales, Swindon, Surrey, Leicester and south London. But on the island itself, WEW has already produced so many £3,000 losers that they are trying to recoup their deficits—often their life savings—by setting up a new pyramid to suck in fresh cash. This week, the Community Investment Club, based in a shopfront in Newport, promised via details in the window to turn £100 into £88,300 but did not mention that one £88,300 winner requires 882 losers. This "club" is open to both sexes.

The public was warned by the authorities, but it is unclear whether the warning was effective.[16]

B. HOW DOES THE PUBLIC VIEW THE *VICTIMS*?

1. With Few Exceptions, People View the Victims of Con Artists Differently Than They View the Victims of Violent Crimes

Almost invariably, the first reaction of people at the mention of Ponzi scheme victims is to blame the victims. The victims of risky investing are deemed "greedy" because they are drawn to enticing offers that are too good to be true; they are gullible and stupid because they ignore investment risk and the risk of possible fraud. Therefore the victims got what they deserved.[17]

This reaction is similar to the reaction toward rape victims, who (so it is said) happened to visit a bar at night or who are viewed as too pretty and sexy for their own good. It is *their* fault that they attract men and entice them into committing rape.[18] However, in the context of investments, not all victims are treated alike. One consideration in judging and differentiating among victims could be the nature of their relationship with the con artist. Mixing business with friendship reduces the arm's-length relationship with the solicitors. Even though people may seek such a mix, they condemn it when friendship blinds the victims to the nature of the con artists and their offerings. Because the relationship between con artists and their victims is important to our understanding of the public's judgment of the victims, we digress somewhat and deal with this relationship here.

In the "friendship context," two reasons may underlie social condemnation of the victims. One reason is, as we have seen, that the victims got what they bargained for. Emotional gratifications are not free. The victims' losses constitute payment for what they received (in hope, excitement, and sometimes money). After all, they should not have expected to receive these benefits without paying for them. The victims have nothing to complain about. Victims may be condemned because they fell for false friendship and false appearances. Rightly or wrongly, it may be assumed that one can easily uncover false expression of feelings.

2. A Related Reason for Condemning the Victims Is That They Did Not Do Their Homework

The victims failed to examine what they were supposed to examine: the transaction itself. First, those who lost their own money should not complain. They should know better than fall for the proposed investments. Thus, in one case, sophisticated victims of a Ponzi scheme lost their claims against the schemers because the investors failed to make inquiries they were capable of making.[19]

Second, representatives of institutions and others who lost *other people's money* are condemned even stronger for having failed to do their job for which investors or employers have paid them. These representatives neglected to evaluate the transaction carefully. Although the individual victims neglected to take care of themselves, the institutional representatives are more blameworthy for having failed to take care of clients who trusted them to take care of the clients' assets. A similar distinction appears with the harsher judgment of legitimate businesses that find themselves in dire straits and "backing into"

Ponzi schemes, compared to the more tolerant judgment of those who started and ended as con artists.

The following cases demonstrate sophisticated investors' follies.

Crigger (a sophisticated investor) was approached by a man called Mason in January 1995. Mason offered to Crigger an investment in a corporation named Rayvon "as a safe investment with a guaranteed return of principal and an assured income stream of six to seven percent *a month*" (court's emphasis). Mason explained that this surefire arrangement was based on a hitherto undiscovered arbitrage opportunity that defendants had identified: Rayvon would use one-year U.S. Treasury bills as security for a loan from a brokerage firm (here, Fahnestock), the proceeds of which they would use to buy and sell certificates of deposit ("CDs") to banks in several countries; profit would be generated by arbitraging the spread in interest rates of the CDs. Crigger was assured that his money would be repaid because it would be held in a brokerage account under instructions "that his investment would not be removed from the account and that Crigger could seek the return of his funds at any time."

The next month, Crigger invested $3 million in Rayvon. He received no disclosure materials and the brokerage instruction were not so reassuring. They gave Rayvon control of Crigger's account and did not ensure repayment of his investment of $3 million, promising "only that he would receive the 'proceeds' from the sale of the Treasury bills—i.e., what was left in his account after all the buying and selling of the CDs." Crigger did not make any independent inquiries or seek any advice before making the investment. In fact, he and other investors were prevented from trying to verify the story or directly contacting the brokerage firm that held his account. If he did that, he was told, he would be "'automatically disqualified' from participation. Crigger and other investors admitted in their testimony in court that the promises of these enormous profits were "too good to be true," and "pretty amazing."[21] The court denied their claims, holding that these investors were not defrauded because they recognized the signals of fraud but did nothing about it.[22] In another case, it was hard to sympathize with investors who paid for a promise of profits up to 4,000 percent.[23] In the year 2000, such profits are not realistic.

Therefore, sympathy for the victims of a Ponzi scheme may dry up if it seems the victims suspected the scheme and suspected that their gain would come from the investments of later investors. Perhaps these victims share some of the characteristics of con artists and adopt the cons' view of the world. If such investor-victims invested early enough, they would indeed gain from the money of those who invested after them. One could view the cons and these "victims" as engaged in a joint venture.[24]

C. IS THERE PROTECTION AVAILABLE FOR SOPHISTICATED POTENTIAL VICTIMS?

Is it really difficult to detect a Ponzi scheme? After all, there are many people who are not caught in the net. If one cares to look, the flags waved by the con artists are bright red warnings. As noted in Chapter 1, although there is an enormous variety of Ponzi schemes, they *all* have a few prominent features in common. First, the con artist always promises very high returns at low risk. Second, in every scheme the source of the payments is costly to evaluate directly and cannot be tested by comparison because the scheme or story is novel. Third, in every Ponzi scheme, even if the con artists are not with a financial institution, they continue to issue their obligations. Fourth, in most of the schemes the salespersons attempt to establish close personal relationships with the investors; and fifth, when the schemes involve securities, there is no compliance with securities law. Stripped of all diversions, feelings, excitements, and fascinations, these elements are quite easy to identify. They earmark the Ponzi scheme. Any one of them should raise a danger sign—a red flag.

1. Red Flag: A Very High Return at Low Risk

Borrowers and issuers who promise extremely high returns are likely to default or fail. The offer to pay very high interest sends a signal of financial stress and need. It also suggests that the borrower or issuer does not care about the level of interest he must pay because he does not intend to pay *any* amount. Not just the interest but the investor's capital is at great risk. Therefore the promise of high return spells high risk. If high return, low risk are offered, then one part of the promise is likely to be a lie. It should raise a red flag.

Even if we believe there is no such thing as a free lunch, some lunches may be literally free (with the salesperson, as a come-on), although the price covers the salesperson's cost. But generally, high return and low risk do not go together. To be sure, in Ponzi schemes the risk does not reside with a business, because there is no business. The risk is that investors may not be told the truth about the use of their invested capital and the source of the returns. In most cases, high return and low risk is a contradiction in terms, and belief in such a possibility is unreasonable. No stories, emotions, good relationships, and friendships should trump the strong signal of danger that high returns and low risk emits. This red flag does not constitute expert advice. Finance and business today are too complex and too time-consuming to truly know, unless one is devoted to acquiring expertise on the topic. Therefore, rather than rely on one's understanding (unless really an expert), it might be desirable to seek a second opinion to determine whether the combined high return and low risk is trustworthy. When an offer looks exceptional, the best thing may be to stop and make no decision, and then seek a reliable, disinterested, expert opinion.

2. Red Flag: The Mystery Source of the Higher Returns

The second signal of a Ponzi scheme is that the purported profits come from a business that is not verified by the con artist and that it would be costly for investors to verify. Regardless of how rational and convincing the sellers' reasons for secrecy are, the facts wrapped in secrecy remain unknown. In addition, one proven fact does not prove others that remain unknown. Lack of information raises a red flag. Many a wise investor has advised time and again never to invest in anything that one does not understand and does not know enough about. The wise investor recognizes a red flag.

3. Red Flag: Continuous Offerings of Obligations

Although financial institutions engage in continuous fundraising (offerings of their obligations or those of others), other businesses hardly ever do so on a regular, short-term basis. If the purported business is not a bank, insurance company, mutual fund, or the like, the fact that the promoters are continuously offering their securities to the public should signal danger. If, in addition, the existence of the proposed business is not verified, and if the promoters offer extremely high returns, the signal becomes a hot red flag indeed.

Enron Corporation, for example, issued its shares continuously. Since it did not purport to be redeeming shares, the question should have been asked, What does the corporation use the ceaseless flow of capital for? In fact, the answer would have illuminated the fraud. The corporation used its own securities as collateral for its own obligations. In fact, it did not even produce the shares but just promised to produce them if it failed. Enron's design was not a classic Ponzi scheme, but it contained the same ingredients. The transaction appears to involve two parties: the corporation's promise and a second party. In fact, there is only one party: the corporation. Its obligations were backed by a collateral of its own obligations, although of a different type. There was a single note in the financial statements that might have pointed the way to further research. But no one asked. The imponderable design should have raised a red flag for investors.

4. Red Flag: Con Artists' Activities Outside the Legal Protections

Ponzi schemes involve offering securities or investment advice. These are regulated activities. Unsophisticated investors may not know the difference between a public offering, which requires registration with the SEC, and a private placement, which requires provision of information but does not pass the scrutiny of government officials. But sophisticated investors do know or should know the difference. If they know, they should note that the information is not provided to them as it is in other cases. Absence of legal compliance should raise a red flag.

5. Other Red Flag Signals

In addition to the nature of the scheme clearly signaling danger, there may be surrounding circumstances that add reasons for caution. First, there may be warnings from insiders who should know. To be sure, the con artists who manage the business are persuasive in calming excited investors, and in convincing even professionals. Yet if professionals, and especially private sector actors who serve as verifiers of information for public investors, receive warnings from insiders (or outsiders), they should take heed. The warnings can come from employees who resigned and who then contact an adviser bank and corporate lawyers.[25] The warning can come to management from insiders, as in the case of Enron, or from employees who left the corporation and contact reporters and analysts to tell the story of the fraud.[26] The recipient of such information should treat it as a red flag, especially if it comes from insiders, regardless of management's response. The more successful the corporation, especially if its rise is fast and exceptional, the higher should the offer raise a red flag.

6. Separating Business, Emotion, and Faith

Investors would see a suspicious scheme more clearly if they did not mix their business decisions with nonbusiness matters, such as religious and personal relationships or the attraction of a mystery. The mix can be deadly because personal relationships, religious influence, and similar influences mute the person's focus on the business and reduce diligence while heightening reliance and trust. Salespeople often seek personal relationships with potential and existing clients. This is not to say that they mean to mislead. But it does mean that an investor should be somewhat on guard, especially if the salesperson is pressing for a closer-than-usual relationship. A salesperson who offers and seeks a personal relationship should raise a red flag. The offer may be genuine, but it might not be.[27]

7. Advice to Investors as Protection Against Affinity Scams Is Similar

The "don'ts" include making an investment one does not understand, or making an investment solely on the recommendation of people you know through an organization, religious, or ethnic group to which a person is a member, as those people may already be victims. Be well aware that if some investors receive a return this does not mean all investors will be so fortunate. The famous "If it's too good to be true, it probably is!" is an extension of the admonition that all investments involve risks, especially if accompanied by a promise of a very high return. It is also a warning against investments that are open to a select few or that one is asked to keep confidential. Investors should ask for documentation. Fraudsters do not like to leave a paper trail; honest people do not mind doing that. Investors should ask for explanations and reject any accounting for why they are not forthcoming. Investors should take time to make a decision even if they are hard-pressed to quickly seize a once-in-a-lifetime opportunity.[28]

Significantly, similar red flags cover specific types of fraud. The Securities and Exchange Commission published a list of signs of banking-related investment frauds.[29] These danger signals include excessive guaranteed returns, fictitious financial instruments, extreme secrecy, and exclusive opportunity. There is nothing new in this list. It could apply effectively to other stories of Ponzi schemes.

In sum: Is it really difficult to identify a potential Ponzi scheme? After identification, is it really difficult to determine whether the scheme is in progress by discovering the real risk, by seeking information about the true source of the returns, and by verifying the offered information?

Chapter 6

The Legal Aftermath

A. COLLECTING THE ASSETS AND MEDIATING AMONG THE VICTIMS

The law comes to the fore when the Ponzi scheme lasts for a long time and the victims lost significant amounts—sometimes their life savings. In such cases, the victims may fight each other to cover their losses. The reason for these conflicts is inherent in the nature of the scheme. A Ponzi scheme starts and ends with three kinds of "players": one is the con artist (or the group of con artists), the second kind is the early group of investors; the third kind is the later investors. Not all investors lose in this scheme because the early investors receive their investments and "profits" from the money paid by later investors. The "unlucky" investors came too late and, rather than gain, lose all or most of their investment.[1] Thus, investors can be divided into those who collected their investments with or without profits and those who received part of their investment or none.

When a Ponzi scheme is uncovered, law plays one role in bringing fraudsters to justice and two additional roles. The first is collecting the fraudsters' remaining assets and claiming funds from those who helped the con artists. The second is dividing the assets fairly among the victims.

B. THE ISSUES

Many legal issues rise upon the discovery and dissolution of a Ponzi scheme. One of these issue, relates to taxation. What if victims paid taxes on the profits they must now repay? How much tax, if any, should the victims recoup? And what if the value of money in the past was more or less than the amount the victims accept or pay now? We are not going to deal with the tax and value issues because these are complicated problems, outside the parameters of this book; and besides, I am neither a tax expert nor an evaluator of money. Therefore, I mention these issues but go no further.

Another legal topic that results from the demise of Ponzi schemes involves the con artist's bankruptcy. This topic raises a number of questions. First, who collects the remaining assets? Second, from whom should the assets be collected? And third, to whom should the assets be distributed?

C. WHO COLLECTS THE REMAINING ASSETS?

Although some of the victims may sue other victims directly, the main scene in a Ponzi scheme case takes place in the bankruptcy court that oversees collection and division of a bankrupt debtor's assets.[2]

The bankruptcy court appoints a trustee to collect the assets that the con artist accumulated or hid. If another agency becomes liable as a guarantor of losses from such Ponzi schemes, such as the Securities Investor Protection Corporation (SIPC), and guarantees against losses of broker-dealers' customers, SIPC may appoint a trustee as well, and the process may differ.

The trustee sues the holders of the con artist's assets and those who helped the con artist in perpetrating fraud, such as feeders (organizations that brought investors to the con artist), persons who received significant gifts from the con artist, and anyone with whom the con artist "parked" substantial amounts of money. The trustee claims the assets these helpers received unlawfully or inequitably from the con artist. Some con artists stash their assets in various bank accounts in the United States and abroad. If the money was hidden and then spent, some institutions might be liable if they knowingly helped to perpetrate the fraud by hiding the money (an action usually to their great benefit).[3] Thus the court supervises the collection of the remaining assets of the con artist and division of the collected assets among the creditors, in this case the victims.[4]

D. WHO, AMONG THE "HELPERS" OF CON ARTISTS, MUST PAY?

1. Who Helps the Con Artists?

Members of the professions such as lawyers and accountants can, and sometimes do, bestow credibility on con artists and their ventures.[5] There are professionals who act as agents of con artists (knowingly or unknowingly) and can induce people to invest in the con artists' schemes.[6]

If such professionals are initially unaware of the nature of the scheme, they usually discover it later. On discovery, some depart and avoid any contact with the con artist. Others might continue to be involved, perhaps because they need the money and perhaps because they hope to extricate themselves from liability later, by pleading ignorance, as one lawyer has done.[7]

Banks can lend credibility to con artists as well. In the case of *Connecticut National Bank v. Giacomi*, a bank approved a loan to a con artist's business.[8] The bank's *approval* sent investors a powerful signal that the con artist's business was creditworthy, on the assumption that the bank had done its "due diligence" and collected information about the borrower. The bank was aware of the investors' assumption, but after approval it is hard for a bank to withdraw approval or publicly announce doubts about the borrower's creditworthiness. There may be a case in which a bank goes further and assists in the fraud, in spite of sufficient facts to suspect a Ponzi scheme and a violation of securities laws.[9]

Regardless of intentions, a respectable bank can feed financial fraud by neglecting to supervise its employees. One bank was found liable for helping a securities fraud that was perpetrated by an employee, to whom the bank provided a false and "severely reckless" reference.[10] A financial institution that hired an independent contractor to create and manage its insurance program was liable for this contractor's management and choice of personnel. Yet, probably without the knowledge of the financial institution's managers, at least one of the hired brokers used this program to operate a Ponzi scheme, adding unaffiliated companies to the policies and retaining the premiums.[11]

Investment companies are not spared con artists' abusive use either. Charles Lewis and his partner conducted a Ponzi scheme by using a number of "ostensible investment companies." The con artists promised investors "that they would be participating in an exclusive program that purchased high-yield notes whose principal was guaranteed by reputable insurers."[12] The names of these reputable companies helped sell fraudulent products.

2. What About Suspecting Helpers?

Assume the employees of a financial institution such as a bank know what is going on in some of the bank's accounts, and they tell a number of their select customers to avoid investing with the con artist. Assume further that, notwithstanding their suspicions, the employees continue to serve the con artist with respect to his or her banking needs. Do these employees and their institutions have a duty to alert the customer-victims, or potential victims, or notify government agencies of their suspicions?

Generally, the answer is no. Institutions may suspect that a customer is conducting a Ponzi scheme, but institutions such as banks generally do not owe a duty of protection from fraud perpetrated by the institutions' customers.[13] Yet even though financial institutions are not the financial police, their position allows them to indirectly offer financial assistance to fraud. The line is not easy to draw, and it is being litigated.[14]

A similar question with a somewhat different answer is posed by feeders to con artists, especially if they richly benefited from investing their clients' money with the con artist. Some of these feeders are the institutions (including advisers) that channel customers' money to the con artist, sometimes on their own initiative, and sometimes on the clients' directives. In both cases, feeders who acted as advisers to the clients may bear responsibility for failing to admonish their clients that the con artist's offers are too good to be true, or failing to examine the con artists' investments, accounting, and custodial services before recommending or investing their clients' money with the con artist.

These feeders are fiduciaries required to serve their clients honestly and well. They may be in a more precarious legal position than banks that shelter the con artists' money because banks generally do not serve the investors as trusted fiduciaries of their customers, while feeders, being investment advisers or money managers, usually do.

In July 2011 Irving Picard, the trustee liquidating Madoff's assets, announced a settlement to the tune of $1 billion with a group of Madoff's feeders. The settlement covered "more than a dozen domestic and foreign investment funds and their affiliates" and needed "approval of the U.S. Bankruptcy Court for the Southern District of New York." In addition, Picard "settled with a former chief executive associated with" a large money management company that operated "the second-largest Madoff 'feeder fund' group." These operations as well as the liquidations by the SIPC and the SEC's involvement and oversight of liquidation, will be evaluated by Congress.[15] In addition to feeders, there may be friends with whom the con artists have "parked" much money for free or for payment. Thus, trustee Picard reached an agreement with the widow of one of Madoff's deceased friends for a repayment of more than $7 billion.[16] And then there are friends who merely received gifts that the rich give to the rich. The question is: under what conditions should these friends return their gifts?

E. HOW TO DIVIDE THE REMAINING ASSETS?

Dividing the remaining con artist's assets among the victims can create conflicts among the trustee in bankruptcy and some of the victims, among receivers of the failing Ponzi business and some of the investors, and sometimes among the victims themselves. There is not enough money to repay all victims. Yet some receive payment not only of their investment with the con artist but also additional money drawn from other victims' payments. Most of this money may be deemed stolen. Therefore, the issues of how much money the victims are entitled to, from whom they can collect, and under what circumstances become complicated. They involve two warring groups of victims whose personal situations may differ. The question is: what is a fair division among them?

As one court noted: "It is clear that the principal invested by any of Madoff's customers 'gave value to the debtor,' and therefore may not be recovered by the Trustee absent bad faith. As for transfers made by Madoff Securities to its customers in excess of the customers' principal—that is, the customers' profits—these were in excess of the 'extent' to which the customers gave value, and hence, if adequately proven, may be recovered regardless of the customers' good faith."[17] Therefore, money that investors paid can be claimed (absent bad faith). Similarly, investors may retain the money that was repaid by the con artist.

Further, usually creditor-investors may *not* keep money the debtor (con artist) gave them within ninety days before the bankruptcy petition was filed.[18] Such a payment would be considered fraudulent (unless the money was made in payment for an ongoing business). This rule can be traced to Charles Ponzi's bankruptcy, and a Supreme Court decision in 1924:

> When news of [Ponzi's] insolvency was published in the paper, the lenders [creditors] rushed to get repaid. Shortly thereafter, a petition in bankruptcy was filed. The trustees then brought an action against the lenders to recover the payments made shortly before bankruptcy as unlawful preferences. When the trial court and the appellate court dismissed the trustees' action, they filed a petition for a writ of certiorari. The Supreme Court held that the payments to the Trustee should recover the payments to the creditors.

A preference to a creditor should be avoided when the creditors could reasonably believe that the payment gave him a greater percentage of his debt than the bankrupt's other creditors of the same class.[19]

So it would seem that those victims who escaped with their money more than ninety days before the bankruptcy filing may keep their money and the profits the con artist gave them.

Well . . . not exactly. One court held that a gift of stolen money cannot vest rights in the recipient even if the gift was made before the ninety-day cutoff point.[20] Stolen money does not change its nature by transfer. It remains stolen money, and a thief cannot bestow ownership that the thief does not have. Therefore, with a few exceptions, people who receive stolen money or stolen goods do not gain owner-ship of the money or goods. One exception to this rule is if the re-ceivers paid value for the property and did not know nor suspect that the money and property were stolen.[21] Similarly, a broker must return the commissions that the con artist paid in connection with the fraudulent scheme.[22]

According to Harold R. Weinberg, the rules concerning stolen goods are shaped by two conflicting public policies. One aims at en-suring that innocent buyers will acquire ownership of assets they buy in an open market. The other policy aims at deterring thieves by making it difficult to sell stolen goods, and deterring buying from thieves. These rules regulate the costs of verifying the source of the goods. If buyers can easily determine whether goods are stolen (for example, if a watch carries personal initials, or its price is very low, and the seller offers the watch in an alley rather than in a shop), then the buyer may be required to return the watch to its rightful owner. The rules may change depending on how much support markets require. Thriving markets might involve stricter rules against trading in stolen goods; in "thin markets" the buyers of stolen property may gain higher protection by law.[23]

One court justified lower protection to the buyers of stolen goods in periods of increasing theft. The court, noted that reduced protection gives people incentives to "prosecute felons, and . . . discourage per-sons from buying stolen goods," even in an open market.[24] The court thus protected good-faith buyers and provided incentives to prosecute those who were aware of the possibility that they were offered stolen goods.

Yet the "net winners," those who collected from the con artists their initial investments and perhaps returns on their investments are fighting to keep some of their winnings and contest the way the collected assets are distributed. They have brought claims in courts as well.[25]

In addition, some courts have limited payments to victims who were negligent or should have known that the con artist's offers were too good to be true. There are arguments that attacked the equitable basis for precluding victims from collecting what is due to them because they were "negligent or worse" with respect to the existence of a Ponzi scheme.[26]

What about victims who "smelled a rat" and decided to withdraw their money after collecting the profits? What if they suspected that the money they received was stolen? What if they knew that they were receiving stolen money? Might they be not entitled to any amount, not even the money they gave the con artist? After all, money is fungible. What they gave the con artist is not the money they received from the con artist upon withdrawal. That money may be stolen as well. On the one hand, we want people to be vigilant and protect themselves against fraud. But on the other hand, what if that protection results in receiving stolen money?

When one Ponzi scheme collapsed and the con artist was convicted, an investor company claimed some of the con artist's assets as a "purchaser" who received the property in "good faith and for value." The government argued that the investor company had reason to believe, or could find out by conducting a reasonable investigation, that the property was subject to forfeiture. Under bankruptcy law, the court determined that the transfer from the con artist to the investor was fraudulent and could not have been an honest purchase for value. This investor had to "wait in line with the rest of the investors that the [con artist] had duped."[27]

Some cases reach a compromise. In one case the court balanced the equities among the defrauded investors. The plaintiff in this case was one of thousands of investors in a Ponzi scheme that promised investors a 20 percent return in ninety days. The investor was requested to return a portion of the payments he received and refused to do so. The court held that comparing the total amount the investor received ($73,290.70), with the amount he had to return ($31,555.32) showed that the investor would be permitted to retain $41,735.38. This amount represented a total return of approximately 83 percent of his investment, while most of the scheme's fifty-two hundred net losers were likely to recover only pennies on the dollar for their initial investment.[28] This investor had to return the money, as required.

The issues become more complex when some victims retrieved their own investments and profits that constitute stolen money but used the money or lost it. They no longer have the money to return. Suppose Lucky invested in a Ponzi scheme fifteen years ago. Having retired, she collected her investment during the ten prior years as well as the profits from these investments. She then purchased a home in one of the islands and invested her savings in an annuity promising to provide her a comfortable income for the rest of her years.

Now suppose that ten years later she receives a demand from the trustee in the con artist's bankruptcy to return the entire amount of her investments and profits, and after pooling this amount with similar others she might receive a pro rata share of the pool. First, she does not know how to get her money from the insurance company. After all, she received the annuity for the amount of $42 million, which is what she paid for it. Second, she will have to offer the entire amount (her own investment and her profits) and might receive very little, depending on the losses of the investors who came after her. With the money she received from the con artist, she bought an expensive house that is now worth less than its purchase price. And she topped it with a mortgage she was paying off from the annuity payments. If the annuity goes, what is she to do?

On the other side of the fence is Angry Investor, who lost all his investments and gained nothing. He is angry because he believes that part, if not all, of Lucky's annuity was bought with his money. If both were imprudent to invest with a con artist, why should Lucky get it all, and he get nothing?

And then there is a third party, Suspicious Investor. She bought into a Ponzi scheme but soon thereafter smelled a rat and decided to reduce her risks, as well as the enormous profits that were offered, and retrieve her investments (perhaps with a little profit). Suspicious Investor may have had some information that supported her suspicions, but she shared it with no one. She just wanted to escape.

Finally there is the *Very* Suspicious Lucky Investor. This person too suspected foul play, imagining that the source of the high profits constituted the payments of new investors. However, he decided to collect as much as he could before demanding his money; being friendly with the con artist, he succeeded in collecting the investments and a significant amount of profits.

How should the law divide the losses among the victims? What role should the suspicions and intentions of the investors play? What role should the effect of the demand on investors for repayment play? What is fair and right in this case? Should the law play the role of a teacher in this case, teaching people not to be gullible, teaching them to be more careful about their investment decisions? How should victimized investors be judged?

In fact, the current evolving spectacle poses all these questions for the courts. The questions are percolating, and many are still unresolved. Yet conflicting principles and policies are emerging.

One way is to look at the source of the money that any of the victims, the feeders, and victims' friends are holding. They distinguish between legitimate and stolen money that they invested with the con artist. "Profits" that constitute stolen money should be repaid. However, because money is fungible, perhaps even the payment that victims invested with the con artist would be viewed as stolen money. In such a case, all victims should return all the money that they received from the con artist, and this amount should be divided as a pro rata share of what they invested.

A second way to resolve the issues is to mitigate the demand for repayment by the years that have passed since the payment and according to the situation of the victims. "Profits" that were paid in stolen money years ago and were spent or lost should not be recovered if the recipient investors did not know or suspect they were receiving stolen money.

A third way is to examine the investors' state of mind. Public policy encourages vigilant investors. But if they suspected foul play, they might not be permitted to collect profits that constituted other people's money. The answers are unclear and, sadly, cannot and will not satisfy everyone.

Epilogue

What can we learn from the stories and analyses in this book?

We can learn that con artists mirror trustworthy people. Deceitful actions can resemble legitimate activities. We noted that there are those who seem to be entrepreneurs and produce nothing. Promises of unbelievable profits can be, and often are, false. Following in the footsteps of others may be beneficial, but also dangerous if we follow blindly. We recognize that some people ignore signs of danger and are overwhelmed by the positive (though misleading) signals that con artists send. For these people it is harder to discover Ponzi schemes before they end up with devastating losses. We can learn that society is populated by people who mimic trustworthiness, who may be self-centered, ruthless narcissists; and that there are true victims as well as foolish or fake victims. We recognize that con artists are addicted to the game and can corrupt their victims, drawing investors into defrauding each other.

America is ambivalent toward con artists. It does not condemn them as it would, say, the slayers of helpless elderly people, even though the actions of con artists may have a similar devastating effect on their victims, and even though their methods may be just as heartlessly cruel. Con artists are gifted, although they do not gift their talents to others or to society. Con artists possess admirable qualities. Had they used their talents differently, society would greatly benefit. Instead they are smart predators who seek to prove that they are smarter than those who trust them.

EPILOGUE

What social factors feed Ponzi schemes? Perhaps these factors arise with "market exuberance" and bubbles, and come to light, like mushrooms popping up after the rain, with the crashes. Perhaps Ponzi schemes percolate as many people become greedy, following other people's unbelievable rise of wealth. In a country where equality is the guiding motto, why should some people have private airplanes and homes all over the world, while others cannot make ends meet? Perhaps the schemes feed a quest for self-satisfaction rather than a search for strength in self-limitation. Recognizing that truth, trust, and honesty are indeterminate, and realizing that people follow many routes with different measures of truth and honesty, we may conclude that "a little dishonesty" will always be there. So a little dishonesty is acceptable or even justified.

Here lies our greatest danger. A society that accepts a little dishonesty as a way of life is headed toward deception and abuse of trust on a grand scale. Because con artists *resemble us*, the true danger is that we might *become like them*. Knowing that fully self-enforced honesty cannot be achieved does not mean that accepting a little fraud, deception, and just a bit of breach of trust is the way to go.

Some people believe that the criminal justice system ought to protect them from fraud. Others believe that once fraud has occurred, the criminal justice system can do very little.[1] It is unclear whether potential prison sentences deter addicted con artists. Nonetheless the frauds that were discovered after the crash of 2008 have shaken the public, regulators, and Congress. Con artists are discovered and jailed. The Securities and Exchange Commission is vigorously pursuing perpetrators of securities fraud. But no one believes that this is enough to stem the tide of fraud.

Some people suggest that the best crime prevention is investor education. Unlike robbery, investors can say "No!" to suspicious investments.[2] Yet this education has been tried for years, without success. Who wants to read copious disclosure documents and evaluate the potential risk and benefit of the financial instruments that they offer? Who can understand these instruments without becoming an expert? And who has the time to become an expert in an area so far from daily life and expertise? Therefore, today, more than in the past, we ask: How can people protect themselves from financial fraud?

It is not as difficult as it seems—that is, provided we maintain self-awareness. Having read the stories of con artists' operations and their victims' reactions, the nature and the characteristics of the actors, we can focus on a number of easy-to-remember and understand questions.

First, who is trying to sell us an investment, and under what circumstances? Are we easily enchanted and charmed by people we do not know well? Do we follow too eagerly our friends' information about a "fabulous investment"? Are we drawn to investments in innovations we do not fully understand, or new ideas that have not been tested? Do we want to belong to an "exclusive investment club"? Let us recognize our own vulnerability to the con artists' allure. After all, very few of us remain entirely insensitive to some aspect of fraudulent schemes.

Knowing our weaknesses constitutes our strength and protection. In Greece, the Temple of Apollo in Delphi carried the inscription "Know thyself." Even the great Achilles had a vulnerable spot: his heel. People who are aware of their weaknesses (such as a tendency to become addicted to gambling, or to alcohol) can either succumb to their tendency or avoid casinos or drinks altogether. We may read, or be told, about a person who became a millionaire in no time. We may wish to become millionaires too. But if someone with the characteristics of a con artist approaches us with a great and tempting offer, or if our friends excitedly tell us about a wonderful once-in-a-lifetime opportunity, we will stop and consider our own tendencies and susceptibilities. And we might remember the stories we read in this book, and say, "Not now, thank you. Let me think about it."

Having paused, notwithstanding the pressure and the attraction of an investment proposal, we will be safer. We might lose a good opportunity but avoid a disastrous investment. Knowing what draws us, we will be more cautious, more questioning, and more skeptical. This approach does not necessarily turn us into suspicious and mistrusting persons. But it helps us remember the power of an enticing story and captivating people. It can raise our awareness of the appeals that induce hasty and risky decisions. This awareness can help us become wiser—and in the long run wealthier.

NOTES

Introduction

1. Merrill v. Abbott (*In re* Independent Clearing House Co.), 41 B.R. 985, 995 (Bankr. D. Utah 1984); subsequent history omitted.
2. Sushil Bikhchandani and Sunil Sharma, *Herd Behavior in Financial Markets*, 47 INT'L MONETARY FUND STAFF PAPERS 279, September 1, 2000, at § 3.
3. Gary Cohen, *Dark Clouds over a Guru to the Stars*, U.S. NEWS & WORLD REP., May 28, 2001, at 35.
4. United States v. Treadwell, 593 F.3d 990 (9th Cir. 2010).
5. Scott Bernard Nelson, *Fleet Writing Off $70M in Ponzi Scam; 4 in N.J. Accused of Bilking 8 Banks With Phony Metals Trading*, BOSTON GLOBE, May 15, 2002, at D1.
6. BankAtlantic v. Coast to Coast Contrs., 22 F. Supp. 2d 1354 (S.D. Fla. 1998).
7. Al Lewis, *Global Finance: Plea in Ponzi That Sacked Elway*, WALL ST. J., November 2, 2010, at C3, LEXIS, News Library, WSJ File.
8. *Id.*
9. *A Century of Ponzi Schemes*, DEALBOOK, December 15, 2008, http://dealbook.nytimes.com/2008/12/15/a-century-of-ponzi-schemes/ (last visited February 21, 2012).
10. Joanne McCulloch, *Cash Plan Director Faces Jail*, SUNDAY TIMES (PERTH), May 26, 2002, at 17.
11. Obsatz, *Con Left Entities Wiser, Poorer*, at B1; *see also* Diana B. Henriques, *$450 Million Fraud by Bill Collector Is Charged by U.S.*, N.Y. TIMES, February 18, 1994, at A1; United States v. Bennett, 161 F.3d 171, 174 n.2 (3d Cir. 1998) ("Later, in 1993, non-profit organizations were also permitted to participate,

and by the end, hundreds had sent funds to New Era."), *cert. denied,* 528 U.S. 819 (1999).

12. *See, e.g.,* United States v. Deters, 184 F.3d 1253, 1255 (10th Cir. 1999); "From a date unknown until August 1994, Ms. Deters operated a Ponzi scheme, in which individuals and church organizations invested money believing their investment returns were generated by profits from legitimate businesses."

13. Diana B. Henriques and Zachery Kouwe, *U.S. Arrests a Top Trader in Vast Fraud,* N.Y. TIMES, December 12, 2008, at A1, LEXIS, News Library, Arcnws File (noting Madoff's confession); *Exhibit A,* http://online.wsj.com/public/resources/documents/madoffclientlist020409.pdf (last visited Feb. 21, 2012) (list of clients); Diana B. Henriques, *Madoff Will Plead Guilty; Faces Life for Vast Swindle,* N.Y. TIMES, March 11, 2009, at A1 (noting length and size of scheme); Diana B. Henriques, *Madoff, Apologizing, Is Given 150 Years,* N.Y. TIMES, June 30, 2009, at A1 (noting sentence).

14. William P. Barrett, *New Mexico Mini-Madoff Case Provides Lesson for Investors,* Forbes, INVESTMENT GUIDE, June 28, 2010, at 90, LEXIS, News Library, Curnws File.

15. Adi Ignatius, *As "Pyramid Scheme" in Russia Begins to Collapse, Rubble May Trap Many,* WALL ST. J., July 27, 1994, at A6.

16. *Furor Fin Does the Vanishing Act with Investors' Rs350 Crore,* INDIA BUS. INSIGHT, December 24, 2001.

17. Chris Jarvis, *The Rise and Fall of the Pyramid Schemes in Albania,* 47 IMF STAFF PAPERS 1 (2000).

18. Katherine Verdery, *"Caritas" and the Reconceptualization of Money in Romania,* ANTHROPOLOGY TODAY, February 1995, at 3 (and authorities cited there).

19. Russell B, *Bottom Lines,* COURIER-MAIL (Brisbane), February 9, 1990, LEXIS, News Library, Arcnws File (noting conviction for aggravated fraud and issuing uncovered checks); *People's Banker Is Put on Trial,* GLOBE & MAIL (Canada), February 19, 1988, LEXIS, News Library, Arcnws File (noting scheme involved at least $13.5 million and ran for fifteen years, ending in 1984); Madeline Prowse, *Where Does Granny the Banker Get Her Money?* GLOBE & MAIL (Canada), August 2, 1984, LEXIS, News Library, Arcnws File (noting that Dona Branca "insists that she runs her business purely out of altruism").

20. Torsten Ove, *Southern Exposure; Investment Operation in Costa Rica Took in Hundreds of Millions, Then It All Fell Apart,* PITTSBURGH POST-GAZETTE, May 11, 2003, at C-1, LEXIS, News Library, Arcnws File.

21. *Cooperative Crisis Continues to Escalate in Haiti,* HAITI PROGRES, July 24–30, 2002, http://www.hartford-hwp.com/archives/43a/467.html (last visited May 2, 2011).

22. *SEC Files Action to Halt International Investment Scheme and Obtains Emergency Asset Freeze and Repatriation Order,* LITIGATION RELEASE No. 21,864 (February 22, 2011), http://www.sec.gov/litigation/litreleases/2011/lr21864.htm (last visited May 2, 2011).

23. Humberto Cruz and Diane Lade, *Don't Lose to Investing Scams—Watch for Signs*, SUN-SENTINEL (Fort Lauderdale, FL), September 18, 2000, at 21; see Curt Anderson, *Ponzi Scheme Collapses Nearly Quadrupled in '09*, BOSTON GLOBE, December 29, 2009, Business, at 6 ("More than 150 Ponzi schemes collapsed in 2009").
24. The list of these cases is with the author.
25. United States v. Reynolds, 643 F.3d 1130 (8th Cir. 2011) ("Reynolds pleaded guilty to conspiracy to commit money laundering . . . and was sentenced by the district court to 130 months' imprisonment. Reynolds appeals from his sentence"; his appeal was affirmed).
26. United States v. Treadwell, 593 F.3d 990 (9th Cir. 2010), *cert. denied*, 131 S. Ct. 280, *and cert. denied*, 131 S. Ct. 281, *and cert. denied*, 131 S. Ct. 488 (2010).
27. *Id.*
28. *A Century of Ponzi Schemes*, DEALBOOK, December 15, 2008, http://dealbook. nytimes.com/2008/12/15/a-century-of-ponzi-schemes/ (last visited February 21, 2012).
29. Joe Dejka, *Thieves to Learn a Lesson; Sarpy County Tries Shoplifting School; Court Cases Diverted; Shoplifting Facts*, OMAHA WORLD-HERALD, June 17, 2002, at 1b.
30. *Id.*
31. Humberto Cruz and Diane Lade, *Don't Lose to Investing Scams—Watch for Signs*, SUN-SENTINEL (Fort Lauderdale, FL), September 18, 2000, at 21.
32. People v. Sandy, 236 A.D. 2d 104 (N.Y. App. Div. 1997); BCCI case.
33. Dejka, *Thieves to Learn a Lesson*, at 1b, *at* Introduction n. 29.
34. Holly Howard Preston, *The Sophisticated Investor's Worst Nightmare; Investment Fraud—A New Bumper Crop*, INTERNATIONAL HERALD TRIBUNE., June 15, 2002, at 13.
35. Paul Palango, *Mountie Misery*, MACLEAN'S, July 28, 1997, at 10.
36. Prepared statement of Debra A. Valentine, General Counsel for the U.S. Federal Trade Commission on "Pyramid Schemes," presented at the International Monetary Fund Seminar on Current Legal Issues Affecting Central Banks, at http://www.ftc.gov/speeches/other/dvimf16.shtm (last visited February 22, 2012).
37. *Noted Banker Chmielinski Among Losers*, DAILY BOSTON GLOBE, June 28, 1957, at 23.
38. See, e.g., Glenn Puit, *Victims Say Beware of Scams*, LAS VEGAS REV.-J., June 27, 1999, at 1B; Richard L. Stern and Reed Abelson, *The Second-Oldest Industry?* FORBES, June 24, 1991, at 236, LEXIS, News Library, Arcnws File (describing a pyramid scheme under the auspices of the Church of God).
39. Arthur A. Leff, *Selling and Swindling* 71 (1976) (Ponzi schemes being preferable to the numbers game or other one-time hits).
40. See, e.g., Floyd v. Dunson (*In re* Rodriguez), 209 B.R. 424, 428 (Bankr. S.D. Tex. 1997) ("The business of debtors was conducted as a Ponzi scheme from about November 1990 until its demise on or about April 23, 1993"); United States v. Londe, 587 F.2d 18, 19 (8th Cir. 1978) ("This finding was based in

part on uncontroverted evidence which showed that from 1969 to 1972 Londe had represented to numerous individuals that he was able to purchase ambulance 'shells' direct from the factory, equip them himself and resell them at a substantial profit"), *cert. denied*, 439 U.S. 1130 (1979); New Jersey v. Childs, 242 N.J. Super. 121, 126 (1990) ("'Between on or about January 1, 1982 and on or about August 31, 1984' defendant used these misrepresentations . . .").

41. *In re* Taubman, 160 B.R. 964, 973 (Bankr. S.D. Ohio 1993).
42. See, e.g., Richard Behar, *Wall Street's Most Ruthless Financial Cannibal*, FORTUNE, June 8, 1998, at 212 ("But Dennis Helliwell, who was sentenced to federal prison last October, ran his Ponzi for 11 years").
43. See *From the "Lectric Law Library" Stacks: How to Avoid Ponzi and Pyramid Schemes*, at http://www.lectlaw.com/files/inv01.htm (last visited February 22, 2012).
44. Terry Greene Sterling, *The Moneychangers; A New Times Investigation; First in a Series*, PHOENIX NEW TIMES, April 16, 1998, LEXIS, News Library, Arcnws File; *From the "Lectric Law Library" Stacks: How to Avoid Ponzi and Pyramid Schemes*, at http://www.lectlaw.com/files/inv01.htm (last visited February 22, 2012). (If new investors constituted the only source of added capital, the number of investors needed to keep the scheme going would be astronomical. It was calculated that at month 11 the number of new investors must exceed the U.S. population and at month 13 it must exceed the world population.)
45. Michael Bacharach and Diego Gambetta, "Trust in Signs," in 2 *Trust and Society* 148, 149 (Karen S. Cook ed., 2001).

Chapter 1

1. Charles Ponzi, *The Rise of Mr. Ponzi* (1935), at http://www.pnzi.com (last visited February 29, 2012).
2. *Id.*
3. *"Ponzi" Schemes*, at http://www.sec.gov/answers/ponzi.htm (last visited July 10, 2001).
4. Ponzi, *The Rise of Mr. Ponzi*, at Ch. 1, n. 1.
5. *Id.*
6. *Id.*
7. *Id.*
8. *Id.*
9. *Id.*
10. *Charles Ponzi, Useless Information*, at http://uselessinformation.org/ponzi (last visited February 22, 2012).
11. United States v. Lindsey, 200 Fed. App'x 902 (11th Cir. 2006), unpublished opinion; see also Stafford v. Giddens (*In re* New Times Sec. Servs., Inc.), 463 F.3d 125 (2d Cir. 2006) ("Goren conducted a Ponzi scheme using the two brokerage houses (the 'Debtor'). He solicited investments in fictional money

market funds; he pretended to invest in genuine money market funds; and he issued fraudulent promissory notes").

12. Binyamin Appelbaum and David S. Hilzenrath, *SEC Didn't Act on Madoff Tips; Regulator Was Warned About Possible Fraud as Early as 1999*, WASH. POST, December 16, 2008, at D01, LEXIS, News Library, Wpost File.

13. *Transcript: The Madoff Affair*, Frontline, http://www.pbs.org/wgbh/pages/frontline/madoff/etc/script.html (last visited February 22, 2012).

14. Some authors noted that Madoff's scheme was unique. See Richard Posner, *Bernard Madoff and Ponzi Schemes—Posner's Comment*, BECKER-POSNER BLOG, December 21, 2008, http://www.becker-posner-blog.com/2008/12/index.html (last visited February 22, 2012); Diana Henriques, *Madoff Scheme Kept Rippling Outward, Crossing Borders*, N.Y. TIMES, December 20, 2008, at A1, http://www.nytimes.com/2008/12/20/business/20madoff.html. But another author disagrees; see Alexander J. Burakoff, *Madoff's Fraud—a "Ponzi Scheme" or a "Madoff Scheme"—The Answer Lies Somewhere in Between: A Classic Ponzi Scheme with a Few Twists* (February 2009) (paper written by a Boston University Law School student with the author; unpublished manuscript, on file with author).

15. Erin E. Arvedlund, *Don't Ask, Don't Tell: Bernie Madoff Is So Secretive, He Even Asks His Investors to Keep Mum*, BARRON'S, May 7, 2001, at 26.

16. Diana Henriques, *Madoff Scheme Kept Rippling Outward, Crossing Borders*, at A1, at Ch. 1, n. 14.

17. Joe Nocera, *Madoff Had Accomplices: His Victims*, N.Y. TIMES, March 13, 2009, at B1.

18. Alistair Barr, *Madoff's Rise Fueled by Leverage, Controversial Fees*, MARKET-WATCH.COM, December 18, 2008, LEXIS, News Library, Arcnws File.

19. *Transcript: The Madoff Affair*, Frontline, http://www.pbs.org/wgbh/pages/frontline/madoff/etc/script.html.

20. M. Corey Goldman, *What Were They Thinking?* INSTITUTIONAL INVESTOR (America's Edition), February 2009, LEXIS, News Library, Arcnws File.

21. Portfolio Staff, *Wiesel Lost "Everything" to Madoff*, PORTFOLIO.COM, February 26, 2009, http://www.portfolio.com/executives/2009/02/26/Elie-Wiesel-and-Bernard-Madoff/#ixzz18mUpirD9 (last visited February 23, 2012).

22. Diana Henriques, *Madoff Scheme Kept Rippling Outward, Crossing Borders*, at A1, at Ch. 1, n. 14.

23. John P. Wise, *"20/20" Interview: Madoff's Former Daughter-In-Law Drops Bomb-shells* (October 22, 2011), http://www.wisn.com/r/29559390/detail.html (last visited February 23, 2012); *Exhibit A*, http://online.wsj.com/public/resources/documents/madoffclientlist020409.pdf (last visited Feb. 21, 2012) (list of clients). http://www.forbes.com/2009/02/05/bernard-madoff-bil-lionaires-business-billionaires-0205_madoff.html.

24. Peterson v. McGladrey & Pullen, LLP, No. 10 C 274, 2010 U.S. Dist. LEXIS 117018 (N.D. Ill. November 3, 2010), unpublished opinion (footnote omitted).

25. State v. Schneider, 148 Ariz. 441, 443 (Ct. App. 1985).

26. BULLETIN: *Man Implicated by Jamaica in Alleged $326 Million Ponzi Known as "Cash Plus" Now Accused by United States of Orchestrating Separate HYIP Scheme That Funneled Cash to Latvian and Jamaican Accounts*, PATRICKPRETTY. COM, February, 24, 2011, http://www.patrickpretty.com/2011/02/24/bulletin-man-implicated-by-jamaica-in-alleged-326-million-ponzi-known-as-cash-plus-now-accused-by-united-states-of-orchestrating-separate-hyip-scheme-that-funneled-cash-to-latvian-and-jamaican-a/.
27. United States v. Moreland, 622 F.3d 1147, 1153 (9th Cir. 2010).
28. Katherine Verdery, "'Caritas' and the Reconceptualization of Money in Romania," *Anthropology Today*, February 1995, at 3.
29. Joanne McCulloch, *Cash Plan Director Faces Jail*, SUNDAY TIMES (Perth), May 26, 2002, LEXIS, News Library, Arcnws File; see also United States v. Cook, 573 F.2d 281 (5th Cir. 1978).
30. United States v. Bach, 172 F.3d 520, 521 (7th Cir.), *cert. denied*, 528 U.S. 950 (1999) (emphasis added).
31. United States v. Mathison, 157 F.3d 541, 544 (8th Cir. 1998).
32. SEC v. JT Wallenbrock & Assocs., 440 F.3d 1109, 1111 (9th Cir. 2006).
33. United States v. Utlaut, 497 F.3d 843 (8th Cir. 2007) (instead of buying seed he used the money to support his gambling addiction. Although he gave the seed orders to his employer, he concealed his "early-pay" program. The employer delivered the seed to the customers but was not aware that the customers had "prepaid" and therefore billed the customers later in the summer. The customers forwarded the invoices to the employee. He then paid the employer from the funds in Agri-Management. Where did the employee receive the money? After all, he spent the money that the customers forwarded to him earlier. He obtained the money to pay the later invoices from new seed orders. In addition he "solicit[ed] direct investment in Agri-Management in exchange for the promise of a guaranteed return." The scheme was discovered in July 2004, when a customer contacted the employer upon noticing that his large payment for seed was not recorded on his invoice. The company investigated, and fired the employee. The fraud cost the employer $3,895,962.90 in reimbursements to customers).
34. Greg Allen, *Florida's Palm Beach Rocked by Madoff Scandal*, NPR, December 16, 2008, http://www.npr.org/templates/story/story.php?storyId=98317793 (last visited February 23. 2012).
35. United States v. Treadwell, 593 F.3d 990 (9th Cir. 2010).
36. United States v. Hayes, 231 F.3d 1132, 1134 (9th Cir. 2000) (emphasis added).
37. CFTC v. M25 Invs., Inc., No.: 3-09-cv-1831-M, 2010 U.S. Dist. LEXIS 118823 (N.D. Tex. October 25, 2010); unpublished opinion.
38. United States v. Gragg, No. 96-5586, 1998 U.S. App. LEXIS 9577, at *3 (6th Cir. May 7, 1998).
39. Lisa Singh, "Fool's Gold," *Dallas Observer*, November 16, 2000, Features, at 1.
40. United States v. Gragg, No. 96-5586, 1998 U.S. App. LEXIS 9577, at *5 (6th Cir. May 7, 1998).

41. Barbara R. Rowe, *Ponzi Schemes*, UTAH STATE UNIVERSITY EXTENSION
FINANCIAL FITNESS FACT SHEET, FL/FF-05 (February 2000).
42. United States v. Londe, 449 F. Supp. 590 (E.D. Mo. 1978).
43. United States v. Munoz, 233 F.3d 1117 (9th Cir. 2000).
44. United States v. Farris, 614 F.2d 634 (9th Cir. 1979).
45. United States v. Anderson, 993 F.2d 1435 (9th Cir. 1993).
46. Alberta Securities Commission Re: Mid West Marketing Group Ltd. Paul
Dennis Charbonneau et al., CANADA NEWSWIRE, November 6, 1997, LEXIS,
News Library, Arcnws File.
47. Singh, *Fool's Gold*, at 1, *at* Ch. 1, n. 39. N. R. Kleinfield, *Unraveling Puzzle of L. I.
Car Dealer Reveals Layers of Personal Mystery*, N.Y. TIMES, April 19, 1992, at A26.
48. Kleinfield, *Unraveling Puzzle*, at A26, *at* Ch. 1, n. 47.
49. United States v. Weiner, 988 F.2d 629 (6th Cir. 1993).
50. Morof v. United Mo. Bank, No. 09-1711, 391 Fed. App'x 534, 2010 U.S. App.
LEXIS 17586 (6th Cir. August 18, 2010); unpublished decision.
51. FTC v. Network Servs. Depot, Inc., 617 F.3d 1127 (9th Cir. 2010).
52. United States v. Midkiff, 614 F.3d 431 (8th Cir. 2010); S. Cherry St., LLC
v. Hennessee Group LLC, 573 F.3d 98 (2d Cir. 2009) (hedge fund researcher).
53. Humberto Cruz and Diane Lade, *Don't Lose to Investing Scams—Watch for
Signs*, SUN-SENTINEL (Fort Lauderdale, FL), September 18, 2000, at 21.
54. Ashby Jones, *Rothstein Draws 50-Year Sentence*, WALL ST. J., June 10, 2010, at
C5 ("Former Florida Lawyer Was Convicted of Running a $1.2 Billion Ponzi
Scheme"; the lawyer was sentenced to fifty years in prison. He used the money
to offer political contributions. The paper has a picture of the lawyer showing a
unique watch collection in 2007).
55. United States v. Wolff (*In re* FirstPay, Inc.), Nos. 09-1076, 09-1107, 2010 U.S.
App. LEXIS 16930 (4th Cir. August 13, 2010); unpublished decision.
56. Adair v. Lease Partners, Inc., 587 F.3d 238 (5th Cir. 2009), *cert. denied*, 130
S. Ct. 3326 (West 2010).
57. Cline v. Reliance Trust Co. 245 Fed. App'x 503 (6th Cir. 2007) (unpublished
opinion; plaintiffs lost on the ground of the statute of limitations).
58. SEC v. JT Wallenbrock & Assocs., 440 F.3d 1109 (9th Cir. 2006).
59. United States v. Sudeen, 434 F.3d 384 (5th Cir. 2005) ("The plant was never
built, because of alleged regulatory difficulties").
60. Jodi Xu, *A Guilty Plea in Ponzi Case*, WALL ST. J., September 16, 2010, at C4,
LEXIS, News Library, WSJ File.
61. Nathan Becker, *Man in Ponzi Scheme Sentenced to 9 Years*, WALL ST. J., September 25, 2010, at A23, LEXIS, News Library, WSJ File.
62. SEC v. Kaleta, Civ. Action No. 4:09-3674, 2011 U.S. Dist. LEXIS 138963 (S.D.
Tex. Dec. 2, 2011), 4:09-3674.
63. Marretta v. Comm'r, 168 Fed. App'x 528 (3d Cir. 2006), unpublished opinion. (Marretta invested "in CNC Trading Company ('CNC'), . . . [which] sold
investments in CNC 'contracts'. . . . Investors were told that CNC used their
money to purchase food products each month for resale to food wholesalers

and supermarket chains. . . . CNC was a Ponzi scheme. Instead of purchasing food products with the money it received from investors, CNC used that money to pay out cash or checks on a monthly basis to prior investors.")

64. United States v. Ramunno, 599 F.3d 1269 (11th Cir. 2010).

65. Carroll v. Stettler, Civ. Action No. 10-2262, Civ. Action No. 10-2262, 2010 U.S. Dist. LEXIS 120672 (E.D. Pa. November 12, 2010); unpublished opinion.

66. Rowe, *Ponzi Schemes.*

67. United States v. Midkiff, 614 F.3d 431 (8th Cir. 2010).

68. Pendergest-Holt v. Certain Underwriters at Lloyd's of London & Arch Specialty Ins. Co., 600 F.3d 562 (5th Cir. 2010).

69. CFTC v. M25 Investments, Inc., No. 3-09-cv-1831-M, 2010 U.S. Dist. LEXIS 118823 (N.D. Tex. October 25, 2010), unpublished opinion; *Forex Ponzi Figure Is Given Probation,* WALL ST. J., September 21, 2010, at C3, LEXIS, News Library, WSJ File ("Federal prosecutors had alleged Bradley D. Eisner was part of a scheme to defraud investors in Razor FX, a financial-services firm that held itself out as being in the business of trading in the currency market, but actually conducted almost no trading").

70. United States v. Hickey, 580 F.3d 922 (9th Cir. 2009), *cert. denied,* 130 S. Ct. 2115 (West 2010).

71. Aubrey v. Barlin, No. A-10-CA-076-SS, 2010 U.S. Dist. LEXIS 103700 (W.D. Tex. September 29, 2010); unpublished opinion.

72. *Fort Lauderdale Attorney Pleads Guilty in Billion Dollar Ponzi Scheme,* PR NEWS-WIRE, January 27, 2010, LEXIS, News Library, Curnws File.

73. Lustgraaf v. Behrens, 619 F.3d 867 (8th Cir. 2010). ("Behrens was President and CEO of 21st Century Financial Group, Inc. . . ." Investors alleged that they "invested money with Behrens through National Investments, Inc., an entity that Behrens controlled. In connection with these investments, Behrens sold promissory notes to Appellants, listing National Investments as the borrower [and investors alleged] that Behrens took their money with the promise that he would invest it and provide them with a steady stream of income. Rather than invest the money, Behrens 'misappropriated the funds for his personal use, spent the money in other ways, or simply transferred money among [Appellants] and other investors to prevent them from discovering the fraud.'")

74. Merrill Scott & Assocs., Ltd., 253 Fed. App'x 756 (10th Cir. 2007), unpublished opinion; United States v. Ramunno, 599 F.3d 1269 (11th Cir. 2010) (a Ponzi scheme relating to commodity futures).

75. United States v. Sudeen, 434 F.3d 384 (5th Cir. 2005).

76. *Id.* ("When a given investor demanded proceeds, Sudeen and Freeman would claim that the investor was ineligible because he had failed to comply with fictitious requirements, that the profits were 'tied up' by the federal government, or that the returns could not be liquidated from overseas assets.")

77. United States v. Treadwell, 593 F.3d 990 (9th Cir. 2010); *Inland Empire Man Who Orchestrated $26 Million Ponzi Scheme Sentenced to 14 Years in Prison,*

STATES NEWS SERVICE, June 7, 2005, LEXIS, News Library, Arcnws File. http://www.justice.gov/usao/cac/pressroom/pr2005/087.html.

78. See SEC v. Bennett, 904 F. Supp. 435, 437 n. 3 (E.D. Pa. 1995); United States v. Bennett, 161 F.3d 171 (3d Cir. 1998), cert. denied, 528 U.S. 819 (1999).

79. Singh, *Fool's Gold*, at 1, *at* Ch. 1, n. 39.

80. Avner Offer, "The Mask of Intimacy: Advertising and the Quality of Life," in *In Pursuit of the Quality of Life*, 211, 225 (Avner Offer ed., 1996); id. at 226 ("Reciprocal giving gives rise to obligation . . .").

81. *Ponzi*, at http://www.crimes-of-persuasion.com/Crimes/InPerson/Major-Person/ponzi.htm (last visited February 25, 2012).

82. *Id.*

83. Keith O'Brien, *Jeff Man Accused of Scam Netting Millions; He Got Rich Prosecutors Say*, TIMES-PICAYUNE (New Orleans), September 16, 2000, Metro, at 1.

84. Terry Greene Sterling, *The Moneychangers; A New Times Investigation; First in a Series*, PHOENIX NEW TIMES, April 16, 1998, LEXIS, News Library, Arcnws File.

85. United States v. Gragg, No. 96-5586, 1998 U.S. App. LEXIS 9577, at *2 (6th Cir. May 7, 1998).

86. United States v. Goheen, No. 98-4033, 1999 U.S. App. LEXIS 4622, at *1 (4th Cir. March 18, 1999).

87. United States v. O'Toole, No. 99-6072, 1999 U.S. App. LEXIS 18192, at *2 (10th Cir. filed August 3, 1999) (in fact, the bonds were close to worthless; investors lost $163,284 in this scheme).

88. *Id.*

89. United States v. Farris, 614 F.2d 634, 637 (9th Cir. 1979).

90. *Inland Empire Man Who Orchestrated $26 Million Ponzi Scheme Sentenced to 14 Years in Prison*, States News Service, June 7, 2005, LEXIS, News Library, Arcnws File. http://www.justice.gov/usao/cac/pressroom/pr2005/087.html.

91. State v. Haas, 138 Ariz. 413 (1983).

92. *Id.* at 417.

93. *Ponzi*, at http://www.crimes-of-persuasion.com/Crimes/InPerson/Major-Person/ponzi.htm (last visited February 26, 2012). The term "units of indebtedness" rings a bell and is remindful of "evidence of indebtedness," contained in the definition of a security in the securities acts. See, e.g., Securities Act of 1933, § 2(a)(1), 15 U.S.C. § 77b(a)(1) (2006) (this scheme earned Ponzi a prison sentence as well).

94. Sterling, *The Moneychangers*, at Ch. 1, n. 84.

95. Perlman v. Delisfort-Theodule, No. 09-80480-Civ-Hurley/Hopkins, 2010 U.S. Dist. LEXIS 116510 (S.D. Fla. November 1, 2010) (memorandum opinion) (unpublished opinion).

96. United States v. Goheen, No. 98-4033, 1999 U.S. App. LEXIS 4622 (4th Cir. March 18, 1999).

97. Gary Cohen, *Dark Clouds over a Guru to the Stars*, U.S. NEWS & WORLD REP., May 28, 2001, at 35.

98. *Assessing the Madoff Ponzi Scheme and the Need for Regulatory Reform: Hearing Before the H. Comm. on Fin. Servs.*, 111th Cong. (2009), FED. NEWS SERVICE, January 5, 2009, LEXIS, News Library, Curnws File (testimony of Allan Goldstein, investor with Bernard L. Madoff Investment Securities).

99. For a description of the complicated structure in Enron, see Tamar Frankel and Mark Fagan, *Law and the Financial System: Securitization and Asset-Backed Securities—Law, Process, Case Studies, and Simulations* 67–82 (2009).

100. United States v. Gragg, No. 96-5586, 1998 U.S. App. LEXIS 9577, at *3 n.1 (6th Cir. May 7, 1998).

101. See Thomas Schelling, CHOICE AND CONSEQUENCES 210–12 (1984); see also Gary Johns, *A Multi-Level Theory of Self-Serving Behavior in and by Organizations*, 21 RES. IN ORGANIZATIONAL BEHAVIOR 1, 16–17 (1999) ("reduction of uncertainty regarding performance leads to less group-serving responses"), citing S. L. Grover, *Why Professionals Lie: The Impact of Professional Role Conflict on Reporting Accuracy*, 41 PERS. PSYCHOL. 55, 251–72 (1993).

102. Iain Pears, *An Instance of the Fingerpost* 502 (1998); Singh, *Fool's Gold*, at 1, *at* Ch. 1, n. 39 (a purported mine owner refused to give details to the reporter. The reporter said that this "reticence made him look suspicious." In this case the con artist defended his reticence. "'Suspicious?' he countered. 'I have projects to protect. I have no use to publicize a project that's in development.'").

103. United States v. Masten, 170 F.3d 790, 792 (7th Cir. 1999).

104. Smith v. Young (*In re* Young), 208 B.R. 189, 194 (Bankr. S.D. Cal. 1997).

105. *Id.* at 201–2.

106. Cruz and Lade, *Don't Lose to Investing Scams*, at 21.

107. Clifford Krauss et al., *Fraud Parade: $8 Billion Case Is Next in Line*, N.Y. TIMES, February 18, 2009, at A1, LEXIS, News Library, Arcnws File.

108. Charles Ponzi, *The Rise of Mr. Ponzi* (1935), at http://www.pnzi.com (last visited February 29, 2012).

109. Singh, *Fool's Gold*, at 1, *at* Ch. 1, n. 39.

110. Greg Allen, *Florida's Palm Beach Rocked by Madoff Scandal*, NPR, December 16, 2008, http://www.npr.org/templates/story/story.php?storyId=98317793 (last visited July 27, 2009).

111. Robert Chew, *How I Got Screwed by Bernie Madoff*, TIME, December 15, 2008, http://www.time.com/time/business/article/0,8599,1866398,00.html (last visited Feb. 27, 2012).

112. *Ex-Conn. Resident Admits Running $100M Ponzi Scam*, ASSOCIATED PRESS FINANCIAL WIRE, Business News, September 14, 2010, LEXIS, News Library, Curnws File (a recent resident "has pleaded guilty to federal charges he operated a $100 million Ponzi scheme that ripped off hundreds of investors." He "stole more than $30 million in 12 years," promising quick high returns on buying and reselling diamonds or buying foreclosed assets from JPMorgan Chase & Co. Bank).

113. United States v. Hickey, 580 F.3d 922 (9th Cir. 2009), *cert. denied,* 130 S. Ct. 2115 (West 2010).

114. *Id.*

115. Scott Bernard Nelson, *Fleet Writing Off $70M in Ponzi Scam; 4 in N.J. Accused of Bilking 8 Banks with Phony Metals Trading,* BOSTON GLOBE, May 15, 2002, at D1.

116. Rose v. Texas, 716 S.W.2d 162 (Tex. 1986).

117. United States v. Van Alstyne, 584 F.3d 803 (9th Cir. 2009).

118. People v. Luongo, 47 N.Y.2d 418, 425 (1979).

119. United States v. Gragg, No. 96-5586, 1998 U.S. App. LEXIS 9577 (6th Cir. May 7, 1998).

120. Katherine Verdery, *"Caritas" and the Reconceptualization of Money in Romania,* ANTHROPOLOGY TODAY, February 1995, at 3 (and authorities cited there).

121. *In re* Taubman, 160 B.R. 964, 971 (Bankr. S.D. Ohio 1993).

122. *Ponzi,* at http://www.crimes-of-persuasion.com/Crimes/InPerson/Major-Person/ponzi.htm (last visited February 27, 2012).

123. *See* Diana B. Henriques, *Court Sets Madoff Case Limitations,* N.Y. TIMES, August 17, 2011, at B1, LEXIS, News Library, Curnws File (noting that some investors in Madoff Ponzi scheme received "fictional profits" from money stolen from other investors).

124. *Charles Ponzi, Useless Information,* at http://uselessinformation.org/ponzi (last visited February 27, 2012) (revealing that Ponzi received enough money to purchase 180 million postal coupons; however there is evidence to prove that only two coupons were actually purchased. Charles Ponzi established a token investment. Of the millions raised from investors, about 1 percent was invested in a legitimate income-producing business; it produced negligible returns).

125. SEC v. Homa, 514 F.3d 661 (7th Cir. 2008).

126. United States v. Calozza, 125 F.3d 687 (9th Cir. 1997).

127. Donn B. Parker, *Fighting Computer Crime* 120 (1983) (describing the rise and fall of Charles Braun).

128. *Id.*

129. *See* Steve Weisman, *The Truth About Avoiding Scams* 181, 185 (2008).

130. United States v. Weiner, 988 F.2d 629, 631 (6th Cir. 1993).

131. Michelle Singletary, *Con Artists Target Retirees with Promissory Note Scam,* SUN-SENTINEL (Fort Lauderdale, FL), June 12, 2000, at 2 (citing Bradley Skolnik).

132. Singh, *Fool's Gold,* at 1, *at* Ch. 1, n. 39.

133. *Walter Edward Scott—"Death Valley Scotty,"* http://www.inn-california.com/articles/biographic/deathvalleyscotty.html (last visited February 27, 2012).

134. Michael Fechter, *Ministries' Top Pitchman Pleads Guilty,* TAMPA TRIB., December 1, 2000, Florida/Metro, at 1 ("Greater created 'the illusion' that it engaged in profit-making investment but employed 'a classic Ponzi scheme'"); Jack Hitt, *The Billion-Dollar Shack,* N.Y. TIMES, § 6, at 123 (December 10, 2000); Lori Pugh, *Heartland Case a Warning to Investors,* INDIANAPOLIS BUS. J., at 23 (August 21, 2000) (offering of investments in offshore banks).

135. Kate Nash, *Up in Smoke*, ADVERTISER (South Australia), April 22, 2002, at 61.
136. United States v. Hayes, Nos. 99-10405, 99-15502, 2000 U.S. App. LEXIS 27329 (9th Cir. filed November 2, 2000), *aff'd.*, 385 F.3d 1226 (9th Cir. 2004).
137. Augustyn v. Superior Court, 186 Cal. App. 3d 1221 (Ct. App. 1986).
138. See, e.g., SEC v. Fitzgerald, 135 F. Supp. 2d 992 (N.D. Cal. 2001); United States v. Griffith, Nos. 89-50581, 89-50626, 89-50241, 1992 U.S. App. LEXIS 24314, at *2 (9th Cir. filed September 18, 1992) (giving investors false financial information and falsely asserting adequate collateral).
139. United States v. Londe, 449 F. Supp. 590 (E.D. Mo. 1978).
140. United States v. Munoz, 233 F.3d 1123 (9th Cir. 2000).
141. Connecticut Nat'l Bank v. Giacomi, Nos. 105860, 105861, 106520, 106992, 1993 Conn. Super. LEXIS 2508 (Super. Ct. September 28, 1993).
142. United States v. Bennett, 161 F.3d 171, 174–75 (3d Cir. 1998), *cert. denied*, 528 U.S. 819 (1999).
143. *Investors Sue Marine Midland for Allegedly Lax Supervision*, BANK & LENDER LIABILITY LITIG. REP., February 4, 1998, at 8.
144. United States v. Goheen, No. 98-4033, 1999 U.S. App. LEXIS 4622 (4th Cir. March 18, 1999).
145. Atty. Grievance Comm'n. v. Martin, 308 Md. 272, 279 (1987).
146. *Transcript: The Madoff Affair*, http://www.pbs.org/wgbh/pages/frontline/madoff/etc/script.html.
147. Kreiger v. United States, 539 F.2d 317 (3d Cir. 1976).
148. Kleinfield, *Unraveling Puzzle*, at A26, *at* Ch. 1, n. 47.
149. United States v. Hein, No. 07-10718, 2010 U.S. App. LEXIS 19311 (11th Cir. September 14, 2010), unpublished decision.
150. KT Group, LLC v. Christensen, Glaser, Fink, Jacobs, Weil & Shapiro, LLP, No. 2:07-CV-790, 2010 U.S. Dist. LEXIS 104166 (D. Utah September 29, 2010), unpublished opinion.
151. Dan Seligman, *The Mind of the Swindler*, FORBES, June 12, 2000, at 425.
152. Kleinfield, *Unraveling Puzzle*, at A26, *at* Ch. 1, n. 47.
153. See generally 1 Tamar Frankel, *Securitization*, part I chap. 5, and especially § 5.8.9 (Ann Schwing ed., 2d ed. 2006).
154. Jim Henderson, *Preacher Has Faith in Pitch*, HOUSTON CHRON., May 26, 2002, at 33.
155. United States v. Van Alstyne, 584 F.3d 803 (9th Cir. 2009).
156. *In re* Taubman, 160 B.R. 964, 973 (Bankr. S.D. Ohio 1993).
157. United States v. Munoz, 233 F.3d 1117 (9th Cir. 2000).
158. *Id.* at 1122–23.
159. *Id.* at 1123.
160. Ponzi, *The Rise of Mr. Ponzi*, at Ch. 1, n. 1.
161. Marion v. TDI Inc., 591 F.3d 137 (3d Cir. 2010), *cert. denied*, 131 S. Ct. 1479 (West 2011).
162. *Id.*

163. U.S. Department of Justice Programs, Office for Victims of Crime, *Providing Services to Victims of Fraud: Resources for Victim/Witness Coordinators* I-1 (July 1998); see also *Boiler Room* (film, 2000) (describing techniques of fraudulent telephone sales).
164. Holly Howard Preston, *The Sophisticated Investor's Worst Nightmare; Investment Fraud—A New Bumper Crop,* INT'L HERALD TRIB., June 15, 2002, at 13.
165. Sanjida O'Connell, *Mindreading: An Investigation into How We Learn to Love and Lie* 139 (1997).
166. *The Producers* (film, 1968); U.S. Department of Justice Programs, *Providing Services to Victims of Fraud* (noting that many victims are home to receive phone solicitations and remain on the phone longer to hear fraudulent sales pitches, due to loneliness); see also *Boiler Room* (film, 2000) (describing techniques of fraudulent telephone sales).
167. *The Producers* (film, 1968).
168. Tim Rutten, *The Moral of Madoff's Tale,* L.A. TIMES, December 17, 2008, pt. A, at 27, LEXIS, News Library, Arcnws File.
169. Steven Wilmsen, *Notorious Boston Con Man Back in Federal Prison,* BOSTON GLOBE, March 23, 2002, at B1, B12.
170. Chad Bray, *Global Finance: Prosecutors Want 19 Years or More for Nadel's Fraud,* WALL ST. J., October 15, 2010, at C3, LEXIS, News Library, Wsj File.
171. "Yellow Kid" Weil and W. T. Brannon, *"Yellow Kid" Weil: The Autobiography of America's Master Swindler* 282 (1948, 2010).

Chapter 2

1. Charles Ponzi, *The Rise of Mr. Ponzi* (1935), at http://www.pnzi.com (last visited February 29, 2012).
2. *Topics: Bernard Madoff,* WALL ST. J., http://topics.wsj.com/person/m/bernard-madoff/1077 (last visited February 29, 2012).
3. Greg Allen, *Florida's Palm Beach Rocked by Madoff Scandal,* NPR, December 16, 2008, http://www.npr.org/templates/story/story.php?storyId=98317793 (last visited February 29, 2012).
4. *Topics: Bernard Madoff,* WALL ST. J., http://topics.wsj.com/person/m/bernard-madoff/1077 (last visited February 29, 2012).
5. *The Owner's Name Is on the Door,* http://en.calameo.com/read/000000007302d949078d1 (last visited February 29, 2012) (mission statement of Madoff firm).
6. Robert Chew, *How I Got Screwed by Bernie Madoff,* TIME, December 15, 2008, http://www.time.com/time/business/article/0,8599,1866398,00.html (last visited February 29, 2011).
7. Dan Reed, *SEC Accuses Fort Worth Pair of Securities Fraud: Suit Alleges Couple Raised $16.5 Million from Investors,* FORT-WORTH STAR TELEGRAM, November 25, 1999, Business, at 1.

8. United States v. Bennett, 161 F.3d 171, 178 (3d Cir. 1998), *cert. denied*, 528 U.S. 819 (1999).
9. N. R. Kleinfield, *Unraveling Puzzle of L. I. Car Dealer Reveals Layers of Personal Mystery*, N.Y. TIMES, April 19, 1992, Section 1, at 26 ("Yet the plan was approved after Mr. McNamara agreed to donate a golf course to the governing town of Brookhaven").
10. Smith v. Young (*In re* Young), 208 B.R. 189 (Bankr. S.D. Cal. 1997).
11. Michael Perlstein, *Accountant Suspect in Fraud Probe: Ex-Boss Says Ponzi Suspect Bilked Firm of $150,000*, TIMES-PICAYUNE (New Orleans), October 23, 2000, National, at 1.
12. *Id.*
13. Alan Feuer and Christine Haughney, *Standing Accused: A Pillar of Finance and Charity*, N.Y. TIMES, December 13, 2008, at B1, LEXIS, News Library, Arcnws File.
14. Katherine Verdery, *"Caritas" and the Reconceptualization of Money in Romania*, ANTHROPOLOGY TODAY, February 1995, at 3 (and authorities cited there).
15. *Id.*
16. Malin Akerstrom, *Crooks and Squares* 146 (1985), quoting Peter Letkemann, *Crime as Work* 45 (1973).
17. *Id.* at 147 (quoting Gerald D. Suttles, *The Social Order of the Slum* 129, 1968).
18. R. J. Brown, *P. T. Barnum Never Did Say "There's a Sucker Born Every Minute,"* HISTORYBUFF.COM, http://www.historybuff.com/library/refbarnum.html (last visited March 1, 2012); M. R. Werner, *Barnum* 56-64 (1923).
19. Prepared statement of Debra A. Valentine, general counsel for the U.S. Federal Trade Commission on "Pyramid Schemes," presented at the International Monetary Fund Seminar on Current Legal Issues Affecting Central Banks, at http://www.ftc.gov/speeches/other/dvimf16.shtm (last visited March 1, 2012); James Walsh, *How Ponzi Schemes, Pyramid Frauds Work*, CONSUMERS' RESEARCH MAG., June 1, 1999.
20. Jim Henderson, *Preacher Has Faith in Pitch*, HOUSTON CHRON., May 26, 2002, at 33.
21. Ponzi, *The Rise of Mr. Ponzi*, at Ch. 2, n. 1.
22. Jennifer Arend, *Slamming Scams*, DALLAS MORNING NEWS, July 12, 1999, Business, at 1D.
23. Ponzi, *The Rise of Mr. Ponzi*, at Ch. 2, n. 1. See also the stories of the insider trader group revealed in court in the case of Galleon Group; they disparaged others but connected among themselves. Michael Rothfeld and Susan Pullman, *Calling Miss Manners: Tapes in Galleon Case Show Some Snark*, WALL ST. J., March 17, 2011, at A1, A16.
24. Ritchie Special Credit Investments, Ltd. v. United States Tr., 620 F.3d 847 (8th Cir. 2010).
25. United States v. Mathison, 157 F.3d 541 (8th Cir. 1998).
26. United States v. Loayza, 107 F.3d 257 (4th Cir. 1996).

27. *Mystery Outlives 'Sicilian Gatsby,'* L.A. TIMES, November 30, 2000, at A1, LEXIS, News Library, Arcnws File.
28. United States v. Weiner, 988 F.2d 629, 632 (6th Cir. 1993).
29. Lisa Singh, *Fool's Gold,* DALLAS OBS., November 16, 2000, Features, at 1.
30. United States v. O'Toole, No. 99-6072, 1999 U.S. App. LEXIS 18192 (10th Cir. filed August 3, 1999).
31. Clifton Leaf, *Enough Is Enough; White-Collar Criminals: They Lie They Cheat They Steal and They've Been Getting Away with It for Too Long,* FORTUNE, March 18, 2002, at 60 (citing the relatively small number of prison sentences for large corporations' white-collar criminals).
32. United States v. Midkiff, 614 F.3d 431 (8th Cir. 2010).
33. *Id.*
34. *Id.*
35. *Id.*
36. *Id.*
37. United States v. Kirschner, No. 09-15785 Non-Argument Calendar, 2010 U.S. Dist. LEXIS 18823 (11th Cir. September 8, 2010); unpublished decision.
38. CFTC v. M25 Investments, Inc., No. 3-09-cv-1831-M, 2010 U.S. Dist. LEXIS 118823 (N.D. Tex. October 25, 2010); unpublished opinion.
39. *Id.*
40. United States v. Treadwell, 593 F.3d 990, 993 (9th Cir. 2010). See also Steve Weisman, *The Truth About Avoiding Scams* 195 (2008).
41. United States v. Ferguson, No. 07-50437, 2011 U.S. App. LEXIS 1908 (9th Cir. January 27, 2011); unpublished opinion.
42. Perlman v. Delisfort-Theodule, No. 09-80480-Civ-Hurley/Hopkins, 2010 U.S. Dist. LEXIS 116510, at *3 (S.D. Fla. November 1, 2010) (memorandum opinion) (unpublished opinion).
43. It may well be that Ponzi's troubles started relatively early because his investment story involved the U.S. Post Office and government investigators visited him frequently. Ponzi, *The Rise of Mr. Ponzi,* at Ch. 2, n. 1.
44. Michael Fechter, *2nd Ministry Called Ponzi Scheme,* TAMPA TRIB., April 13, 1998, Florida/Metro, at 1.
45. Paul Whittaker, *Police "Put Millions" into Failed Loans Plan,* ADVERTISER (South Australia), May 8, 1998, LEXIS, News Library, Arcnws File.
46. State v. Blair, 579 P.2d 1133 (Colo. 1978).
47. Terry Greene Sterling, *The Moneychangers; A New Times Investigation; First in a Series,* PHOENIX NEW TIMES, April 16, 1998, LEXIS, News Library, Arcnws File.
48. Kuran and Sunstein suggest two types of herding, which they name "cascades." One is an informational cascade, in which people follow what other people do even if it conflicts with information they themselves have. This is the herding referred to in the text. Informational cascade is usually the province of the investors; they buy and sell on the assumption that the aggregate information

is better than their own. The other type is "reputational cascade." In this case, people conform to the behavior of others as well, but for different reasons. The followers do not necessarily rely on the information of the groups they emulate. Rather, they follow others in order to maintain their own reputation, or to curry favor with these groups because they live in the same communities or depend on them. These followers may say in private what they would not utter in public or would avoid repeating in front of the group members. That is one way in which social culture is fashioned. In both cases people follow the crowd and forgo their own convictions. Both con artists and their victims may follow a reputational cascade. Timur Kuran and Cass R. Sunstein, *Availability Cascades and Risk Regulation*, 51 STAN. L. REV. 683 (1999).

49. Robert H. Frank, *Passions Within Reason* 155–56 (1988).
50. See, e.g., Lisa M. Fairfax, *"With Friends Like These . . .": Toward a More Efficacious Response to Affinity-based Securities and Investment Fraud*, 36 GA. L. REV. 63 (2001).
51. *Id.*
52. See, e.g., Fox Butterfield, *This Way Madness Lies: A Fall from Grace to Prison*, N.Y. TIMES, April 21, 1996, § 1, at 14 (Ms. Redd hosted many fundraisers for the church).
53. United States v. Luca, 183 F.3d 1018, 1027 (9th Cir. 1999).
54. *Id.* at 1027.
55. *Id.*
56. *Id.*
57. *Id.*
58. Sterling, *The Moneychangers*, at Ch. 2, n. 47.
59. Chuck Fager, *Federal Authorities Collar Greater Ministry Leaders*, CHRISTIANITY TODAY, April 26, 1999, at 22.
60. *Id.*
61. Jim Henderson, *Preacher Has Faith in Pitch*, HOUSTON CHRONICLE, May 26, 2002, at 33.
62. *Id.*
63. *Video: Madoff Victims Speak Out, Rabbi Gellman*, VANITY FAIR, March 4, 2009, http://www.vanityfair.com/politics/features/2009/04/madoff-victims-speak-video200904 (last visited March 2, 2012).
64. *Investors' Stories: The Madoff Affair*, FRONTLINE, http://www.pbs.org/wgbh/pages/frontline/madoff/investors/ (last visited March 2, 2012).
65. See, e.g., Fairfax, "With Friends Like These. . . ." *at* Ch. 2, n. 50.
66. See, e.g., Gary L. Tidwell, *Anatomy of a Fraud* 3 (1993), describing the venture of Jim and Tammy Bakker, a television evangelist couple who raised more than $66 million to build lifetime shared vacation and religious activities. Only 52 percent of this amount was used for that purpose. The rest of the money was used for operating expenses and a lavish style of living for the Bakkers and their entourage. United States v. Bakker, 925 F.2d 728 (4th Cir. 1991), noting that the Bakkers were indicted on December 5, 1988, describing the Jim and

Tammy Bakker story, affirming Bakker's conviction and remanding in part; Mary T. Schmich, *Bakker Guilty on All Counts*, CHICAGO TRIB., October 6, 1989, at 1, noting the conviction on October 5, 1989; United States v. Luca, 183 F.3d 1018, 1024 (9th Cir. 1999); "The district court . . . concluded that 'many of the victims' were vulnerable based on their ages and their membership in the church in which Luca held a leadership position."

67. Butterfield, *This Way Madness Lies*, at 14, *at* Ch. 2, n. 52.

68. See, e.g., United States v. Bennett, 161 F.3d 171 (3d Cir. 1998), *cert. denied*, 528 U.S. 819 (1999).

69. Brigid McMenamin, *The Banker and the Nun*, FORBES, October 6, 1997, at 100.

70. *Id.*

71. United States v. Rasheed, 663 F.2d 843, 845 (9th Cir. 1981); see Bruce C. Smith, *Congregation Prepares to Celebrate a Miracle, Faith Baptist Church Rises from Mountain of Debt*, INDIANAPOLIS STAR, November 20, 2000, at A1 (pastor took investors' money to help church and instead lived lavish lifestyle, leaving church indebted).

72. United States v. Rasheed, 663 F.2d 843, 845–46 (9th Cir. 1981).

73. *Id.* at 845. "In early 1977, Rasheed formed the Church of Hakeem. The Church was incorporated under California law, and received tax exempt status as a religious organization."

74. Gary Cohen, *Dark Clouds over a Guru to the Stars*, U.S. NEWS & WORLD REP., May 28, 2001, at 35. *But see* United States v. Spirk, 503 F.3d 619 (10th Cir. 2007): "Unlike most operators of Ponzi schemes, Spirk did not live the high life while the money rolled in; he plowed the cash into LASCO and ASA, even reducing his salary so that he could pay the staff's wages. This is cold comfort to the investors, however, many of whom lost their retirement savings."

75. Michael Gillard, *Copperfingers "Took Pounds 35m Hit,"* OBSERVER, January 1998, at 1, LEXIS, News Library, Arcnws File.

76. United States v. Hall, 349 F.3d 1420 (11th Cir. 2003), *aff'd sub nom.* Whitfield v. United States, 543 U.S. 209 (2005).

77. United States v. Luca, 183 F.3d 1018, 1027 (9th Cir. 1999).

78. *Id.*

79. Dan Reed, *SEC Accuses Fort Worth Pair of Securities Fraud: Suit Alleges Couple Raised $16.5 Million from Investors*, FORT-WORTH STAR TELEGRAM, November 25, 1999, Business, at 1.

80. Singh, *Fool's Gold*, at 1, *at* Ch. 2, n. 29.

81. Henderson, *Preacher Has Faith in Pitch*, at 33, *at* Ch. 2, n. 61.

82. See *Pyramid Schemes*, http://www.crimes-of-persuasion.com/Crimes/Delivered/pyramids.htm (last visited March 3, 2012).

83. Verdery, *"Caritas,"* at 3 (and authorities cited there), *at* Ch. 2, n. 14.

84. Kate Nash, *Up in Smoke*, ADVERTISER (South Australia), April 22, 2002, at 61.

85. Peter Fimrite, *Did He Have a Deal for You*, S. F. CHRON., February 15, 1998, at 1/Z1.

NOTES TO PAGES 78–82

86. Don Jacobs, *Telemarketing Con Artists Do Not See Selves as Criminals: 47 Convicted of Fraud Subject of UT Study*, KNOXVILLE NEWS-SENTINEL, December 10, 2001, at A1.

87. *The Scam That Fell to Earth*, AUSTRALIAN, July 18, 2001, Finance Section, at 30, LEXIS, News Library, Arcnws File. *See also Former Alta Businessman Pleads Guilty to Bilking 15,000 People out of $60 M*, CANADIAN PRESS NEWSWIRE, May 6, 2003, LEXIS, News Library, Arcnws File.

88. Matthew Gifford, *Pyramid Scheme*, http://www.matthewgifford.com/2002/08/23/PyramidScheme/ (last visited March 4, 2012).

89. See, e.g., Kathleen Lynn, *15-Year-Old Settles Stock Fraud Charges*, RECORD (Bergen County, N.J.), September 21, 2001, at A1.

90. *See* Tamar Frankel, *Trusting and Non-Trusting on the Internet*, 81 B.U. L. REV. 457, 469 (2001).

91. Martha Graybow and Grant McCool, *UPDATE 1-SEC Charges Madoff Recruiter with Fraud*, REUTERS, June 22, 2009, http://www.reuters.com/article/2009/06/22/madoff-sec-idUSN2250993920090622 (last visited March 5, 2012).

92. Iain Pears, *An Instance of the Fingerpost* 309 (1998).

93. United States v. Kirschner, No. 09-15785 Non-Argument Calendar, 2010 U.S. Dist. LEXIS 18823 (11th Cir. September 8, 2010); unpublished decision.

94. Brian Trumbore, *Charles Ponzi*, at http://www.buyandhold.com/bh/en/education/history/2000/ponzi.html (last visited March 5, 2012), citing Robert Sobel, *The Great Bull Market: Wall Street in the 1920s*; Stockschlaeder & McDonald, Esqs. v. Kittay (*In re* Stockbridge Funding Co.), 145 B.R. 797 (Bankr. S.D.N.Y. 1992).

95. *Man Pleads Guilty to Federal Charges After Swindling More than $24 Million from Local Victims*, US FED NEWS, November 16, 2005, LEXIS, News Library, Arcnws File. "Aware he was under suspicion, Edmundo fled the United States." "The investors [in the "Knight Express" program], who were told their funds would be used to purchase and resell Federal Reserve notes, were promised a six percent monthly return."

96. People v. Luongo, 47 N.Y.2d 418, 425 (1979).

97. Nash, *Up in Smoke*, at 61, *at* Ch. 2, n. 84.

98. Frankel, *Trusting and Non-Trusting on the Internet*, *at* Ch. 2, n. 90.

99. See Ponzi, *The Rise of Mr. Ponzi*, *at* Ch. 2, n. 1.

100. *Transcript: The Madoff Affair*, FRONTLINE, http://www.pbs.org/wgbh/pages/frontline/madoff/etc/script.html (last visited March 5, 2012).

101. United States v. Van Alstyne, 584 F.3d 803 (9th Cir. 2009).

102. Jack Sirard, *Promissory Note Scheme Spreading Fast in State*, SCRIPPS HOWARD NEWS SERVICE, June 4, 2000, *available at* LEXIS, News Library, Curnws File; Singletary, *Con Artists Target Retirees with Promissory Note Scam*, at 2, *at* Ch. 2, n. 102.

103. Singletary, *Con Artists Target Retirees with Promissory Note Scam*, at 2, *at* Ch. 2, n. 102.

104. Perlstein, *Accountant Suspect in Fraud Probe*, at 1.

105. United States v. Gold Unlimited, 177 F.3d 472, 478 (6th Cir. 1999).
106. See, e.g., SEC v. Blackwell, 211 F.3d 602 (4th Cir. 2000).
107. Henderson, *Preacher Has Faith in Pitch*, at 33, at Ch. 2, n. 61.
108. See *Pyramid Schemes*, http://www.crimes-of-persuasion.com/Crimes/Delivered/pyramids.htm (last visited March 5, 2012).
109. Douglas Rushkoff, *Coercion: Why We Listen To What "They" Say* 215–55 (1999). See also Carmelina Prete, *Women Let off Hook in Pyramid Schemes*, HAMILTON SPECTATOR, April 16, 1998, at N1, LEXIS, News Library, Arcnws File.
110. See *Pyramid Scheme, at* http://www.skepdic.com/pyramid.html (last modified December 9, 2010).
111. See *Pyramid Schemes*, http://www.crimes-of-persuasion.com/Crimes/Delivered/pyramids.htm (last visited March 5, 2012).
112. *Id.* http://www.crimes-of-persuasion.com/Crimes/Delivered/pyramids.htm. A pyramid scheme can also be distinguished from a legal distribution system as a system "which pays override commissions on more than five levels of participation. Even the largest corporation cannot stretch the markups on products beyond the hierarchy of sales person, branch manager, district manager, regional manager and national manager without becoming uncompetitive with standard retail outlets.").

Chapter 3

1. Sanjida O'Connell, *Mindreading: An Investigation into How We Learn to Love and Lie* 245 (1997).
2. *Id.* at 128.
3. *Id.* at 244.
4. *Id.* at 171; *id.* at 172.
5. *A Brief History of Lie Detection*, FIN. SECTOR TECH., January/February 2004, LEXIS, News Library, Arcnws File. "Scientists at Manchester Metropolitan University claim they have developed the most accurate lie detector yet, using a new technique which interprets facial gestures. 'Silent Talker' detects and analyses the thousands of 'microgestures' which indicate someone might be telling untruths. According to the team at MMU, Silent Talker is 80 per cent reliable."
6. Daniel McNeill, *The Face* 242 (1998).
7. Julia McKinnell, *Tips from a Professional Lie Spotter*, MACLEAN's, August 16, 2010, at 75, LEXIS, News Library, Arcnws File (describing Pamela Meyer, *Liespotting: Proven Techniques to Detect Deception* (2010)).
8. O'Connell, *Mindreading*, at 60, *at* Ch. 3, n. 1.
9. *Id.* at 110.
10. *Id.* at 116.

NOTES TO PAGES 89–99

11. Robert H. Frank, *Passions Within Reason* 151 (1988).
12. O'Connell, *Mindreading*, at 139, at Ch. 3, n. 1.
13. *Id.* at 225.
14. See M. R. Werner, *Barnum* (1923).
15. 57 SLAVIC REV. 774 (1998).
16. Dan Seligman, *The Mind of the Swindler*, FORBES, June 12, 2000, at 426; *If It's Too Good to Be True*. . . . *Pyramid Schemes in Cyberspace: Same Old Deal*, http://www.cbintel.com/pyramidfraud.htm (last visited March 5, 2012), emphasizing fraud on the Internet in the form of pyramid schemes.
17. *Dale Carnegie's Secrets of Success*, http://www.dalecarnegie.com/secrets_of_success/ (last visited March 5, 2012).
18. United States v. Aptt, 354 F.3d 1269 (10th Cir. 2004).
19. *The Scam That Fell to Earth*, AUSTRALIAN, July 18, 2001, Finance Section, at 30, LEXIS, News Library, Arcnws File.
20. James Long and Jeff Manning, *Losses Dig Pit That Founder of Capital Consultants Is Unable to Escape*, SUNDAY OREGONIAN, September 24, 2000, at A01.
21. *Id.*
22. Edmund H. Mahony, *Hedge Fund Manager Pleads Guilty of Fraud*, HARTFORD COURANT (Connecticut), March 8, 2011, at A7, LEXIS, News Library, Curnws File.
23. United States v. Carpenter, 359 Fed. App'x 553 (6th Cir. 2009), unpublished decision.
24. United States v. Helbling, 209 F.3d 226 (3d Cir. 2000), *cert. denied*, 531 U.S. 1100 (2001).
25. United States v. Hartstein, 500 F.3d 790 (8th Cir. 2007), *cert. denied*, 552 U.S. 1102 (2008).
26. It is not surprising that Ponzi dreamed of transforming his scheme into a legitimate banking business. He had believed for some time that his business would produce the promised returns. The securitizers of loans also started with the belief that they could collect more money than others do. Only when they realized that there was no hope of such collection did they begin "empty refinancing." *See* Amended Complaint, Am. Int'l Life Assurance Co. v. Bartmann, No. 99-CV-0862-C (N.D. Okla. 1999).
27. Holly Howard Preston, *The Sophisticated Investor's Worst Nightmare; Investment Fraud—A New Bumper Crop*, INT'L HERALD TRIB., June 15, 2002, at 13.
28. See, e.g., Peter Byrne, *Double Injustice*, SF WKLY., July 12, 2000, LEXIS, News Library, Arcnws File; N. R. Kleinfield, *Unraveling Puzzle of L. I. Car Dealer Reveals Layers of Personal Mystery*, N.Y. TIMES, April 19, 1992, at A26.
29. Everett L. Shostrom, *Man, The Manipulator: The Inner Journey from Manipulation to Actualization* 13 (1967); *id.* at 36–39 (describing various types of manipulators).

212

30. Avner Offer, "The Mask of Intimacy: Advertising and the Quality of Life," in *In Pursuit of the Quality of Life* 211, 225 (Avner Offer ed., 1996) ("A gift is an exchange in which a transfer is not mediated by price, but is rather reciprocated at the discretion of the receiver"); *id.* at 226 ("Reciprocal giving gives rise to obligation . . .").

31. Douglas Rushkoff, *Coercion: Why We Listen To What "They" Say* 33–35 (1999).

32. Eugene Linden, *The Parrot's Lament* 50–51 (1999).

33. *Id.* at 70–72.

34. Avishalom Tor, *The Fable of Entry: Bounded Rationality and the Efficacy of Competition* (unpublished manuscript, Harvard Law School, September 2001); on file with author.

35. *Id.* part III.

36. Charles Ponzi, *The Rise of Mr. Ponzi* (1935), at http://www.pnzi.com (last visited March 6, 2012). As he himself attested, Ponzi was called "a dreamer, a visionary, and everything else, including a crook, probably on account of the fact that I didn't get away with it, like many of the bankers I know of and like some of the big corporations I know of. If I had, they would have called me a genius; a wizard, without the quotation marks."

37. United States v. Spirk, 503 F.3d 619 (7th Cir. 2007).

38. Armstrong v. Guccione, 470 F.3d 89 (2d Cir. 2006).

39. Gary Johns, *A Multi-Level Theory of Self-Serving Behavior in and by Organizations*, 21 RES. IN ORGANIZATIONAL BEHAVIOR 1, 22 (1999).

40. Ponzi, *The Rise of Mr. Ponzi*, at Ch. 3, n. 36.

41. *Id.*

42. *Id.* Describing his failed promotion of a large water and light project Charles Ponzi wrote: "Even at those days I was no slouch at promoting. For the very good reason that money with me is always the last consideration instead of being the first. The money is always around to be had. The main thing is to have an idea. A plausible idea which can be dressed up and sold."

43. See Daniel Kahnman and Amos Tversky, *On the Psychology of Prediction*, 80 PSYCH. REV. 237, 238, 241 (1973) ("[I]ntuitive predictions are dominated by [the representation of certain select facts] and are relatively insensitive to prior probabilities." Such decisions "violate the statistical rules of prediction in systematic and fundamental ways."); David Hirshleifer, *Investor Psychology and Asset Pricing*, 56 J. FIN. 1533, 1545 (2001) ("[U]se of the representativeness heuristic can cause trend chasing, because people are too ready to believe that trends have systematic causes.").

44. *Ponzi*, at http://www.crimes-of-persuasion.com/Crimes/InPerson/Major-Person/ponzi.htm (last visited March 6, 2012).

45. Lisa Singh, *Fool's Gold*, DALLAS OBS., November 16, 2000, Features, at 1.

46. *Id.*

47. *Id.*

48. Ponzi, *The Rise of Mr. Ponzi*, at Ch. 3, n. 36.

49. *Id.*

50. Michael Bacharach and Diego Gambetta, "Trust in Signs," in 2 *Trust and Society* 148, 153 (Karen S. Cook ed., 2001).

51. Aaron Richardson, *Ponzi Schemer's Exotic Car Collection Being Auctioned by Feds on Tuesday,* AUTOBLOG, February 28, 2011, http://www.autoblog.com/2011/02/28/ponzi-schemers-exotic-car-collection-being-auctioned-by-feds-on/ (last visited March 6, 2012).
52. Bacharach and Gambetta, "Trust in Signs," 148, 155, *at* Ch. 3, n. 50.

Chapter 4

1. Deborah and Gerald Strober, *Catastrophe: The Story of Bernard L. Madoff, the Man Who Swindled the World* 83 (2009).
2. Elan Golomb, *Trapped in the Mirror* 18–19 (1992).
3. *Id.* at 17–18.
4. This definition of a disorder is due for elimination in the 2013 edition of *DSM.* The change has raised a controversy among psychiatrists; http://well.blogs.ny-times.com/2010/11/29/narcissism-no-longer-a-psychiatric-disorder/.
5. Golomb, *Trapped in the Mirror,* at 21, *at* Ch. 4, n. 2.
6. *Id.* at 21.
7. *Id.* at 22.
8. *Id.* at 23.
9. Paul Legall, *Croft Has "Psychopath" Written All over Him: Psychologist,* HAMILTON SPECTATOR, June 24, 1997, at N4.
10. Keith Nuthall, *Making a Killing; To Those Who Met Him, Albert Walker Seemed Such a Nice Man. How Wrong They Were . . .,* INDEPENDENT (London), July 12, 1998, at 20, LEXIS, News Library, Arcnws File.
11. *Id.,* at 20.
12. *Id.*
13. *Id.*
14. *Id.*
15. Nick Brown, *Alleged Ponzi Schemer Ducks Murder Plot Charges,* LAW 360, March 17, 2011, http://www.law360.com/topnews/articles/232977 (last visited May 2, 2011). The agreement with the prosecutors included repayment to the victims.
16. Eslaminia v. White, 136 F.3d 1234 (9th Cir. 1998).
17. Sanjida O'Connell, *Mindreading: An Investigation into How We Learn to Love and Lie* 138–39 (1998); see also Tamar Frankel, *Trust and Honesty: America's Business Culture at a Crossroad* 111–33 (2006).
18. Martin L. Hoffman, *Empathy and Moral Development* 54 (2000).
19. *Id.* at 222, 228–29.
20. *Id.* at 222–23.
21. Ezra Stotland, *White Collar Criminals,* 33 J. SOCIAL ISSUES 179, 188–89 (1977).
22. Laura Reider, Comment, *Toward a New Test for the Insanity Defense: Incorporating the Discoveries of Neuroscience into Moral and Legal Theories,* 46 UCLA L. REV. 289, 322–24 (1998).

23. State v. Sarchman, 34 P.3d 1107 (Ct. App. Idaho 2001); Ayers v. Doth, 58 F. Supp. 2d 1028 (D.C. Minn. 1999), lack of control demonstrating a danger of repeat offense combined with "the lack of any victim empathy or belief that his actions were wrong"; see also Thorgaard v. State, 876 P.2d 599 (Ct. App. Idaho 1994).

24. Kimberlin v. Dewalt, 12 F. Supp. 2d 487 (D. Md. 1998).

25. United States v. Raymond Thomas No. 10-4277 (6th Cir. 11a0667n.06; 437 Fed. Appx. 456; 2011 U.S. App. LEXIS 18847; 2011 FED App. 0667N (6th Cir.); 108 A.F.T.R.2d (RIA) 6254.

26. United States v. Gordon B. Grigg 11a0670n.06; 434 Fed. Appx. 530; 2011 U.S. App. LEXIS 19019; 2011 FED App. 0670N (6th Cir.).

27. United States v. Shawn Richard Merriman (10-1439 10th Cir)) 647 F.3d 1002; 2011 U.S. App. LEXIS 15403 July 27, 2011, Filed.

28. Peter Fimrite, *Did He Have a Deal for You*, S. F. CHRON., February 15, 1998, at 1/Z1.

29. Reider, Comment, 322-24, *at* Ch. 4, n. 22.

30. Lewis Beale, *An Heir-Raising Enterprise*, L.A. TIMEL.A. TIMES, November 18, 1992, at E1.

31. See Frankel, *Trust and Honesty* 111, *at* Ch. 4, n. 17.

32. Reider, Comment, 322-24, *at* Ch. 4, n. 22. In one case, "The State's expert concluded that [the offender's] condition, in combination with the personality disorder, the span of time during which [he] committed his crimes, his recidivism, *his persistent denial, and his lack of empathy* or remorse, made it more likely than not that he would commit further sexually violent acts." Seling v. Young, 531 U.S. 250 (2001).

33. Don Jacobs, *Telemarketing Con Artists Do Not See Selves as Criminals: 47 Convicted of Fraud Subject of UT Study*, KNOXVILLE NEWS-SENTINEL, December 10, 2001, at A1.

34. *Id.*

35. Golomb, *Trapped in the Mirror*, at 12-13, *at* Ch. 4, n. 2.

36. See, e.g., Lisa Davis, *Jamba Liar*, SF WKLY., October 27, 1999, LEXIS, News Library, Arcnws File; Peter Byrne, *Double Injustice*, SF WKLY., July 12, 2000, LEXIS, News Library, Arcnws File.

37. Andrew McIntyre, *Ponzi Schemes Flourish During Tough Times*, POST & COURIER (CHARLESTON, SC), April 20, 2009, http://www.postandcourier.com/news/2009/apr/20/ponzi_schemes_flourish_during_tough_time79229/?wap (last visited March 18, 2011).

38. Michael Benson and Francis T. Cullen, *The Special Sensitivity of White-Collar Offenders to Prison: A Critique and Research Agenda*, 16 J. CRIM. JUSTICE 207, 211-12 (1988).

39. Gary Johns, *A Multi-Level Theory of Self-Serving Behavior in and by Organizations*, 21 RES. IN ORGANIZATIONAL BEHAVIOR 1, 10-11 (1999).

40. Jim Henderson, *Preacher Has Faith in Pitch*, HOUSTON CHRON., May 26, 2002, at 33.

41. *Mystery Outlives "Sicilian Gatsby,"* L.A. Times, November 30, 2000, at A1, LEXIS, News Library, Arcnws File.

42. *Id.*

43. *Id.*

44. Malin Akerstrom, *Crooks and Squares* 176 (1985).

45. Charles Ponzi, *The Rise of Mr. Ponzi* 96, 99 (1935), at http://www.pnzi.com (last visited March 6, 2012).

46. Benson and Cullen, *The Special Sensitivity of White-Collar Offenders to Prison,* at Ch. 4, n. 38.

47. Akerstrom, *Crooks and Squares* 156–57, *at* Ch. 4, n. 44. (quoting William H. Whyte, *The Organization Man* 1956).

48. *Id.* at 157.

49. *Id.* at 168.

50. Henderson, *Preacher Has Faith in Pitch,* at 33, *at* Ch. 4, n. 40.

51. Benson and Cullen, *The Special Sensitivity of White-Collar Offenders to Prison,* 4, *at* Ch. 4, n. 46.

52. Jacobs, *Telemarketing Con Artists Do Not See Selves as Criminals* at A1, *at* Ch. 4, n. 33.

53. *Id.* at A1; Frankel, *Trust and Honesty,* 111–33, *at* Ch. 4, n. 17.

54. Joe Clements, *Kaan, "Condo King" Lilly Float Message: We Won,* Banker & Tradesman, September 13, 2004, at 1, 11.

55. Benson and Cullen, *The Special Sensitivity of White-Collar Offenders to Prison,* 207, 211, *at* Ch. 4, n. 46.

56. Johns, *A Multi-Level Theory of Self-Serving Behavior in and by Organizations,* 22, *at* Ch. 4, n. 39.

57. Robert H. Frank, *Passions Within Reason* 159 (1988).

58. Jennifer Wells, *The Small Price of Big-Time Fraud,* Toronto Star, May 22, 2002, at A03, LEXIS, News Library, Arcnws File.

59. Lisa Singh, *Fool's Gold,* Dallas Observer, November 16, 2000, at 1. See also generally Gillian Tett, *Fool's Gold: How the Bold Dream of a Small Tribe at J. P. Morgan Was Corrupted by Wall Street Greed and Unleashed a Catastrophe* (2009).

60. P. Whittaker, *Investors Knew Risks, Says Loans Scheme Creator,* Courier-Mail (Queensland, Australia), May 8, 1998, at 2, LEXIS, News Library, Arcnws File.

61. SEC v Economou, 830 F.2d 431, 435 (2d Cir. 1987).

62. Singh, *Fool's Gold,* at 1, *at* Ch. 4, n. 59.

63. Donn B. Parker, *Fighting Computer Crime* 124 (1983) describing the fall of Charles Brown.

64. Marshall B. Clinard and Peter C. Yeager, *Corporate Crime* 67–73 (1980).

65. United States v. Masten, 170 F.3d 790, 794 (7th Cir. 1999).

66. The World's Greatest Con Artists, http://greatestconartists.webs.com/josephweil. htm (last visited March 13, 2012).

67. Jake Bernstein, *Madoff Calls Big Investors 'Complicit' in Jailhouse Interview*, PRO-PUBLICA, April 8, 2011, http://www.propublica.org/article/madoff-calls-big-investors-complicit-in-jailhouse-interview-110408 (last visited May 2, 2011).

68. Whittaker, *Investors Knew Risks*, at 2, at Ch. 4, n. 60.

69. Jacobs, *Telemarketing Con Artists Do Not See Selves as Criminals*, at A1, at Ch. 4, n. 33.

70. Akerstrom, Crooks and Squares 16, 20–25, at Ch. 4, n. 47.

71. *Id.* at 71–99.

72. Johns, *A Multi-Level Theory of Self-Serving Behavior in and by Organizations*, 14, at Ch. 4, n. 39; see also Iain Pears, *An Instance of the Fingerpost* 253 (1998).

73. Pears, *An Instance of the Fingerpost*, at Ch. 4, n. 72.

74. See Marshall B. Clinard and Peter C. Yeager, *Corporate Crime* 67 (1980); Frankel, *Trust and Honesty*, 31.

75. Parker, *Fighting Computer Crime* 124, at Ch. 4, n. 63.

76. Whittaker, *Investors Knew Risks*, at 2, LEXIS, News Library, Arcnws File, at Ch. 4, n. 60.

77. Patrick J. Kiger, *In Enron's Wake, Time for a Review of Nonqualified Plans*, WORKFORCE MGMT., March 2004, at 70, http://www.workforce.com/section/benefits-compensation/feature-enrons-wake-time-review-nonqualified-plans/index. html; "In the Enron case, shortly before the Houston-based energy giant went bankrupt in December 2001, the corporate nonqualified benefits plan was used to illegally funnel $53 million in early distributions to a handful of executives, according to a February 2003 report by the staff of the congressional Joint Committee on Taxation."

78. Diana B. Henriques, *Madoff Suits Add Details About Fraud*, N.Y. TIMES, June 23, 2009, sec. B, at 1, LEXIS, News Library, Curnws File.

79. *Id.*

80. Joe Nocera, *Was LinkedIn Scammed?* N.Y. TIMES, May 20, 2011, at A19.

81. Bayou Superfund, LLC v. WAM Long/Short Fund II, L.P. (*In re* Bayou Group, LLC), 362 B.R. 624 (Bankr. S.D.N.Y. 2007).

82. Frankel, *Trust and Honesty*, 91–94, at Ch. 4, n. 31.

83. Ezra Stotland, *White Collar Criminals*, 33 J. SOCIAL ISSUES 179, 186 (1977).

84. David Tennant, *Why Do People Risk Exposure to Ponzi Schemes? Econometric Evidence from Jamaica*, 21 Journal of International Financial Markets, Institutions, and Money (July 2011).

85. NASD INVESTOR FRAUD STUDY, May 12, 2006, at 5. "Additionally a subgroup of 'likely active investors' was created within the larger group of non-victims to determine if the difference in financial literacy score had to do with the number of active investors in the non-active group. The investment victims outscored even this subgroup of likely active investors on the financial literacy questions." *Id.* at 5–6.

86. Michèle Belot et al., *Can Observers Predict Trustworthiness?* (January 26, 2010), abstract, http://www.econ.au.dk/fileadmin/site_files/filer_oekonomi/seminarer/

NOTES TO PAGES 137-144

Economics/10/JeroenVanDeVen.pdf. "We investigate whether experimental subjects can predict behavior in a prisoner's dilemma played on a TV show. Subjects report probabilistic beliefs that a player cooperates, before and after the players communicate. Subjects correctly predict that women and players who make a voluntary promise are more likely to cooperate. They are able to distinguish truth from lies when a player is asked about her intentions by the host. Subjects are to some extent able to predict behavior; their beliefs are 7 percentage points higher for cooperators than for defectors. We also study their Bayesian updating. Beliefs do not satisfy the martingale property and display mean reversion." But see Felicia Smith, *Madoff Ponzi Scheme Exposes "The Myth of the Unsophisticated Investor,"* 40 U. BALT. L. REV. 215 (2010).

87. Tennant, *Why Do People Risk Exposure to Ponzi Schemes?* at Ch. 4, n. 84.
88. Frankel, *Trust and Honesty* 49–55, at Ch. 4, n. 21.
89. *Id.*, 49, 53.
90. Gabriel Cohen, *For You, Half Price*, N.Y. TIMES, November 27, 2005, § 14, at 4, http://www.nytimes.com/2005/11/27/nyregion/thecity/27brid.html?ex=12 90747600&en=d5b19f580f176c64&ei=5090&partner=rssuserland&emc=rss (last visited May 3, 2011).
91. *The Scam That Fell to Earth*, AUSTRALIAN, July 18, 2001, Finance Section, at 30, LEXIS, News Library, Arcnws File.
92. *Id.*
93. Killion v. Huddleston, No. M2000-02413-COA-R3-CV, 2001 Tenn. App. LEXIS 695 (Tenn. Ct. App. September 19, 2001).
94. Tennant, *Why Do People Risk Exposure to Ponzi Schemes?* at Ch. 4, n. 84.
95. *Id.*
96. *Id.*
97. *Id.* See also John R. Nofsiger, *The Psychology of Investing* at 35 (4th ed. 2010).
98. Tennant, *Why Do People Risk Exposure to Ponzi Schemes?* at Ch. 4, n. 84.
99. Scott Halford, *The Successful Optimist*, ENTREPRENEUR, Jul. 27, 2010, http://www.entrepreneur.com/management/managementcolumnistscotthalford/article207648.html (last visited May 3, 2011).
100. Tennant, *Why Do People Risk Exposure to Ponzi Schemes?* at Ch. 4, n. 84.
101. *Id.*
102. *Id.*
103. Michael Lynn and C. R. Snyder, "Uniqueness Seeking," in *Handbook of Positive Psychology* 395, 396 (C. R. Snyder and Shane J. Lopez eds., 2001).
104. Shelley E. Taylor et al., "Toward a Biology of Social Support," in *Handbook of Positive Psychology* 556.
105. Lynn and Snyder, "Uniqueness Seeking," 395, 401, *at* Ch. 4, n. 103.
106. *Id.* at 402.
107. *Id.* at 395.
108. Tennant, *Why Do People Risk Exposure to Ponzi Schemes?* at Ch. 4, n. 84.
109. NASD INVESTOR FRAUD STUDY, May 12, 2006, at 5. "Additionally a subgroup of 'likely active investors' was created within the larger group of non-victims to

determine if the difference in financial literacy score had to do with the number of active investors in the non-active group. The investment victims outscored even this subgroup of likely active investors on the financial literacy questions." *Id.* at 5–6.

110. See Deanna M. Barch et al., *Anterior Cingulate and the Monitoring of Response Conflict: Evidence from an fMRI Study of Overt Verb Generation*, 12 J. COGNITIVE NEUROSCIENCE 298, 298 (2000), abstract, http://www.mitpressjournals.org/doi/abs/10.1162/089892900562110 (last visited March 18, 2011); "Studies of a range of higher cognitive functions consistently activate a region of [the brain]" when the subjects had to be engaged in choices. See also Nofsinger, *The Psychology of Investing* 11–22.

111. Adam Smith, *Wealth of Nations*, book 1, chap. X, at 107 (1776).

112. NASD INVESTOR FRAUD STUDY, May 12, 2006, at 6.

113. Robert Prentice, *Whither Securities Regulation? Some Behavioral Observations Regarding Proposals for Its Future*, 51 DUKE L.J. 1397 (2002).

114. *Video: Madoff Victims Speak Out, Irwin and Steven Salbe*, VANITY FAIR, March 4, 2009, http://www.vanityfair.com/politics/features/2009/04/madoff-victims-speak-video200904 (last visited July 26, 2009).

115. *Id.*

116. The World's Greatest Con Artists, http://greatestconartists.webs.com/josephweil.htm (last visited March 13, 2012).

117. *Video: Madoff Victims Speak Out*, at Ch. 4, n. 114.

118. Kate Nash, *Up in Smoke*, ADVERTISER (South Australia), April 22, 2002, at 61 (describing the same attitude in Australia).

119. Joanne McCulloch, *Cash Plan Director Faces Jail*, PERTH SUNDAY TIMES, May 26, 2002, LEXIS, News Library, Curnws File.

120. Adair v. Lease Partners, Inc., 587 F.3d 238 (5th Cir. 2010).

121. I am indebted to Peter Tufano of the Saïd Business School at Oxford University for this comment.

122. *Id.*

123. Dodds v. Cigna Sec., Inc., 12 F.3d 346, 350 (2d Cir. 1993).

124. Cohain v. Klimley, Nos. 08 Civ. 5047 (PGG), 09 Civ. 4527 (PGG), 09 Civ. 10584 (PGG) 2010 U.S. Dist. LEXIS 98870 (S.D.N.Y. September 20, 2010), unpublished decision, violations of Section 10(b) of the Securities Exchange Act of 1934 and Section 12 of the Securities Act of 1933; see, e.g., *In re* Nova-Gold Res. Inc. Sec. Litig., 629 F. Supp. 2d 272 (S.D.N.Y. 2009), applying the storm warnings doctrine in dismissing Securities Act claims, including those asserted under Section 12, as time-barred.

125. Michael Perlstein, *Accountant Suspect in Fraud Probe: Ex-Boss Says Ponzi Suspect Bilked Firm of $150,000*, TIMES-PICAYUNE (New Orleans), October 23, 2000, National, at 1.

126. Fimrite, *Did He Have a Deal for You*, at 1/Z1, *at* Ch. 4, n. 28.

127. See, e.g., Sherm Robbins, *What Is a Ponzi*, at http://adv-marketing.com/business/008-a.htm (last visited March 18, 2011).

128. Terry Greene Sterling, *The Moneychangers; A New Times Investigation; First in a Series*, PHOENIX NEW TIMES, April 16, 1998, LEXIS, News Library, Arcnws File.

129. See, e.g., *Judge Freezes Assets of Securities Firm Accused of Scheme*, DALLAS MORNING NEWS, November 25, 1999, at 51A.

130. Bob Cox, *Worried Cornerstone Investors Await Receiver's Report*, FORT WORTH STAR-TELEGRAM, February 13, 2000, Business, at 1.

131. *The Scam That Fell to Earth*, at 30, *at* Ch. 4, n. 91.

132. David Baines, *The Little Bank That Isn't*, CANADIAN BUS., June 24, 2002, Money, at 36.

133. United States v. Gragg, No. 96-5586, 1998 U.S. App. LEXIS 9577 (6th Cir. May 7, 1998).

134. Charles A. Jaffe, *Risky Business*, CHI. TRIB., December 30, 1999, Zone C, at 1.

135. "Compulsive gamblers live in a fantasy world and deny reality...." The problem of gambling is similar to drug addiction. John G. Edwards, *Former Broker Warns About the Dangers of Gambling Addiction*, LAS VEGAS REV. J., November 9, 1999, at 3D (listing the results of investor addiction, including attempted suicides double those of drug addicts, and resort to crime, including violent crime).

136. Jim Kelly, *Gambling's Social Costs Are Not Being Addressed*, MORNING CALL (Allentown, PA), March 17, 1997, at B2. See also *Getting Hooked: Rationality and Addiction* (Jon Elster and Ole Jørgen-Skog eds., 1999).

137. James Daw, *Sinner Sent to Prison for Swindle*, TORONTO STAR, February 6, 2001, LEXIS, News Library, Arcnws File.

138. Brendan Moynihan, *Knowing When to Hold . . . and Fold; Advice for Traders*, FUTURE, September 1995, at 34.

139. Ken Kurson, *Las Vegas Rules: Sports Betting Isn't Like the Market. It Is the Market*, ESQUIRE, April 1998, at 138.

140. Moynihan, *Knowing When to Hold*, at 34, *at* Ch. 4, n. 138.

141. Liss v. Al Manuel, 296 N.Y.S.2d 627 (Misc. Civ. Ct. 1968).

142. See N.Y. Const. art. 1 § 9 (prohibiting gambling; authorizing legislatures to pass laws prohibiting gambling); N.Y. Penal Law §§ 225.00–30 (McKinney 2008 & Supp. 2011), making it a crime to promote gambling or to possess gambling records and devices. It is not a crime just to participate in the game). N.Y. General Obligations Law § 5–401 (McKinney 2001), providing that wagers made to depend on gambling are unlawful); id. § 5–411, providing that contracts for such wagers are void.

143. *Merriam-Webster's Collegiate Dictionary* 689 (10th ed. 1999).

144. *Id.* at 478. Another part of the definition is "to play a game for money or property."

145. David M. Halbfinger and Daniel Golden, *The Lottery's Poor Choice of Locations; Boom in Instant Games, Keno Widens Sales Gap Between White and Blue Collar; The Lottery at 25; Last of Four Parts*, BOSTON GLOBE, February 12, 1997, at A1.

146. Pythia Peay, *Uncontrolled Gambling Is Poor Bet*, STUART NEWS (Stuart, FL), July 20, 1996, at D4.

147. Charles Osgood, *Easy Money*, CBS NEWS TRANSCRIPTS, March 7, 1999, LEXIS, News Library, Arcnws File.

148. Liz Pulliam Weston, *Talk Is Vital in Planning Family Finances*, L.A. TIMES, April 28, 2000, pt. C, at 1.

149. Ron Ziegler, *Net Trading Catches Fire: Don't Get Burned by Easy-to-Execute, Technology-Driven Transactions*, NAT'L POST, May 22, 1999, at 4.

150. See John Seigenthaler, *Some Stock Market Investors Are Gambling Addicts*, NBC NIGHTLY NEWS, LEXIS, News Library, Arcnws File, December 24, 2000; Tom Rhodes, *Inside New York*, SUNDAY TIMES (London), February 20, 2000 LEXIS, News Library, Arcnws File.

151. Paul Sloan, *Can't Stop Checking Your Stock Quote?* U. S. NEWS & WORLD REP., July 10, 2000, at 40; David Ferrell, *Going for Broke*, L.A. TIMES, December 13, 1998, part A, at 28, noting that "a small but significant" percentage of investors, between 1 and 4 percent, are addicted to trading.

152. See Ponzi, *The Rise of Mr. Ponzi* 107, *at* Ch. 4, n. 45.

153. *Id.* at 107, 110–11.

154. *Id.* at 114–15.

155. Akerstrom, *Crooks and Squares* 156–57, *at* Ch. 4, n. 47.

156. Jacobs, *Telemarketing Con Artists Do Not See Selves as Criminals*, at A1.

157. Joe Dejka, *Thieves to Learn a Lesson; Sarpy County Tries Shoplifting School; Court Cases Diverted; Shoplifting Facts*, OMAHA WORLD-HERALD, June 17, 2002, at 1b.

158. http://www.answers.com/topic/calculating.

159. David Weisburd et al., *White-Collar Crime and Criminal Careers: Some Preliminary Findings*, 36 CRIME & DELINQUENCY 342, 349 (1990).

160. *Id.* at 347.

161. Robbie Whelan, *Guilty Plea Ends Tale of Redemption*, WALL ST. J., April 5, 2011, at C1, LEXIS, News Library, WSJ File.

162. United States v. Gold Unlimited, 177 F.3d 472, 478 (6th Cir. 1999).

163. Henderson, *Preacher Has Faith in Pitch*, at 33.

164. Peter Gosnell, *Fraudster Winged off with $2m*, DAILY TELEGRAPH (Sydney), April 25, 2002, at 41, LEXIS, News Library, Arcnws File.

165. See Marianne Lavelle et al., *Payback Time?* U.S. NEWS & WORLD REP., March 11, 2002, at 36.

Chapter 5

1. Crigger v. Fahnestock & Co., 443 F.3d 230 (2d Cir. 2006).

2. Marshall B. Clinard and Peter C. Yeager, *Corporate Crime* 21 (1980).

3. On this subject, see Paul W. Bonapfel et al., *The Business Bankruptcy Panel: Ponzi Schemes—Bankruptcy Court v. Federal Court Equity Receivership*, 26 EMORY BANKR. DEV. J. 207 (2010); Mark D. Sherrill, *Limitations of Market*

Participants' Protections Against Fraudulent-Conveyance Actions, 28–4 ABIJ 28 (2009); "Investors are the most obvious victims of Ponzi schemes and similar frauds, whether they lose their investment or face a clawback after a successful redemption." "Warren Buffet famously observed, 'It's when the tide goes out that you find out who has been swimming naked.'" See also Tally M. Wiener, Essay, *On the Clawbacks in the Madoff Liquidation Proceeding*, 15 FORDHAM J. CORP. & FIN. L. 221 (2009).

4. Susan Pulliam, Jenny Strasburg, and Michael Rothfeld, *The Galleon Case: Defense Worked—to a Point*, WALL ST. J., May 18, 2011, at C1, LEXIS, News Library, WSJ File (Raj Rajaratnam, found guilty of insider trading).

5. Lewis Hyde, *Trickster Makes This World* 216–17 (1998).

6. *Id.* at 8.

7. *Id.* at 7.

8. Nancy Dillon, *SEC Using Lifetime Ban as Weapon Against Fraud*, DAILY NEWS (New York), October 7, 2002, at 30, LEXIS, News Library, Arcnws File; Alf Young, *Balancing Act: Why Modern-Day Capones May End up on Easy Street*, SUNDAY HERALD (GLASGOW), August 25, 2002, at 3, LEXIS, News Library, Arcnws File.

9. Jennifer Wells, *The Small Price of Big-Time Fraud*, TORONTO STAR, May 22, 2002, at A03, LEXIS, News Library, Arcnws File.

10. Matt Ridley, *The Origins of Virtue, Human Instincts and the Evolution of Cooperation* 29 (1996); id. at 32–33 (dealing with parasite cells).

11. http://www.alibris.com/booksearch?author=Jerome+Schneider (last visited February 29, 2012).

12. Indictment, United States v. Schneider, Eric Witmeyer. File No. CR 02 0403 (N.D. Cal. December 19, 2002); *Offshore Gurus Jerome Schneider and Eric Witmeyer Indicted*, December 19, 2002, http://www.quatloos.com/Jerome_Schneider_indicted.htm (last visited October 19, 2004).

13. Josh Richman, *Tax Shelter Guru's Partner Pleads Guilty, Will Testify*, January 21, 2003, http://www.quatloos.com/guru_pleads_guilty.htm (last visited October 1, 2004).

14. Christopher Albert, Talk at Boston University School of Law class re: Federal Strategies Against Financial Fraud: Techniques to Detect and Recover Hidden Assets (October 1, 2003).

15. Tony Levene, *Curse of the Pyramids Haunts Isle of Wight*, GUARDIAN (London), July 6, 2001, http://www.guardian.co.uk/money/2001/jul/07/personalfinancenews.jobsandmoney.

16. *Id.*

17. Tamar Frankel, *Trust and Honesty: America's Business Culture at a Crossroad*, 35 (2006).

18. See Sricki, *The Politics of Victim Blaming*, MOTLEY MOOSE, June 7, 2010, http://motleymoose.com/diary/2544/the-politics-of-victim-blaming (last visited March 18, 2011); "Sadly, blaming the victims of rape is a frightfully

common occurrence, which contributes . . . to the social stigma associated with rape."

19. Crigger v. Fahnestock & Co., 443 F.3d 230 (2d Cir. 2006).

20. *Id.*

21. *Id.* The court held that the insurance company was a sophisticated institutional investor and that investments were an important part of its business. It specifically acknowledged that it was sophisticated. Even though the insurance company had little experience in the particular type of transaction, the court found that it still was capable of evaluating the risk involved. Therefore, the insurance company could not claim to have been defrauded.

22. National Western Life Ins. Co. v. Merrill Lynch, Pierce, Fenner & Smith., 213 F. Supp. 2d 331 (S.D.N.Y 2002).

23. U.S. Dept. of Justice, Press Release, *Inland Empire Man Who Orchestrated $26 Million Ponzi Scheme Sentenced to 14 Years in Prison* (June 7, 2005). http://www.justice.gov/usao/cac/pressroom/pr2005/087.html (last visited 2/29/2012), STATE NEWS SERVICE, LEXIS, News Library, Curnws File.

24. This issue is debated heatedly among investors, some of whom have received more than their investments while others have lost not only returns but their investments as well. See, e.g., Eric Konigsberg, *Investors in a Competition for a Piece of the Madoff Pie*, N.Y. TIMES, June 29, 2009, at B1, LEXIS, News Library, Curnws File.

25. See Amended Complaint, Am. Int'l Life Assurance Co. v. Bartmann, No. 99-CV-0862-C (N.D. Okla. 1999).

26. See Dirks v. SEC, 463 U.S. 646 (1983).

27. See John R. Nofsinger, *The Psychology of Investing*, chap. 10 (4th ed. 2010).

28. *Regulators Sound Alarm on Affinity Scams*, CANADA NEWSWIRE, January 29, 2002, LEXIS, News Library, Curnws File.

29. *How Prime Bank Frauds Work*, http://www.sec.gov/divisions/enforce/prime-bank/howtheywork.shtml.

Chapter 6

1. Merrill v. Abbott (*In re* Independent Clearing House Co.), 41 B.R. 985, 995 (Bankr. D. Utah 1984), subsequent history omitted; Susan Spencer-Wendel, *Madoff Victims Doubt Payouts*, PALM BEACH POST, July 18, 2011, at 1B, LEXIS, News Library, Curnws File (noting that critic of Madoff trustee "believes 80 percent of the money will be paid out to the wealthiest 20 percent of investors").

2. 28 U.S.C. § 157(a) (2006), saying district courts may refer Bankruptcy Code cases and proceedings to bankruptcy judges; 28 U.S.C. § 157(b)(1) (2006), providing that bankruptcy courts may hear Title 11 cases and "core proceedings"; 28 U.S.C. § 157(b)(2)(A), (B) (2006), providing that "core proceedings" include matters concerning administration of estate, allowance or disallowance

of claims against estate, or exemptions from property of estate. Another form of legal process is establishment of an equity receivership for Ponzi schemes. See David A. Gradwohl and Karin Corbett, *Equity Receiverships for Ponzi Schemes*, 34 SETON HALL LEGIS. J. 181 (2010).

3. 18 U.S.C. § 152(7) (2006), prohibiting concealment of assets in contemplation of bankruptcy case or intent to defeat provisions of Bankruptcy Code; Chad Bray, *Madoff Trustee Goes After Safra*, WALL ST. J., May 11, 2011, at C3, LEXIS, News Library, Wsj File, noting that Madoff trustee sought to recover transfers to bank from Madoff feeder funds; lawsuit alleged bank knew or should have known of irregularities concerning Madoff. See also, e.g., *Trustee Sues Real Estate Exec for $115M; Williams Realty Founder Accused of Luring Friends into Ponzi*, INDIANAPOLIS BUS. J., July 12, 2010, LEXIS, News Library, Curnws File.

4. 28 U.S.C. § 157(b)(1), (2)(A), (B) (2006).

5. See, e.g., Dan McAllister, *Tripping over the Past*, AM. LAW., November 2000, at 78 (Locke Liddell & Sapp, a Texas law firm, was accused of aiding a client, a former football player, along with three of its lawyers); Terry Greene Sterling, *Accountants Down*, PHOENIX NEW TIMES, December 14, 2000, LEXIS, News Library, Arcnws File.

6. See, e.g., People v. Luongo, 47 N.Y.2d 418, 423 (1979).

7. Jason Spencer, *100 Investors Sue Law Firm over Losses in Alleged Scam*, AUSTIN AM.-STATESMAN, September 15, 2000, at B3.

8. Connecticut Nat'l Bank v. Giacomi, 699 A.2d 101 (Conn. 1997).

9. State *ex rel.* Goettsch v. Diacide Distribs., 561 N.W.2d 369 (Iowa 1997). See also *In re* Agape Litig., Nos. 09-CV-1606 (ADS)(AKT), 09-CV-1782 (ADS) (AKT), 2011 U.S. Dist. LEXIS 33587 (E.D.N.Y. 2011). "Accepting the well-pleaded allegations in the Second Amended Complaints as true, the Plaintiffs may have plausibly alleged that Bank of America was negligent or acted with disregard to the seemingly obvious signs that Agape was defrauding investors. While this may highlight a need for greater oversight and accountability from financial institutions, it is not enough to overcome the hurdle of pleading that BOA plausibly had actual knowledge or provided substantial assistance to the Agape Ponzi scheme."

10. Woods v. Barnett Bank of Fort Lauderdale, 765 F.2d 1004 (11th Cir. 1985).

11. Apartment Inv. & Mgmt. Co. v. Nutmeg Ins. Co., 593 F.3d 1188 (10th Cir. 2010).

12. United States v. Lewis, 594 F.3d 1270 (10th Cir. 2010); the investors' money was never used to buy these notes but rather to pay the con artists and pay off earlier investors. The scheme lasted from April 1999 until late 2004 and the estimated losses to investors were over $40 million.

13. MLSMK Inv. Co. v. JP Morgan Chase & Co., No. 10-3040-cv, 2011 U.S. App. LEXIS 11425 (2d Cir. June 6, 2011).

14. *Id.*; *In re Terrorist Attacks on September 11, 2001*, 349 F. Supp. 2d 765, 830 (S.D.N.Y. 2005), aff'd., 538 F.3d 71 (2d Cir. 2008).

15. Melanie Waddell, *Madoff "Feeder Fund" Settlement Reached*, ADVISORONE, July 28, 2011, http://www.advisorone.com/2011/07/28/madoff-feeder-fund-settlement-reached (last visited November 18, 2011).

16. Tom Hays, *$7.2b Settlement OK'd by Judge in Madoff Case*, BOSTON GLOBE, January 14, 2011, at 7, LEXIS, News Library, Curnws File.

17. Picard v. Katz. 11 Civ. 3605 (JSR) [Adv. Pro. No. 10-05287], 2011 U.S. Dist. LEXIS 109595 (S.D.N.Y. September 27, 2011).

18. Tally M. Wiener, Essay, *On the Clawbacks in the Madoff Liquidation Proceeding*, 15 FORDHAM J. CORP. & FIN. L. 221 (2009).

19. Cunningham v. Brown, 265 U.S. 1 (1924). The court reasoned that the lenders were creditors because their money could not be traced in the bank accounts. The court noted that an unlawful payment to a minor constituted a preference.

20. Christian Bros. High Sch. Endowment v. Bayou No Leverage Fund, LLC (*In re Bayou Group, LLC*), 2010 U.S. Dist. LEXIS 99590 (S.D.N.Y., September 17, 2010).

21. The relationship between net losers and net winners in a Ponzi scheme is very complicated and involves both interpretation of statutes and judicial decisions. For a great detailed legal analysis of the issues, see Andrew Kull, "Common Law Restitution and the Madoff Litigation" (unpublished manuscript, on file with author).

22. Sec. Inv. Protection Corp. v. Old Naples Sec., Inc. (*In re Old Naples Sec., Inc.*), 343 B.R. 310 (M.D. Fla. 2006).

23. Harold R. Weinberg, *Markets Overt, Voidable Titles, and Feckless Agents: Judges and Efficiency in the Antebellum Doctrine of Good Faith Purchase*, 56 TUL. L. REV. 1 (1981).

24. *Id.*, 10 n. 38 (1981), quoting Hosack v. Weaver, 1 Yeates 478, 479 (Pa. 1795), quoting J. Kelyng, *A Report of Divers Cases in Pleas of the Crown* 48 (1708).

25. United States v. $7,206,157,717 on Deposit at JP Morgan Chase Bank, N.A., 274 F.R.D. 125 (S.D.N.Y. 2011).

26. Tanvir Alam, *Fraudulent Advisors Exploit Confusion in the Bankruptcy Code: How In Pari Delicto Has Been Perverted to Prevent Recovery for Innocent Creditors*, 77 AM. BANKR. L.J. 305 (2003).

27. United States v. Frykholm, 362 F.3d 413 (7th Cir. 2004).

28. Donell v. Kowell, 533 F.3d 762 (9th Cir. 2008).

Epilogue

1. Humberto Cruz and Diane Lade, *Don't Lose to Investing Scams—Watch for Signs*, SUN-SENTINEL (Fort Lauderdale, FL), September 18, 2000, at 21.

2. *Id.*

INDEX

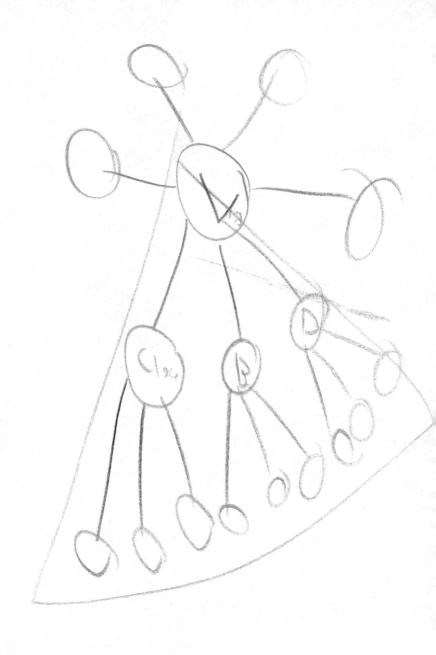